THE MODERN THEATRE
Volume Two

Eric Bentley is the author of *What is Theatre?* and other volumes.

THE
MODERN THEATRE

Volume Two
Edited by

ERIC BENTLEY

Five Plays

FANTASIO

THE DIARY OF A SCOUNDREL

LA RONDE

PURGATORY

MOTHER COURAGE

Doubleday Anchor Books

DOUBLEDAY & COMPANY, INC., GARDEN CITY, N.Y.

ACKNOWLEDGMENTS

Acknowledgment of permission to reprint is to be found on the title page of each play.

Beyond these thanks to my authors and translators, I owe thanks to many secret collaborators. Theodore Hoffman helped me extensively with the dialogue of *Mother Courage*, and W. H. Auden suggested a number of lines for the songs that would fit Dessau's music better. Desmond Vesey went so far as to let me read his version of *Mother Courage* before I made my own. Mr. Louis Simpson gave me an idea for one of the songs.

I also owe thanks to those of my authors who let me suggest—and even execute—changes in *their* scripts.

Many of the suggestions for titles in my modern anthologies come to me, unsolicited, from strangers. I would urge readers of the present volume to send me their ideas. Here and now I must confine myself to thanking those whom I regularly "pump" for their opinions and even persuade to read plays which they might otherwise have lived happily without: Jacques Barzun, William Becker, and Theodore Hoffman.

My own editorial labors have been shared cheerfully—I should say gaily—by my wife, Joanne Davis Bentley. We, in turn, were assisted by Miss Violet Serwin, who can type from copy which your modern printer would probably take for prehistoric cave drawings.

That this series should exist at all was the idea of Mr. Jason Epstein, of Doubleday and Company. The form it has finally taken was devised by him and myself in constant consultation—when not at length, then at long distance. If the result is something to be grateful for, it is clear that the gratitude should go, in a very large measure, to him.

E.B.

CONTENTS

FANTASIO

A Play in Two Acts by
ALFRED DE MUSSET
English version by Jacques Barzun

THE DIARY OF A SCOUNDREL
A Comedy in Three Acts by
ALEXANDER OSTROVSKY
English version by Rodney Ackland

LA RONDE
Ten Dialogues by
ARTHUR SCHNITZLER
English version by Eric Bentley

PURGATORY
A Play in One Act by
W. B. YEATS

MOTHER COURAGE
A Chronicle of the Thirty Years' War
in Twelve Scenes by
BERTOLT BRECHT
English version by Eric Bentley

THE MODERN THEATRE
Volume Two

FANTASIO

A Comedy in Two Acts
by

ALFRED DE MUSSET

English version by
Jacques Barzun

Characters

THE KING OF BAVARIA
THE PRINCE OF MANTUA
MARINONI, *His Aide-de-Camp*
RUTTEN, *the King's Secretary*

Young Men about Town
FANTASIO
SPARK
FACIO
HARTMANN

ELSBETH, *daughter of the King*
HER GOVERNESS
FLAMEL, *a Page*
ANOTHER PAGE

THE PLACE: *Munich*

ACT ONE

SCENE 1 THE COURT

The KING *surrounded by his courtiers;* RUTTEN.

THE KING. Dear friends, I announced to you quite some time ago the betrothal of my dear Elsbeth with the Prince of Mantua. Today I apprise you of the arrival of that prince. Tonight possibly, tomorrow at latest, he will be in our palace. Let it be a day of rejoicing for everyone; let the prisons be opened and let the people pass the night in entertainment. Rutten, where is my daughter?

The courtiers withdraw.

RUTTEN. Sire, she is in the park with her governess.

THE KING. Why have I not yet seen her today?

RUTTEN. It seemed to me that the Princess's countenance was somewhat touched with melancholy. What young girl is not pensive on the eve of her wedding? And the death of St. John has upset her.

THE KING. How can you say so! The death of my buffoon, of a court fool who was hunchbacked and nearly blind?

RUTTEN. The princess loved him.

THE KING. Tell me, Rutten, you've seen the Prince. What sort of man is he? I am giving him what is most precious to me in the world and, alas, I do not know him.

RUTTEN. I stayed but a very short while in Mantua.

THE KING. Speak freely. Through whose eyes can I learn the truth if not through yours?

RUTTEN. In truth, Sire, I am unable to say anything as to the mind and character of the noble prince.

THE KING. Is that the way it is? You, a courtier, hesitate? With what eulogies the air of this room would be filled, what hyperboles and flattering comparisons, if the prince who tomorrow will be my son-in-law had seemed to you worthy of the title. Have I made a mistake, dear friend? Have I made a bad choice?

RUTTEN. Sire, the prince has the reputation of being the best of rulers.

THE KING. Politics is a gossamer web, in which more than one broken fly struggles helplessly. I shan't sacrifice my daughter's happiness to any interest.
Exeunt.

SCENE 2 A STREET

SPARK, HARTMANN, *and* FACIO, *drinking around a table.*

HARTMANN. Since today is the princess's wedding-day, let's drink and smoke and try to make some noise.

FACIO. It might be a good idea to mix with this mob that overruns the streets and snuff out a few Chinese lanterns on the heads of these good burghers.

SPARK. Nonsense! Let us smoke quietly.

HARTMANN. I shall do nothing quietly. Even if I have to act as clapper in a bell, I must ring out on a holiday. Where the devil is Fantasio?

SPARK. Let's wait for him, let's not do anything without him.

FACIO. Oh, he'll find us anyway. He must be getting tipsy in some hole on the Lower Street. Hey there! another round!
He raises his glass.

OFFICER, *entering.* Gentlemen, I must beg you to move along if you don't want to be disturbed in your merrymaking.

HARTMANN. Why so, Captain?

OFFICER. The princess is just now on the terrace that you can see from here. You can understand that it is not fitting your cries should reach her ears.

FACIO. This is intolerable!

SPARK. What difference does it make to us whether we laugh here or elsewhere?

HARTMANN. How do we know that elsewhere we'll be allowed to laugh? You'll see, some fellow in a green uniform will spring out of every cobblestone and tell us to go laugh in the moon.
Enter MARINONI, *in a cloak.*

SPARK. The princess has never done a tyrannical act in her life, God keep her! If she doesn't want us to laugh, it must be that she is sad, or perhaps singing. Let's leave her in peace.

FACIO. Humph! Here is some foreign cloak sniffing for news. The traveling gull looks as if to accost us.

MARINONI, *approaching.* I am a stranger, gentlemen; what is the reason of this holiday?

SPARK. Princess Elsbeth is about to be married.

MARINONI. Ah! Ah! She is beautiful, I presume?

HARTMANN. As beautiful a woman as you are handsome a man.

MARINONI. Beloved of her people, if I may venture, for it seems to me everything is illuminated.

HARTMANN. Right again, good stranger, all these lighted lanterns, as you have wisely remarked, are nothing else than an illumination.

MARINONI. I meant to say, is the Princess the cause of this rejoicing?

HARTMANN. The sole cause, great logician; we could all of us get married at once and there would not be the slightest sign of joy in this ungrateful town.

MARINONI. Happy is the princess who knows how to make her people love her!

HARTMANN. A few lighted lanterns do not constitute the happiness of a people, dear primitive, which does not prevent the aforementioned Princess from being as whimsical as a lady-bird.

MARINONI. Indeed! You said "whimsical"?

HARTMANN. I did, dear unknown, I used that very word.
Marinoni salutes and withdraws.

FACIO. What the deuce is that stammering Italian after? He left us only to approach another group. I can smell a spy a league away.

HARTMANN. I smell nothing at all. He is stupid to perfection.

SPARK. Here is Fantasio.

HARTMANN. What's the matter with him? He waddles like a justice of the peace. Either I mistake very much or some lunacy ripens in his brain.

FACIO. Well, friends, what shall we do tonight?

FANTASIO. Absolutely everything except give birth to another novel.

FACIO. I was saying that we should mingle with this rabble and amuse ourselves a bit.

FANTASIO. The great thing would be to procure false noses and firecrackers.

HARTMANN. You mean put our arms around the girls, pull the burghers' wigs, and break the lanterns! Come, let's go. It's settled.

FANTASIO. Once upon a time there was a Persian king——

HARTMANN. Come on, Fantasio.

FANTASIO. Count me out, count me out.

HARTMANN. Why?

FANTASIO. Give me a glass of wine.
He drinks.

HARTMANN. You have the month of May on your cheek—

FANTASIO. True, and the month of January in my heart. My head is like an old chimney without a fire—only wind and ashes. Ouf!
Sits down.

How bored I am that everybody should be gay. I wish that this heavy sky were an immense nightcap pulled down to the ears so as to extinguish this dull town and its dull inhabitants. Come, for pity's sake tell me some old joke, something faded and threadbare.

HARTMANN. Why?

FANTASIO. To make me laugh. I can't laugh any more at what's made-up new. Perhaps I shall laugh at what I've heard before.

HARTMANN. You seem to me a trifle misanthropic—inclined to melancholy.

FANTASIO. Not in the least.

FACIO. Are you with us, yes or no?

FANTASIO. I'm with you if you're with me. Let us bide here awhile and talk of this and that, while we admire our new clothes.

FACIO. Good Lord, no! If you're weary of standing up, I'm weary of sitting still. I must exert myself—out in the open.

FANTASIO. Oh, I couldn't exert myself. I am going to smoke under these old chestnuts, with my good friend Spark who'll keep me company. Won't you, Spark?

SPARK. Just as you like.

HARTMANN. In that case, good-bye. We're going to see the fun.

HARTMANN *and* FACIO *leave*.

FANTASIO *sits down with* SPARK.

FANTASIO. What a failure this sunset is! Nature does wretchedly tonight. Look at the valley down there, those four or five measly clouds climbing the mountain. I used to do landscapes like that when I was twelve years old, on the cover of my schoolbooks.

SPARK. The tobacco is first-rate and so is the beer.

FANTASIO. I must bore you horribly, Spark?

SPARK. No, why do you think so?

FANTASIO. You bore *me* horribly. Doesn't it bother you to see

the same face day after day? What the deuce will Hartmann and Facio find to do in town?

SPARK. They're two sprightly fellows who can't sit still.

FANTASIO. What a wonderful thing, the Arabian Nights! Oh
Spark, my dear Spark, if you could transport me to China!
If I could only quit my own skin for an hour or two!
If I could only be that gentleman passing by!

SPARK. That seems to me rather difficult.

FANTASIO. That gentleman passing by is charming. Look! what
a fine pair of silk breeches! What pretty red flowers on his
waistcoat! His watch fob swings on his stomach in counter-
rhythm to his coat tails, which flit about his calves. I am
sure that man has in his head a thousand thoughts that are
absolutely foreign to me. His essential character is his
alone. Alas! Everything men say to one another is the
same; the ideas they exchange are the same in all their
conversations; but inside all these isolated machines, what
hidden recesses, what secret compartments! It is a world
apart each one bears with him! An unknown world which
is born and dies in silence. What solitudes these human
bodies!

SPARK. Why don't you drink, old man, instead of racking your
brain uselessly?

FANTASIO. Only one thing has amused me these three days
past: my creditors have got a judgment against me and if
I set foot within my house, four marshals will grab me by
the collar.

SPARK, *soberly*. That is very amusing news indeed.

FANTASIO. Do you realize that my furniture will be sold
tomorrow morning? We'll go and buy a few pieces, shall we?

SPARK. Do you need money, Henry, do you want my purse?

FANTASIO. Idiot! If I had no money I would have no debts.
Have you noticed something, Spark? We have no status,
we practice no profession.

SPARK. Is that what makes you sad?

FANTASIO. Well, there is no such thing as a melancholy fencing
master.

SPARK. You seem to me to be sick of the world.

FANTASIO. Ah, my dear fellow, to be sick of the world one must have tasted of it, traveled all over it.

SPARK. Well?

FANTASIO. Well, where can I go? Look at this old smoky town: there is no square, street, or alley I haven't roamed thirty times over; there are no stones that I haven't dragged my worn heels upon; no house of which I do not know what girl's or old woman's stupid head is to be seen eternally behind the windowpane; I cannot take a step without treading on my steps of yesterday. Still, dear friend, this town is nothing compared to my mind. All its corners are to me a hundred times more familiar; all the streets, all the holes of my imagination are a hundred times more worn. I've roamed through it in a hundred times more ways, this dilapidated mind; I, its sole occupant! I've intoxicated myself in all its wineshops, I've wallowed there like a despotic king in a golden litter; I've trotted through it like a good merchant on a jaded mule; and now I dare enter only like a robber with a dark lantern in his hand.

SPARK. I don't understand it at all, this perpetual working over yourself; I, when I smoke, for example, my thoughts go up in smoke; when I drink, they flow as Spanish wine or Flemish beer; when I kiss my mistress's hand, they enter at her graceful fingers to spread through all her being like currents of electricity; I want the perfume of a flower to divert me, and of all things in nature or the universe the smallest suffices to change me into a bee and make me flit hither and thither with every new pleasure.

FANTASIO. Clinching the point, then, you *could* enjoy fishing?

SPARK. If it amuses me, I can do anything.

FANTASIO. Even take the moon between your teeth?

SPARK. That wouldn't be amusing.

FANTASIO. Ho ho! How do you know? Taking the moon between your teeth is not to be despised. Let's play baccarat.

SPARK. No indeed!

FANTASIO. Why not?

SPARK. We'd lose all our money.

FANTASIO. Oh, good God! What are you thinking of now! It is you who don't know what to invent to torture your mind. Does everything look black to you, you wretch? Lose all our money! Is there no faith or hope of God in your breast? Are you an abominable atheist, capable of drying up my soul and disillusioning me about everything—me who am full of youthful sap?
He starts to dance.

SPARK. You know, there are times when I shouldn't take my oath that you're not crazy.

FANTASIO, *still dancing.* Let me have a bell, a crystal bell!

SPARK. Now what in heaven's name do you want a bell for?

FANTASIO. Didn't Jean-Paul say that a man absorbed in a great thought was like a diver under his bell at the bottom of the great ocean? I want a bell, Spark, a bell; for I am dancing on the great ocean.

SPARK. Become a journalist or a man of letters, Henry. It's about the most effective way left to uproot misanthropy and deaden the imagination.

FANTASIO. Oh I wish I could have a passion for lobster with mustard sauce, or some pretty girl, or the classification of minerals. Spark, let's try, between the two of us, to build a house.

SPARK. Why don't you write down all your reveries. They would make a pretty volume.

FANTASIO. A sonnet is better than a long poem and a glass of wine better than a sonnet.
He drinks.

SPARK. Why don't you travel? Go to Italy.

FANTASIO. I've been there.

SPARK. Well, isn't it a beautiful country?

FANTASIO. There are a great many flies—large as grasshoppers—they sting you all night long.

SPARK. Go to France.

FANTASIO. There is no decent wine between the Rhine and
  Paris.

SPARK. Go to England.

FANTASIO. That's where I am: the English have no country.
  I'd as soon see them here as at home.

SPARK. Go to the devil, then!

FANTASIO. Ah, if there only were a devil in the sky! if there
  were a hell, how soon I'd blow my brains out to go and see
  it all! What a wretched thing is man! Not even able to jump
  out of the window without breaking his legs! Forced to
  practice the violin for ten years to be a tolerable musician!
  To have to learn in order to be a painter, or a stable boy;
  learn to make an omelet! I swear, Spark, there are times
  when I yearn to sit on a parapet, look at the river flowing
  by and start counting one, two, three, four, five, six, seven,
  and so on until I die.

SPARK. What you're saying would make most people laugh.
  As for me, it makes me shudder: it's the history of our
  age. Eternity is a great eagle's nest whence every century,
  like a young eaglet, flies out to cross the heavens and disappear. Our age, in its turn, has come to the edge of the
  nest, but its wings have been clipped and it awaits death,
  gazing at the sky in which it cannot soar.

FANTASIO, *singing*.
  Thou callst me thy life,
  Oh call me thy soul.
  For thy life lasts a day
  But thy soul cannot die.
  Do you know a more divine love song than that, Spark?
  It's Portuguese. I can never think of it without wanting to
  fall in love with someone.

SPARK. Who, for example?

FANTASIO. Who? I don't know: some beauty, splendidly round
  like the women of Mieris; something sweet like the west
  wind, pale like the rays of the moon; pensive like the
  little maids in Flemish inns that one sees in their paintings;
  they give the stirrup cup to some tall-booted traveler,
  straight as a pike on a big white horse. What a glorious
  thing, the stirrup cup! A young woman on the threshold,

the lighted fire seen at the back of the room, supper laid out, the children asleep—all the tranquillity of peaceful and contemplative life in a corner of paint! And there the traveler, still breathless but firm in his saddle, twenty leagues done and thirty to do, a swallow of spirits and good-bye. The night is deep beyond; the weather threatening, the forest full of danger. The good woman watches you for a moment, then as she returns to her fire, she gives forth the sublime charity of the poor "God be with him!"

SPARK. If you were in love, Henry, you'd be the happiest of men.

FANTASIO. Love no longer exists, my dear fellow. Religion, its mother, has pendulous breasts like an old purse with a copper penny in the bottom. Love is the holy wafer that must be broken in half at the foot of the altar and swallowed together in a kiss. The altar is no more; love is no more. Long live nature, there is still wine.
He drinks.

SPARK. You are getting tipsy.

FANTASIO. I am getting tipsy, you are quite right.

SPARK. It's a bit late for that.

FANTASIO. What do you call late? Is midday late? Midnight, is that early? Where do you take hold of the day? Let's stay here, Spark, I beg of you. Let's drink, talk, analyze, nonsensify, let us talk politics and invent governmental combinations; let us catch all the gnats flitting about this candle and put them in our pockets. Do you know that shotguns operated by steam are a great thing, philanthropically speaking?

SPARK. How do you make that out?

FANTASIO. There was once upon a time a king who was very wise, very wise; very, very happy. . . .

SPARK. And then?

FANTASIO. The only thing lacking to his happiness was children. He ordered public prayers to be said in every temple.

SPARK. What are you getting at?

FANTASIO. I'm thinking of my beloved Arabian Nights. That's the way they all begin. I say, Spark, I'm tipsy. I must do something. Tra la, tra la. Come, let's get up!

A funeral passes by.

Hallo, good people, whom are you burying there? Now's not the time to inhume properly.

THE PALLBEARERS. We're burying St. John.

FANTASIO. St. John is dead? The king's jester is dead? Who's taken his place—the Lord Chancellor?

THE PALLBEARERS. The fool's place is vacant! You can have it if you like.

Exeunt.

SPARK. That's the kind of insolence you expose yourself to. What did you mean by stopping them?

FANTASIO. There's nothing insolent in what he said. It's a piece of friendly advice that man gave me. And I'm going to act on it at once.

SPARK. You're going to be the court jester?

FANTASIO. This very night, if they want me. You know I can't go back home. Besides, I want to enjoy the royal comedy that's to be played tomorrow, and from the royal box itself.

SPARK. Clever, aren't you? You'll be recognized and thrown out by the flunkeys. Are you forgetting you're the godson of the late queen?

FANTASIO. Stupid, aren't you? I'll put on a hump and a red wig like St. John's and nobody will recognize me, even if they set three dozen godmothers after me.

He knocks at the door of a shop.

Ho! Good fellow, open up, if you're not out—you, your wife and your little pups!

TAILOR, *coming out.* What is your lordship's desire?

FANTASIO. Aren't you the court tailor?

TAILOR. At your service.

FANTASIO. Aren't you the one who made for St. John?

TAILOR. Yes, your Honor.

FANTASIO. You knew him? You know on which side he carried his hump? How he curled his moustache, what kind of wig he wore?

TAILOR. Ha Ha! Your Honor is joking.

FANTASIO. Fellow! I am in no mood for joking. Lead the way into your back shop, and if you do not care to be poisoned tomorrow in your breakfast coffee, strive to be silent as the grave on what is about to take place.

Exit with tailor, SPARK *follows.*

SCENE 3   AN INN ON THE MUNICH ROAD

Enter the PRINCE *of* MANTUA *and* MARINONI.

PRINCE. Well, Colonel?

MARINONI. Your Highness?

PRINCE. Well, Colonel?

MARINONI. "Melancholy, whimsical, giddily gay, obedient to her father and very fond of green peas."

PRINCE. Write that down; and remember I can make out writing only when it's round and sloping.

MARINONI, *writing.* Melanch——

PRINCE. Write in a low voice; I've been pondering an important scheme since dinner.

MARINONI. Here, Highness, is what you require.

PRINCE. Good.
Reading.
I don't know in my entire kingdom of any neater hand-writing. I appoint you my intimate friend. Sit down please, but some distance away. So you think, my friend, that the character of the princess, my future wife, is secretly known to you?

MARINONI. Yes, your highness. I have roamed through the

environs of the palace, and these tablets contain the principal points of the various conversations I engaged in.

PRINCE, *looking in his glass*. Seems to me I am as badly powdered as any mean fellow.

MARINONI. But the costume is magnificent.

PRINCE. What would you say, Marinoni, if you saw your master in a simple olive drab frock coat?

MARINONI. Your Highness mocks my credulity.

PRINCE. No, Colonel. Learn that your master is the most romantic of men.

MARINONI. Romantic, your Highness?

PRINCE. Yes, my friend (that *is* your title), the important scheme I ponder is something unheard of in the history of my house. I intend to arrive at the court of the King, my father-in-law, in the dress of an ordinary aide-de-camp. It is not enough that I sent a man of my suite to collect reports on the future princess of Mantua (that man, Marinoni, was yourself), I want to observe her with my own eyes.

MARINONI. Do you mean it, Highness?

PRINCE. Don't stand there petrified. A man like me must have as his intimate friend a vast and enterprising intellect.

MARINONI. Only one thing seems to me to prevent your Highness's design.

PRINCE. What is that?

MARINONI. The idea of such a disguise could occur only to the glorious prince who governs us, but if my gracious sovereign mingles with the royal attendants, to whom will the King of Bavaria tender the honors of the gorgeous feast that is to take place in the great Hall?

PRINCE. You are right, if I am disguised, someone must take my place. And that is impossible! I had not thought of that.

MARINONI. Why impossible, Highness?

PRINCE. I can indeed lower the princely dignity to the rank of colonel; but how can you think that I would consent to raise any man alive to my station? Do you think, moreover, that my future father-in-law would forgive me?

MARINONI. The King is said to be a man full of common sense and intelligence, with a pleasant disposition.

PRINCE. H'm, I am truly reluctant to give up my plan. To penetrate into this new court without pomp or noise, observe everything, approach the princess under a false name, and perhaps make her love me! Oh! My mind wanders. It is impossible—Marinoni, my friend, I cannot resist it: try on my full dress uniform!

MARINONI. Highness!
Bows.

PRINCE. Think you the centuries to come will forget a like circumstance?

MARINONI. Never, gracious Prince.

PRINCE. Come, try on my suit.
Exeunt.

ACT TWO

SCENE 1 THE GARDEN OF THE KING OF BAVARIA

Enter ELSBETH *and her* GOVERNESS.

GOVERNESS. My poor eyes have wept, wept a heavenly torrent.

ELSBETH. You are so kind! I, too, was fond of St. John. He had so much wit. He was no ordinary jester.

GOVERNESS. To think that the dear soul is gone above on the eve of your wedding day. He who spoke only of you, at dinner and supper, all the live long day. So gay and amusing a fellow that he made his ugliness lovable; one's eyes always sought him out in spite of themselves.

ELSBETH. Don't talk to me of my wedding. That's an even greater calamity.

GOVERNESS. Didn't you know that the Prince of Mantua arrived today? They say he is an Adonis.

ELSBETH. What are you talking about, my dear? He is horrible and stupid, everybody here knows it by now.

GOVERNESS. Indeed? I had been told he was an Adonis.

ELSBETH. I didn't especially want an Adonis, but it is cruel sometimes to be only the daughter of a king. My father is the best of men; the union he contemplates insures the peace of the kingdom and he will be rewarded with the blessings of his people, but I, alas! I shall have *his* blessing and nothing more.

GOVERNESS. How sad you seem!

ELSBETH. If I refused the prince, war would soon break out anew. What a pity that these peace treaties are always written with tears. I wish I were a great mind and could find happiness in marrying anyone at all when policy required it. To be the mother of a people consoles a great heart, but not a weak head. I'm only a poor dreamer. Perhaps it's because of the novels you always carry about in your pockets.

GOVERNESS. Lord! Don't speak of it.

ELSBETH. I know very little of life but I've dreamed a great deal.

GOVERNESS. If the Prince of Mantua is such as you say, God will not let this affair be consummated, I'm sure.

ELSBETH. You think not? God lets men alone, my dear, and takes no more note of our complaints than of the bleating of sheep.

GOVERNESS. I'm sure that if you refuse the Prince, your father will not force you.

ELSBETH. No, of course he won't force me, that's why I'm sacrificing myself. Do you want me to tell my father he must break his word, cross out with a stroke of the pen his respectable name from a contract that will make thou-

sands happy? What matters one unhappy soul? I shall let
my good father be a good king.

GOVERNESS. OO-hoo.

Weeps.

ELSBETH. Don't weep for me, dear. You would only make me
weep, and a royal fiancée must not show red lids. Don't
take on so. After all, I shall be a queen. Perhaps it's amusing. Perhaps I shall take a fancy to my jewels—how do I
know?—to my coaches and my new court. Luckily, for a
princess there is something in marriage besides a husband.
I shall perhaps find happiness at the bottom of my wedding
basket.

GOVERNESS. You are a true sacrificial lamb.

ELSBETH. Come, my dear, let us begin by laughing about it,
and keep our tears for the time when we'll need them. They
say the Prince of Mantua is the most ridiculous thing in
the world.

GOVERNESS. If only St. John were here!

ELSBETH. Oh, St. John, St. John!

GOVERNESS. You were very fond of him, my child.

ELSBETH. It was strange; his mind bound me to him by in-
visible threads that seemed to lead from the heart. His
perpetual mocking at my storybook ideas pleased me dearly,
for I can only with difficulty tolerate people who agree
with me. I do not know what there was about him, his
eyes, gestures, the way he took snuff—a singular man. When
he spoke to me, delightful images passed before my eyes;
his words gave life as if by magic to the strangest things.

GOVERNESS. He was a genuine Triboulet.

ELSBETH. I don't know about that but his mind was a jewel.

GOVERNESS. There are pages coming and going; I think the
Prince will soon appear; it is time for you to go in and dress.

ELSBETH. I beg of you, leave me a quarter of an hour more;
go get ready what I'll need; dear, dear friend, I haven't
much longer to dream.

GOVERNESS. God in Heaven! Is it possible that this marriage

take place an it displease Thee? A father, sacrifice his daughter! The King would be a Jephtah to do it.

ELSBETH. Don't speak badly of my father and lay out my things; go, my dear, go.

Exit GOVERNESS.

ELSBETH, *alone.* I think there is someone behind these bushes. Is it the ghost of my poor jester that I see sitting on the grass among the flowers? Answer me. Who are you? What are you doing there, pulling flowers?

She walks towards a flower bed.

FANTASIO, *sitting, dressed in cap and bells with a hump and a wig.*

I am only a poor flower puller who wishes good day to your pretty eyes.

ELSBETH. What means this travesty? Who are you to parade under a large wig in the guise of a man whom I loved? Are you a student of buffoonery?

FANTASIO. Please your Serene Highness, I am the new jester of the King; the Majordomo received me favorably; I was introduced to the groom of the Bed Chamber, the pastry cooks are my protectors—since last evening—and I am now modestly pulling flowers while waiting for wit to come to me.

ELSBETH. I very much doubt whether you will ever pull *that* flower.

FANTASIO. Why not? Wit can come to an old man as readily as to a young girl. It is so difficult sometimes to distinguish between a witty thought and a great blunder. To talk a great deal, that's the secret. The worst pistol shot, if he fires 780 shots a minute, can hit a fly just as easily as he who shoots once or twice with careful aim. I ask only to be comfortably fed for the size of my stomach, and I shall look at my shadow to see if my wig is growing.

ELSBETH. With the result that you are now dressed in the weeds of St. John. You are right to speak of your shadow; so long as you wear this costume, the shadow will look more like him than like you.

FANTASIO. I am just now composing an elegy which will decide my fate.

ELSBETH. How so?

FANTASIO. It will clearly prove that I am the greatest poet in
the world, or else it will be worthless. I am engaged in taking
apart the universe to fit into an acrostic; the moon, the sun
and the stars are struggling to enter my rimes, like school
children at the door of a theater.

ELSBETH. Poor fellow! What a trade you are taking up! To be
witty at so much an hour. Have you nor arms nor legs?
Wouldn't you do better digging the soil instead of your
brain?

FANTASIO. Poor little girl! What a trade you are taking up! To
marry an oaf that you have never seen! Have you nor heart
nor head? Wouldn't it be better to sell your dresses rather
than your body?

ELSBETH. You are rather audacious, Sir Jester!

FANTASIO. What is the name of this flower, please?

ELSBETH. That's a tulip. What are you going to prove?

FANTASIO. A red tulip or a blue tulip?

ELSBETH. Blue, it seems to me.

FANTASIO. Not at all, it is a red tulip.

ELSBETH. Are you putting a new dress on an old adage? You
really don't need it to tell me that of tastes and colors there
is no disputing.

FANTASIO. I am not disputing. I tell you that this tulip is a red
tulip and at the same time I admit that it is blue.

ELSBETH. How do you manage that?

FANTASIO. Like your marriage contract. Who under the sun
can know if he is born blue or red? The tulips themselves
don't know it. Gardners and politicians are such extraordinary grafters that apples become pumpkins, and that
thistles emerge from the maw of a donkey to be drowned
in gravy on the plate of a bishop. This tulip which I see
expected to be red, but it has married and is quite astonished
to find itself blue. It is thus the entire world is metamor-
phosed under the hand of man. Poor Dame Nature must

laugh in her own face when she sees in her lakes and oceans her eternal masquerade! Do you think there was a smell of roses in Moses' paradise? No, it was of new-mown hay. The rose is a daughter of civilization. She is a duchess like you and me.

ELSBETH. The pale flower of the hawthorn can become a rose, and a thistle may turn into an artichoke; but one flower cannot change into another. So what does nature care? We cannot change her: we embellish or we kill her. The most puny violet would die rather than give in, if one tried to change its shape by a single petal.

FANTASIO. Which is why I care more about a violet than a king's daughter.

ELSBETH. There are certain things even jesters themselves have no right to mock. Take care! If you heard me converse with my governess, watch out for your ears.

FANTASIO. Not my ears, my tongue. You mistook the sense and there is therefore no sense in your words.

ELSBETH. Don't make puns if you want to earn your wages, and don't compare me to a tulip if you don't want to earn something else.

FANTASIO. Who knows? A pun is a consolation for many ills and playing with words is as good a way as any other of playing with thoughts and deeds and persons. Everything is a pun here below and it is as difficult to understand the glance of a four-year old child as the drivel in any three modern plays.

ELSBETH. You seem to me to look at the world through a revolving prism.

FANTASIO. Everyone has his eyeglass but nobody knows exactly what color it is. Who will tell me whether I am happy or unhappy, good or bad, sad or gay, witty or stupid?

ELSBETH. You are ugly, in any case, that is certain.

FANTASIO. Not any more than your beauty. Here comes your father with your future husband. Who shall say whether you will marry him or not?
Exit.

ELSBETH. Since I can't avoid meeting the Prince of Mantua,
I might as well come out to greet him.

Enter the KING, MARINONI *dressed as the* PRINCE *and the*
PRINCE *dressed as an aide-de-camp.*

KING. Prince, here is my daughter. Forgive her gardening
attire. You are here in the home of a bourgeois who governs
other bourgeois, and our etiquette is as indulgent to ourselves as to them.

MARINONI. Allow me to kiss this fair hand, madam, if it be not
too great a favor to my lips.

PRINCESS. Your Highness will excuse me if I return to the
palace. I shall see your Highness, in a more fitting state,
I hope, at the presentation tonight.

AIDE-DE-CAMP. The Princess is right. Such modesty is divine.

KING, *to* MARINONI. Who is this aide-de-camp who follows you
like your shadow? It is unbearable to hear him add asinine
remarks to everything we say. Please send him away.

MARINONI *whispers to the* PRINCE.

PRINCE. Very clever of you to have persuaded him to send me
away. I shall try to join the Princess, and offer her a few
delicate words without seeming to.
Exit.

KING. This aide-de-camp is a fool, my friend. What use can you
have for him?

MARINONI. Hm, Hm. Let us proceed a little further, if your
Majesty will be so good; I seem to see a perfectly delightful
shrubbery on this side.
Exeunt.

SCENE 2   ANOTHER PART OF THE GARDEN

PRINCE, *entering.* My disguise is a success. I observe and I make
myself loved. So far everything is as I could wish. The
father seems to me a great king, though too informal; and I
should be surprised if he hadn't liked me from the first.
Ah, I see the Princess on her roundabout way to the palace.
Luck is with me indeed.

Enter ELSBETH; *the* PRINCE *accosts her.*

Your Highness, permit a faithful servant of your future consort to offer you the sincere felicitations which his humble and devoted heart cannot but be filled with on seeing you. Happy are the great ones of the earth! They can marry you! I cannot. It is quite impossible. I am of obscure birth. I have as my sole patrimony a name that is feared by our enemies. A heart pure and without stain beats under this modest uniform. I am a poor soldier riddled with bullets from head to foot. I have not a ducat; I am solitary and exiled from my native land as from my celestial home, that is to say, the paradise of my dreams. There is no woman's heart I can press to my own; I am accurst and silently brooding.

ELSBETH. Sir, what do you want with me? Are you crazy or begging for alms?

PRINCE. Oh, how difficult it would be to find words to express what I feel! I saw you passing alone in this alley; I thought it was my duty to throw myself at your feet, and to offer you my company as far as the postern gate.

ELSBETH. I am much obliged to you. Do me the favor of leaving me alone.

Exit.

PRINCE, *alone.* Did I do wrong to approach her? It had to be done, though. Yes, I was right to approach her. Nonetheless she answered me very disagreeably. Perhaps I shouldn't have spoken to her in so lively a manner. Still, it had to be done; for her marriage is almost settled and I am then to supplant Marinoni who is now taking my place. Yes, I was right to speak with her in lively fashion. But the answer was disagreeable. Could her heart be false and hard? It might be wise to ascertain the fact cunningly.

Exit.

SCENE 3   AN ANTEROOM IN THE PALACE

FANTASIO, *lying on a rug.* What a delightful trade, that of jester! I was tipsy, I think, when I put on this costume last night, and offered my services at the palace, but in truth, never did sane reason inspire me to any better step than this one stroke of folly. I appeared, and here I am, settled, pampered,

registered—and what is better still—forgotten. I come and go
in this old palace as if I had lived in it all my life. A few
moments ago I ran into the King. He did not even have the
curiosity to look at me; his jester was dead; he was told,
"Sire, here is a new one." Wonderful! At last, thank God,
my brain is relaxed. I can play all the pranks imaginable
without being admonished or stopped by anybody. I am
one of the domestic animals of the King of Bavaria and if
I want to—as long as I keep my hump and wig—I shall be
let live between a spaniel and a canary till the day of my
death. Meanwhile my creditors can break their heads
against my door at leisure. I am as safe here under this wig
as in the West Indies.

But isn't that the Princess I see in the next room through
this glass door? She is fixing her marriage veil; two heavy
tears drop down her cheeks, and one rolls off like a pearl
to her breast. Poor child! This morning I heard her talk
with her governess, truly it was by chance; I was sitting
on the grass without any other purpose than to sleep there.
Now she is weeping, not suspecting that I see her again.
Ah, if I were a student of rhetoric, how deeply I would reflect on this crowned misery, this poor lamb with a pink
ribbon about her throat to lead her to the slaughter. This
little girl no doubt is sentimental. She finds it cruel to marry
a man she does not know. And yet she is sacrificing herself
in silence. How capricious is chance! I had to be tipsy, run
across the funeral of St. John, take his place and his clothes,
in short, I had to commit the greatest folly in the world in
order that I might see, through this door, perhaps the only
two tears that this child will let fall on her sorrowful marriage veil.

SCENE 4   THE GARDEN

THE PRINCE *and* MARINONI.

PRINCE. You are a fool, colonel.

MARINONI. Your Highness is mistaken about me in the most
painful manner.

PRINCE. You are a master-fool. Couldn't you prevent it? I entrust you with the greatest scheme that has been conceived for an incalculable number of years, and you, my best friend, my most faithful servitor, pile up one blunder on top of another. No, really, say what you like, it is unforgivable.

MARINONI. How could I prevent your Highness from drawing upon your head the unpleasantnesses which are the necessary consequence of the role being played? You command me to take your name and to act exactly as if I were the Prince of Mantua. How can I prevent the King of Bavaria from giving affront to my aide-de-camp? You were wrong to intrude into our affairs.

PRINCE. I'd like to see a varlet like you presume to give me orders.

MARINONI. Consider, Your Highness, that in any event I must be either the Prince or the aide-de-camp. It is by your order that I act.

PRINCE. Calling me "impertinent fellow" in front of the assembled court because I wanted to kiss the hand of the Princess! I'm ready to declare war on him, hasten back to my domains and take command of my armies.

MARINONI. But reflect, Highness—that that unfortunate compliment was addressed to the aide-de-camp and not to the Prince. Do you pretend to be respected under that guise?

PRINCE. Enough! Give me back my coat.

MARINONI, *taking off the coat.* If my sovereign requires it, I am ready to die for him.

PRINCE. Truth to tell, I do not know what to decide. On the one hand, I am furious at what happened; on the other, I am heartbroken to have to abandon my scheme; for the Princess does not seem to respond indifferently to the speeches with double meanings that I cease not to pursue her with. Already I have succeeded in whispering in her ear the most incredible things. Come, let us reflect on our situation.

MARINONI, *holding the coat.* What am I to do, Highness?

PRINCE. Put it on again, put it on, and let us go back to the palace.
Exeunt.

SCENE 5 ELSBETH; THE KING.

KING. Daughter, you must answer frankly the question I am going to ask you. Does this marriage displease you?

ELSBETH. It is for you, Sire, to answer that yourself. I am pleased if it pleases you. I am displeased if it displeases you.

KING. The Prince seems to me an ordinary man, of whom it is difficult to say anything. The stupidity of his aide-de-camp is the only thing against him, in my opinion; as for him, he may be a good prince but he is not an outstanding man. There is nothing there that repels or attracts me. What can I say to you? The heart of a woman has secrets that I cannot know; women sometimes take such singular heroes; they so strangely seize upon one or two sides of a man who is presented to them, that it is impossible to judge for them, so long as one is not guided by some tangible clue. Why don't you tell me clearly what you think of your intended?

ELSBETH. I think that he is Prince of Mantua, and that war will break out tomorrow if I do not marry him.

KING. That is certain, my child.

ELSBETH. I therefore think that I shall marry him and that war will be averted.

KING. May the blessings of my people shower gratitude upon thee on thy father's behalf! O, dearest daughter! I am happy about this marriage, but I would not want to see in these beautiful eyes a sorrow that betrays their resignation. Think it over a few days more.

Exit.

Enter FANTASIO.

ELSBETH. Here you are too, poor fellow! How do you like it here?

FANTASIO. Like a bird in freedom.

ELSBETH. Your answer would have been better had you said, "Like a bird in a cage." The palace is pretty enough, but it is a cage just the same.

FANTASIO. The dimensions of a palace or a room do not make

a man more or less free. The body moves where it can; but the imagination sometimes opens wings wide as the sky in a cell not larger than the hand.

ELSBETH. And so, you are a happy fool?

FANTASIO. Very happy. I make small talk with the pastry cooks and the little dogs. There is in the kitchen a little cur not higher than that who has told me charming things.

ELSBETH. In what tongue?

FANTASIO. In the purest idiom. He could not make a grammatical mistake in the space of a year!

ELSBETH. Could I hear a few words in that vein?

FANTASIO. Indeed, I would rather you didn't. It is a special tongue, spoken only by little curs. Trees and wheatsheaves also know it, but King's daughters do not. When is your wedding?

ELSBETH. In a few days everything will be over.

FANTASIO. That is to say, everything will have begun. I intend to give you a gift made by my own hand.

ELSBETH. What sort of gift? I am curious to know.

FANTASIO. I mean to give you a pretty little stuffed canary, which sings like a nightingale.

ELSBETH. How can he sing if he is stuffed?

FANTASIO. He sings beautifully.

ELSBETH. You persist in making fun of me most indefatigably.

FANTASIO. Not at all. My little canary has a little music-box in his little belly. Very genty you push a little spring under his left foot and he sings all the new operas like Jenny Lind.

ELSBETH. An invention of your brain, no doubt?

FANTASIO. By no means. It is a court canary; there are a great many well-brought-up little girls who can boast no other device than that. They have a little spring under their left arm, a pretty little spring with fine jewels like a dandy's watch. Their governor or governess works the spring and immediately you see the lips open with the most gracious

smile: a charming stream of honeyed words bursts forth with
the sweetest murmur, and all the social conventions, like
sprightly nymphs, at once begin their pretty ballet around
the miraculous fountain. The betrothed opens astonished
eyes; the audience whispers indulgently, and the father,
filled with secret happiness, looks down with pride upon
the golden buckles of his shoes.

ELSBETH. You seem most readily to harp on certain subjects.
Tell me, jester, what did the young ladies do to you that
you should always so gaily satirize them? Can respect for
duty of any kind find favor in your eyes?

FANTASIO. I greatly respect ugliness. That is why I respect
myself so profoundly.

ELSBETH. You seem, at times, to know more than you utter.
From where do you come and who are you, that in one day
here you should already have penetrated mysteries that
the princes themselves will never suspect? Is it to me you
address your folly or do you speak by chance?

FANTASIO. By Chance and to Chance. I speak a great deal to
Chance: she is my dearest confidant.

ELSBETH. She seems, indeed, to have told you what you should
not know. I am inclined to believe that you spy on my words
and acts.

FANTASIO. God knows them. What matters it to you?

ELSBETH. More than you think. This afternoon, in that room,
while I was putting on my veil, I heard steps behind the
hangings. I should be greatly surprised if that wasn't you.

FANTASIO. Be assured that it will remain between your handker-
chief and me. I am no more indiscreet than I am curious.
What pleasure could I take in your sorrow? What pain could
your pleasure give me? You are there and I am here. You are
young, I am old; beautiful, I ugly; rich, and I poor. You
see there is no connection between us. What matter to you
that Chance on her highroad should have brought to one
crossing two wheels that do not turn in the same rut, that
cannot make prints in the same dust? Is it my fault if
while I slept one of your tears fell on my cheek?

ELSBETH. You speak to me in the shape of a man whom I loved.

That is why I listen in spite of myself. My eyes believe they see St. John. But maybe you are nothing but a spy?

FANTASIO. What good would it do me? Even if it were true that your wedding has cost you a few tears, and even if I had learned this by chance, nobody would give me a ducat for it nor would you be put in a dark closet. I understand quite well that it must be unpleasant to marry the Prince of Mantua; but after all, I am not the one who has to do it. Tomorrow or the day after you will have left for Mantua with your wedding dress and I shall still be here on my stool and in my old breeches. Why will you have it that I wish you harm? I have no reason to desire your death: you have never lent me any money.

ELSBETH. But if chance has made you see what I want to be kept secret, should I not send you away to prevent another accident?

FANTASIO. Is it your idea to compare me to the attendant in a five act tragedy, and are you afraid that I will follow your shadow, declaiming verses? Don't send me away, I beg of you. I am very happy here. See, there is your governess approaching with her pockets full of mysteries. Proof of the fact that I won't listen to her is that I'm going to the pantry to eat the wing of a chicken that the Majordomo has set aside for his wife.
Exit.

GOVERNESS. Do you know something terrible, my dear Elsbeth?

ELSBETH. What do you mean? You are trembling all over.

GOVERNESS. The Prince is not the Prince, and neither is the aide-de-camp the aide-de-camp. It's a regular fairy tale.

ELSBETH. What plot are you spinning now?

GOVERNESS. Sh-sh! One of the officers of the Prince himself just told me. The Prince of Mantua is a perfect Almaviva; he is disguised and hidden among the aides-de-camp; no doubt he wanted to see and know you as in a story book. He is disguised, the noble lord, he is disguised—as in the *Barber of Seville.* The one who has been presented to you as your future husband is only an aide-de-camp named Marinoni.

ELSBETH. I don't believe it!

GOVERNESS. It is a fact, a thousand times a fact. The noble lord is disguised. It is impossible to recognize him. It is altogether wonderful.

ELSBETH. You were told by an officer?

GOVERNESS. One of the Prince's officers. You can ask himself.

ELSBETH. And he didn't point out among the aides-de-camp the true Prince of Mantua?

GOVERNESS. Just imagine, my dear, that he was trembling also, the poor man, while he was telling me. He has confided his secret only because he wishes to please you, and he knew I would tell you. As to Marinoni, it is positive fact, but the true Prince he did not point out to me.

ELSBETH. If it were true it would be at least something to think about. Do bring me that officer.

Enter a Page.

GOVERNESS. What is it, Flamel? You're all out of breath.

PAGE. Ah, my lady, it was so funny I nearly died. I dare not speak before Her Highness.

ELSBETH. Speak; what's happened?

PAGE. Well, just when the Prince of Mantua came into the courtyard at the head of his suite, his wig rose up into the air and all of a sudden disappeared.

ELSBETH. What do you mean? How silly!

PAGE. Madam, I hope to die if it isn't true. The wig rose up into the air on a fishhook. We found it in the pantry, beside a broken bottle. No one knows who played the joke. But the Duke is none the less furious and he swears that if the criminal is not sentenced to death he will declare war on the King, your Father, and will put everything to fire and sword.

ELSBETH. Come, my dear, let's hear all the details of this story. My seriousness is beginning to desert me.

Enter another Page.

ELSBETH. Well, what news?

PAGE. Madam, the King's jester is in prison. It's he who lifted the Prince's wig.

ELSBETH. The jester, in prison? And on the prince's orders?

PAGE. Yes, Highness.

ELSBETH. Come, mother dear. I must speak with you.
Exit with GOVERNESS.

SCENE 6 THE PRINCE; MARINONI.

PRINCE. No, no, let me drop the mask, it is time I exploded. I won't let the thing go unpunished. Death and damnation! A royal wig suspended on a fishhook! Are we among barbarians? Is this Siberia? Is there no longer under the sun any civilized behavior? I am foaming with anger, my eyes are starting from my head.

MARINONI. You will ruin everything by your violence.

PRINCE. And this father—this King of Bavaria—this monarch vaunted in all last year's almanacs, this man whose exterior is so decent, who talks in such proper language—bursts out laughing when his son-in-law's wig soars in the air! For after all, Marinoni, I admit it was your wig that was lifted, but it is still the Prince of Mantua's, since it is he whom they believe to be you. When I think it might have been I in flesh and blood, *my* wig perhaps—Ah, there is a Providence! When God sent me suddenly the notion of disguising myself; when that flash of genius, "I must disguise myself" crossed my mind, this fatal event must have been foreordained by Destiny. This it is which saved from an intolerable affront the head of my people. But by heaven, everything shall come to light! Too long have I betrayed my dignity. Since human and divine majesty is ruthlessly violated and lacerated, since among men there are no notions left of good and evil, since the king of several thousand men bursts out laughing like a stableboy at the sight of a wig, Marinoni, give me back my coat.

MARINONI *takes off the coat.* If my sovereign commands it, I am ready to suffer for him a thousand tortures.

PRINCE. I know your devotion. Come, I shall tax the king with his guilt without mincing words.

MARINONI. You refuse the Princess's hand? Yet she ogled you throughout dinner in the most obvious fashion.

PRINCE. You think so? I am lost in a morass of perplexities. Come, let's go to the king anyway.

MARINONI, *holding the coat*. What am I to do, Highness?

PRINCE. Put it on again for the moment. You'll give it back to me presently. They will be all the more petrified when they hear me assume my customary tone in this drab coat.

Exeunt.

SCENE 7   A PRISON

FANTASIO. I don't know whether there is a Providence, but it's amusing to believe in it. Now here was a poor little princess who was going to marry against her will a disgusting animal, a provincial boor, on whom chance had let fall a crown, as the eagle of Æschylus let fall the tortoise. Everything was prepared, the candles lit, the bridegroom powdered, the poor child confessed. She had wiped away the two charming tears I saw this morning. Nothing but two or three pieces of hocus-pocus were lacking for her life's unhappiness to be settled. There ran through all this the fate of two kingdoms, the peace of two peoples; and I had to think of disguising myself as a hunchback, and to tipple once again in the pantry of our good king in order to fish up on the end of a string the wig of his dear ally. In very truth, I believe that when I am tipsy I have something of the superhuman. Here is the wedding spoiled and everything once more in debate. The Prince of Mantua asks for my head in exchange for his wig. The King of Bavaria finds the penalty a trifle severe and consents only to imprisonment. The Prince of Mantua, God be praised, is so stupid that he would be hacked to pieces rather than give in; and thus the princess remains a maid, at least for the time being. If there isn't in all this the matter for an epic in twelve cantos, then I am a fool. Pope and Boileau have written admirable verse on subjects of far less importance. Ah, were I a poet, how I would depict the scene of the wig flitting about in the upper air! But the man who would be capable of writing such things will not deign to write them. Well, posterity will have to do without.

He falls asleep. Enter ELSBETH *and the* GOVERNESS, *lamp in hand.*

ELSBETH. He sleeps. Shut the door quietly.

GOVERNESS. Do you see: there is no doubt about it. He has taken off his false wig; his deformity has disappeared at the same time. Here he is such as his people see him on his triumphal chariot: that is the noble Prince of Mantua.

ELSBETH. Yes, 'tis he. Now my curiosity is satisfied. I wanted to see his face, nothing more; let me bend down to look.
She takes the lamp.
Psyche, be careful of the drop of oil.

GOVERNESS. How handsome he looks!

ELSBETH. Why did you give me so many fairy tales and novels to read? Why did you plant in my poor brain so many strange and mysterious flowers?

GOVERNESS. How you tremble on the tip of your little toes!

ELSBETH. He's waking up; let us go.

FANTASIO, *waking.* Is it a dream? I am holding the hem of a white dress?

ELSBETH. Let me go, let me—

FANTASIO. Ah, it is you, Princess. If it is the pardon for the king's jester you bring me so divinely, let me resume my hump and my wig; it will be done in a trice.

GOVERNESS. Oh Prince, how unbecoming of you to deceive us so! Do not put on your disguise again. We know everything!

FANTASIO. Prince! Where do you see a prince?

GOVERNESS. Pray, why dissemble?

FANTASIO. I do not dissemble in the least, by what mischance do you call me Prince?

GOVERNESS. I know my duties towards Your Highness.

FANTASIO. Madam, I beg of you to explain the words of this good lady. Is there really some extraordinary misapprehension or am I the object of some mockery?

ELSBETH. Why ask when it is you who are mocking us?

FANTASIO. Am I perchance a prince?

ELSBETH. Who are you if you are not the Prince of Mantua?

FANTASIO. My name is Fantasio; I am a resident of Munich.
He shows a letter.

ELSBETH. A resident of Munich? Then why your disguise and
what are you doing here?

FANTASIO. Madam, I beg you to forgive me.
On his knees.

ELSBETH. What means this? Get up, man, and go. I grant you
pardon from a penalty you doubtless deserved. What made
you do it?

FANTASIO. I cannot tell you my motive in coming here.

ELSBETH. You cannot? Yet I want to know it.

FANTASIO. You must excuse me. I dare not confess it.

GOVERNESS. Let us go, Elsbeth; do not expose yourself to hearing speech unworthy of you. This man is a thief, or an up-
start who will talk to you of love.

ELSBETH. I want to know the reason that made you assume
this garb.

FANTASIO. I beg you, spare me.

ELSBETH. No, no! Speak or I shall shut this door on you for ten
years.

FANTASIO. Madam, I am riddled with debts. My creditors have
got a judgment against me; at this very moment, my effects
have been sold and if I were not in this prison I should be
in another. They must have called to arrest me last night.
Not knowing where to spend the night, nor how to evade the
pursuit of the marshals, I hit upon this disguise and this
refuge at the feet of the king. My uncle is an old skinflint
who lives on potatoes and radishes, and who lets me starve
in all the wineshops of the kingdom. If you must know, I
owe 20,000 pounds.

ELSBETH. Is all this true?

FANTASIO. If I lie I'm willing to pay them.
A noise of horses is heard outside.

GOVERNESS. Some carriage is going by; it is the king himself. If I could catch the Page's eye. Ho there! Flamel, where are you off to?

PAGE, *from outside.* The Prince of Mantua is about to leave.

GOVERNESS. The Prince of Mantua!

PAGE. Yes, war is declared. There was a terrible scene between him and the king in front of the whole court. The Princess' marriage is off.

ELSBETH. War is declared! What a calamity!

FANTASIO. You call it a calamity, Highness? Would you prefer a husband who makes life and death revolve about his wig? I say, Madam, if war is declared, we shall know what to do with our hands. The idlers in the parks will put on their uniforms; I myself shall take up my musket—if it hasn't yet been sold at auction. We'll take a little tour through Italy, and if ever you enter Mantua, it will be as a veritable queen, without need of any votive candles other than our swords.

ELSBETH. Fantasio, won't you stay as my father's jester? I'll pay your 20,000 pounds.

FANTASIO. I should like nothing better, but, to tell the truth, if I *had* to stay, I should some fine day jump out of the window and run away.

ELSBETH. Why? You know that St. John is dead. We really must have a jester.

FANTASIO. I like the position better than any other, but then, I am not fit to hold any position at all. If you think it worth 20,000 pounds to have been rid of the Prince of Mantua, give them to me and don't pay my debts. A gentleman without debts would not want to be seen anywhere. It has never occurred to me to be without debts.

ELSBETH. Well, I'll give you the money. But take the keys to my garden. Whenever you are tired of being pursued by creditors, come and hide among the tulips where I found you this morning; be careful to have on your wig and your striped suit; don't ever appear before me without your

twisted back and your silver bells, for that's the way I like
you. You'll be my jester for as long as you wish, and then
you'll go back to your affairs. Now you can go; the door
stands open.

GOVERNESS. I can hardly believe that the Prince of Mantua has
come and gone without my ever setting eyes upon him!

THE DIARY
OF
A SCOUNDREL

A Comedy in Three Acts

by

ALEXANDER
OSTROVSKY

English version by
Rodney Ackland

Characters

YEGOR DIMITRICH GLOUMOV,
a young man

GLAFIRA KLIMOVNA GLOUMOVA,
his mother

STYOPKA,
their servant

NEEL FEDOSEITCH MAMAEV,
a wealthy gentleman, a distant relative of Gloumov

KLEOPATRA ILVOVNA MAMEVA,
his wife

KROUTITZKY,
an old man of importance

IVAN IVANOVITCH GORODOULIN,
a young man of importance

SOFIA IGNATIEVNA TOUROUSINA,
a wealthy widow, the daughter of a merchant

MASHENKA,
her niece

YEGOR VASSILITCH KOURCHAEV,
a Hussar

GOLUTVIN,
a man without an occupation

MANIEFA,
a seeress

Companions to Madame Tourousina:
MATRIOSHA
LUBINKA

MAMAEV'S MANSERVANT
GRIGORI,
Madame Tourousina's manservant

THE TIME: 1860.
THE PLACE: *Moscow and outside Moscow.*

ACT ONE

SCENE 1

The living-room of the GLOUMOV *apartment in Moscow. It is rather poorly furnished except for one or two articles which would be more in place in a fashionable drawing-room. There are two doors, one on right, opening on to the hall, the second into the other rooms of the apartment.* STYOPKA, *the servant, lolls in his shirt sleeves, picking his teeth.* GLOUMOV *is pacing the room. Going to the door up-stage, he calls out:*

GLOUMOV. Get on with those letters, Mamma!

MADAME G., *off*. There's not a bite to eat in the house!

GLOUMOV. We'll have plenty to eat if you do what I tell you.

MADAME G., *entering*. I wish you'd find someone else to write them.

GLOUMOV. Oh, don't argue!

MADAME G. *to* STYOPKA. Get up! Lolling about in here! Your place is in the kitchen. The samovar's not been polished for weeks.

STYOPKA. No, and I've not been paid for weeks. Not since the old man died.

MADAME G. Don't speak of your sainted master like that! God rest his soul. Go on, go away, I hate the sight of you.
Going to the desk she gets out paper, pen and ink.

STYOPKA. Well, I don't like it here. I'm not used to living in pokey apartments. I'm the only one that stayed on with you when you moved to this place. You ought to be grateful to me.

41

MADAME G. The greatest calamity that ever happened to this country was the freeing of the serfs!

STYOPKA. I wouldn't stay at all if it wasn't for the young master. It's only a matter of time before he'll put us on our feet in a fine mansion again.

GLOUMOV. Well, go and arrange that business with Mr. Mamaev's manservant. How much of your savings have you got left?

STYOPKA. Only about 200 roubles, sir.

GLOUMOV. Nonsense. You've got at least 500. Lend me another fifty.

STYOPKA, *grumbling under his breath, produces an old purse and fumbles in it.*

MADAME G., *who has been copying out a letter.* What's this word, Yegor? I can't understand your writing. Kourchaev is a *what?*

GLOUMOV, *looking over her shoulder.* "Vile seducer."
Taking the money from STYOPKA.
Thanks. . . . Here you are, here's five for the Mamaev job, five to replenish the larder, and two for yourself.

STYOPKA. Thank you very much, sir.
He goes towards the door upstage.

GLOUMOV. And don't pay for the food unless you have to.

STYOPKA, *off.* Very good, sir.

MADAME G., *looking after him.* Disgusting dolt!
To GLOUMOV.
Give me ten of those roubles. I haven't had a new hat since your father died, and then I only had one every three months. Stingy old devil!
GLOUMOV *gives her the money. She grabs it from him.*

GLOUMOV. Get on with the letters, do!

MADAME G. What's the good? Madame Tourousina will never let you marry her niece. The dowry of 20,000 roubles——

GLOUMOV. That's exactly why I've chosen her.

MADAME G. They could get a prince or at least a general for that. Kourchaev won't get her either, so I can't see the point of these anonymous letters about him. Your own second cousin, too!

GLOUMOV. As if that mattered to you! You know his type—a typical Hussar—if he had money he'd only lose it at cards.

MADAME G. If I could see any *good* coming of them.

GLOUMOV. That's my business.

MADAME G. What chance do you think there is?

GLOUMOV. Every sort of chance. My dear Mamma, you know me: I'm intelligent and malicious, envious of anyone better off than myself. In fact, I take after you. Yet what did I do when Papa was alive and we had money? Nothing but hang about feeling bored and bad-tempered and writing lampoons on everybody in Moscow. Now that I've got to make a place for myself I've realised it's not enough to make fun of all the stupid people who run this city. One must know how to take advantage of their idiocies. Unfortunately it's no good thinking of a career in Moscow. The only thing they do here is talk. All one can hope for is a bride with a fat dowry and an important job with no work and a fat salary.

MADAME G. Where are you going to get that?

GLOUMOV. In the Civil Service, of course. But how do people succeed in Moscow? Not by doing anything, merely by talking. Talk is the only thing that matters here. And nobody likes talking better than I do. So what is to prevent my success in the hot air spouters' Paradise? Nothing.

MADAME G. Well, stop talking and let me write these anonymous letters.

GLOUMOV, *moving about the room looking for something.* Have you moved my diary, Mamma?

MADAME G. It's on the table over there.

GLOUMOV, *taking it.* Thank you. What a mistake I made with my lampoons and malicious epigrams! I've finished with all that!
Throwing himself into a chair.

From now on it's to be nauseating, toadying flattery, the only language the élite of Moscow understand. I shall begin with Madame Tourousina's circle. When I've squeezed that dry, I shall move on to the next.

MADAME G. Oh stop, my head's aching. What's this? Kourchaev's a what? "Well-known"
trying to decipher it.
"criminal?"

GLOUMOV. No, liberal, liberal. . . . But do you know what I intend to do, Mamma, while I'm flattering these stupid fools? I must have some outlet for my feelings or I should go mad.
Holding up the book.
It will be this, my diary. All the bitterness that boils up in my soul I shall get rid of here, and there'll be nothing but honey on my lips. Alone, in the silence of the night, I shall write these chronicles of human triviality entirely for myself. I shall be both author and reader.
There is a loud peal at the front door bell.

MADAME G. Styopka!

STYOPKA *lounges in, pulling on his jacket.*

STYOPKA: It's that military gentleman in the Hussars. I saw him getting out of a cab with another gentleman. They both looked tipsy to me.

MADAME G., *to* GLOUMOV. Kourchaev! What does he want?

GLOUMOV. Nothing, I dare say. To show off his stupidity.

MADAME G., *following* STYOPKA. Do up your coat, take those sunflower seeds out of your mouth! Ten years ago you'd have got a good beating!

STYOPKA, *going into the hall.* Well, it's not ten years ago.

MADAME G., *hurrying back to the table.* I'd better hide those letters! And Yegor, put that diary away. You don't want people prying into it.

GLOUMOV. Leave them, leave them, Mamma.

STYOPKA, *announcing.* Mr. Kourchaev and Mr. Golutvin.

KOURCHAEV *is a typical Hussar of the period. Tall, slim,*

with a military bearing and vacuous expression. He is in that pleasant stage of intoxication which shows itself in an unwonted enthusiasm and expansiveness. His friend, a few years older, dressed in an exaggeration of the latest fashion which borders on the ludicrous, has had an equal amount to drink.

KOURCHAEV. Gloumov, my dear fellow, I want you to meet a very great friend of mine—oh, a thousand pardons, Madame Gloumova.

Clicking his heels and kissing her hand.

Are you keeping in the best of health?

MADAME G. Not too well. . . . It's only six weeks since my sainted husband was taken from me, God rest his soul. But I'm bearing up somehow for the sake of Yegor, poor boy I'm bearing up. . . .

KOURCHAEV. Allow me to present a very great friend of mine—Golutvin.

GOLUTVIN, *kissing* MADAME GLOUMOVA's *hand.* Enchantée, Madame.

GLOUMOV, *to* STYOPKA, *idly watching in the doorway.* Styopka, go and attend to that job. At once, do you hear me?

STYOPKA. Very good, sir.

Goes out.

KOURCHAEV, *leading* GOLUTVIN *towards* GLOUMOV. I know you'll like each other. Golutvin's a devilish clever fellow. Gloumov —Golutvin.

Almost pushing GOLUTVIN *into* GLOUMOV's *arms.*

There, I'm entrusting him to you.

GLOUMOV, *turning and putting his diary into a drawer.* I can't accept the responsibility.

He adds.

This isn't the first time I've met Mr. Golutvin.

GOLUTVIN. I don't think I cared for the tone of voice.

MADAME G., *sotto voce.* The poor boy's not himself since he lost his sainted father, God rest his soul. Pray be seated both of you. If you'll excuse me, I have some correspondence to finish.

She seats herself at the desk and continues writing during the following scene, occasionally glancing up at KOURCHAEV.

GOLUTVIN. } Merci, merci, Madame. Trop gentille, trop aimable.

KOURCHAEV. } Certainly, certainly.... Sit here, Golutvin.

GLOUMOV. May I ask to what I'm indebted for this visit? I have very little time to spare, gentlemen. What's it about?
He sits down.

GOLUTVIN, *after exchanging glances with* KOURCHAEV. Mon cher ami, have you any verses?

GLOUMOV. Verses? You must have come to the wrong place.

GOLUTVIN. Mais non, mais non! Vous êtes trop modeste, mon cher.

GLOUMOV, *to* KOURCHAEV, *who, seated at the table, has picked up a pencil and is drawing something.* I say, do you mind not scribbling on my papers?

KOURCHAEV. My dear Yegor, apologies. . . . Now look here, we know perfectly well you've got some of those—what are they called? Um, you know, funny verses about fellows.

GOLUTVIN. Lampoons.
Turning to GLOUMOV.
In a word, my dear sir, we want lampoons—you've got them.

GLOUMOV. I'm sorry. I've none at all.

KOURCHAEV. Now, now, come on, we know. . . . Several fellows have told us. You've got a lot of devilish funny lampoons on everybody in town. Be a good fellow and help my very dear friend, Golutvin here. He wants to get a job writing the gossip column in a newspaper.

GLOUMOV. Oh, does he?
To GOLUTVIN.
Have you ever written anything?

GOLUTVIN. *Anything?* I've written everything. Novels, stories, plays, articles, epics——

GLOUMOV. Have you had them published?

GOLUTVIN. Oh no, they've none of them been published.

KOURCHAEV. They're much too good, that's the trouble.

GLOUMOV. Have you read them?

KOURCHAEV. No, but he's told me about them——

GOLUTVIN, *to* GLOUMOV, *interrupting.* Nobody's interested in anything but scandal today. So I want to start on that now. Writing scandalous paragraphs.

GLOUMOV. Oh, I shouldn't do that. It might be dangerous.

GOLUTVIN. Dangerous? What do you mean—that I might be set upon at night, attacked on my way home?

GLOUMOV. You'd undoubtedly get a few horsewhippings.

GOLUTVIN, *after a slight pause.* Never in Moscow, my dear friend, we leave that sort of thing to other—less civilised cities.

GLOUMOV. Well, go on then, write.

GOLUTVIN. But whom am I to write about? I don't know anybody.

KOURCHAEV. Look here, Yegor, we've heard that you've got some sort of diary in which you've pulled everybody to pieces——

GOLUTVIN. I hear it's the most delicious, malicious gossip in Moscow. *Do—do* lend it to me.

GLOUMOV. I haven't a diary.

KOURCHAEV. Now come on, you can't keep up this pretence with us.

GOLUTVIN. All I want is the material. Think of the money we could make with your material and my talent.

KOURCHAEV. Be a good fellow, Yegor. He really needs the money. He has to drink at other fellows' expense. It's humiliating for him.

GOLUTVIN. And I want to work—to work! All I need is the material.

GLOUMOV, *getting up.* I have none.

Taking up a paper from in front of KOURCHAEV.

What's this picture of a hippopotamus?

KOURCHAEV. It's not a hippopotamus. It's my respected uncle, Neel Fedoseitch Mamaev. Drawn as a hippopotamus, of course.

GOLUTVIN. Tell me, is he an interesting personality? Would he be of interest to me, for instance?

KOURCHAEV. He's a horrible old bore. He thinks himself the brainiest man in Moscow and all he does is lecture people for their own good.

GOLUTVIN. Is he rich? Important?

KOURCHAEV. That's the trouble, he's got a lot of money to leave so I'm always having to ask him for advice. Nothing gives him greater pleasure.

GOLUTVIN, *taking the drawing from* GLOUMOV. Excusez moi, monsieur. Now all we need is an amusing title for this picture and we'll sell it to the papers. Write underneath, er, now let me think of something really witty. . . . Write . . .

A flash of inspiration.

The Talking Hippopotamus.

KOURCHAEV *does so, laughing.* Talking hippopotamus. . . . But look here, we can't have it published. After all, he is my uncle.

GLOUMOV, *taking the paper from him, he slips it into his pocket.* And my cousin, incidentally.

GOLUTVIN. Tell me more about him. Has he other characteristics that I could satirise?

KOURCHAEV. In my opinion he's not all there. For three years he's been looking for a new apartment. He doesn't really want one. It's simply an excuse to go about talking and boring people—but it looks as if he's doing something, at least. He drives off in the morning, looks over about ten apartments, has a talk with the landlords and the porters, then he makes a round of the grocers' shops to taste the caviar and smoked herrings. He plants himself down and starts to bore the unfortunate shop assistants. The poor fellows don't know how to get him out of the shop, but he's delighted with himself and thinks he's spent a profitable morning.

Turning to GLOUMOV.

By the way, his wife, my Aunt Kleopatra, is in love with you.

GLOUMOV. Oh, really?

KOURCHAEV. She saw you at the opera the other day. "Who's that? she kept asking me. Her eyes were nearly popping out of her head and she practically twisted her neck off. . . . I mean it. . . . This is no joke, you know.

GLOUMOV. I'm not joking. It's you who treat everything as a joke.

KOURCHAEV. Well, anyway, you take my advice.

With a glance at MADAME GLOUMOVA, *then sotto voce*.

I should follow that up if I were you. . . . Now, are you going to let us see that diary of yours?

GLOUMOV. No.

KOURCHAEV. Be a good fellow.

GOLUTVIN. Just a tiny peep.

GLOUMOV *doesn't answer*.

Some lampoons then. . . .

Diminuendo.

Just one lampoon . . . an epigram.

GLOUMOV. I've told you I have none.

GOLUTVIN, *suddenly springing up and making for the door*. Oh, what's the use of talking to him? Let's go and get some dinner.

Bowing to MADAME GLOUMOVA *on his way out*.

Bonjour, madame. Merci.

MADAME G., *smiling politely*. Going so soon?

Turning to KOURCHAEV.

Oh, this correspondence! My poor brain! Even my spelling goes. How many l's are there in "villainous"?

KOURCHAEV. Villainous—er—let me see . . . two.

MADAME G. Of course. Thank you.

KOURCHAEV. Can I be of assistance? Shall I have the letters delivered for you?

MADAME G. You're too kind. I couldn't put you to so much trouble. Good-bye. Come and see us again soon. Always delighted to see you.
She holds out her hand which he kisses.

KOURCHAEV. Indeed I will.
He clicks his heels, and is on his way out when GLOUMOV *stops him.*

GLOUMOV. What on earth are you doing with a creature like that?

KOURCHAEV. Devilish clever fellow. I like clever people.

GLOUMOV. You've most certainly found one there.

KOURCHAEV. Clever enough for us anyway. Really intelligent fellows wouldn't bother with fellows like us.
He goes.
GOLUTVIN *has been waiting for him outside the front door. As soon as the door is closed* GLOUMOV *drops his stiff attitude, bursts into laughter and strides about the room in a high state of elation.*

GLOUMOV. It's working, it's all working, Mamma! Exactly as I'd planned. I knew Cousin Kleopatra had seen me from her box. I took good care that she should. She got an excellent view of my profile and I tried to look exceedingly romantic.

MADAME G. This Mamaev, her husband, he's the person you must get hold of. Why should Kourchaev get a legacy from him? *You* must get it instead, Yegor. Shall I send an anonymous letter to *him?*

GLOUMOV. No, no, I've got everything planned. I know all about Mamaev. He has at least fifty nephews and cousins, including myself whom he hasn't met yet. He picks on one of them, makes a will in his favor until he gets sick of him, then he forbids him the house, chooses another one and renames his will again. . . . But Kourchaev won't last long. This little drawing of a hippopotamus

taking it from his pocket
should prove very useful.
Replaces it carefully.
You see, once I'm friendly with the Mamaevs I'm on the first rung of the ladder. Through them I can meet Kroutitzky and Gorodoulin who are not only extremely important in the Civil Service—*but*—they are intimate friends of Madame Tourousina. And once I've gained entrance to her house, there's nothing to stop me.

MADAME G. That's all very well, dear, but the most difficult step is the first.

GLOUMOV. Don't worry, I've taken it. Mamaev's coming here this morning.

MADAME G. What do you mean?

GLOUMOV. He likes looking over apartments. I found that out some days ago. Styopka is out arranging with Mamaev's servant to bring the old fellow here.
The front door bell rings.
Going towards the door.
If this is Madame Maniefa, be as nice to her as possible. In fact, be more than nice to her.

MADAME G. Indeed I won't! Why should I lower myself in front of a disgusting, common, creature? A low fortune-teller reeking of vodka!

GLOUMOV. A "clairvoyante", Mamma. And a very useful ally. She's going to tell fortunes at Madame Tourousina's next Wednesday. Time enough for you to play the grand lady when I'm married to Tourousina's niece. For the moment all I ask is your help. You must treat Maniefa as if she were an archbishop. When she moves about the room we must support her under the armpits like acolytes when a bishop's saying Mass. She expects that. And give her what's left of the vodka.
He opens the door. An enormous woman with a florid complexion, a magnificent shawl wrapped round her, is revealed on the threshold. She is holding on to the doorpost and breathing heavily.
Madame Maniefa! Mamma! It *is!* It's Madame Maniefa!

Our prayers are answered. Will you come in, Madame Maniefa? Isn't this a great honour, Mamma?

MANIEFA, *coming ponderously into the room.* Are you fleeing the vanities of the world, young man?

GLOUMOV. Oh, indeed I am. But I need your help, dear Madame Maniefa—your holy influence. Mamma, get Madame Maniefa a chair.

MANIEFA, *lowering herself into it with painful groans and grunts.* Oh, my back! Ah! . . . that's better.

Rubs her diaphragm and belches.

It's that tea they gave me where I called last. Something told me that would be an evil house.

She takes no notice whatever of MADAME GLOUMOVA *who has been madly bowing and curtseying.*

GLOUMOV. Do you think a little drop of vodka would put you right? Mamma, bring the vodka for Madame Maniefa.

MADAME GLOUMOVA *goes to get it.*

GLOUMOV. You do too much, you know. You ought to think of yourself more.

MANIEFA, *her eyes fixed on the bottle which* MADAME GLOU-MOVA *has produced.* Flee—flee from the vanities of the world. . . . At one pious household I was in today they gave me money for charity. They gave alms through my hands. The holy saints prefer alms to flow through holy hands instead of sinful ones.

She watches intently as MADAME GLOUMOVA *pours her out some vodka.*

GLOUMOV. And *such* holy hands! . . .

Taking out some money.

May I humbly offer twenty roubles?

MANIEFA, *putting the money in her bag.* Blessed are they that give. . . . Could you make it thirty?

GLOUMOV. Twenty-five.

MANIEFA *without replying, holds out her hand for the other five roubles and drains the vodka in one gulp.* STYOPKA *comes in, his arms filled with provisions—loaves, cooked sausages, smoked herrings, a bottle of wine.*

STYOPKA. It's all arranged, sir. The gentleman's on his way here now.

GLOUMOV. Madame Maniefa, will you stay and share our humble meal?

MANIEFA, *her eyes greedily on the food.* A few crusts—that's all I need.

GLOUMOV. Perhaps you'd like to rest first? . . . Mamma, take Madame Maniefa to your room.

Placing a hand under the Prophetess's armpit and signalling to his mother to do the same on the other side—which she does with a surreptitious grimace.

MANIEFA. Ooooh . . . my back. . . . God's chosen ones are sorely afflicted. . . .

They lead her to the door.

Flee . . . from the vanities of the world.

She glances over her shoulder at the vodka bottle.

GLOUMOV. Mamma! Take the vodka bottle with you! Madame Maniefa is worn out with her holy work.

MADAME GLOUMOVA gives her son a look of suppressed fury, darts back, and snatches up the bottle and glass. They lead MANIEFA off. STYOPKA *lays out the food on a table.* GLOUMOV *comes back.*

You didn't *pay* for that, Styopka?

STYOPKA. Bless you no, sir. It's from Smirnoff's where Mr. Kourchaev shops. I put it down to his account.

GLOUMOV, *tasting a piece of smoked herring.* Good. How much did you give Mr. Mamaev's servant?

STYOPKA. Three roubles.

GLOUMOV. I must put all this down.

Gets his diary and sits at the table with it.

Let's see, Maniefa—twenty-five roubles, Mamaev's servant —three roubles. . . .

The front door bell rings.

STYOPKA, *going to answer it.* That'll be him. . . .

MADAME G., *putting her head round the door.* Lying on my bed! I shall have to have it disinfected now.

GLOUMOV. Don't come in till I call you. Go back and stay with her.

MADAME G., *withdrawing*. Disgusting creature—I was saving that vodka for my birthday.

SERVANT, *appearing*. I've brought Mr. Mamaev—I don't know how he'll take it. I told him this was a *nice* apartment.

GLOUMOV. Here you are—here's another rouble.

SERVANT. Very good, sir.
Goes out.

GLOUMOV. Go on, Styopka—into the kitchen.

STYOPKA, *going*. Good luck, sir. . . .
Sotto voce.
He's a silly old fool. I've seen him.
GLOUMOV *sits at the desk and pretends to be working. MAMAEV, a short fat gentleman, overcome with the heat and the climb up the stairs, enters followed by his servant.*

MAMAEV, *mopping his brow*. What's this—a bachelor's apartment?

GLOUOV, *bowing to him and continuing with his work*. Yes, it is.

MAMAEV, *ignoring him*. Wouldn't be so bad, decently furnished, but what's the good of a bachelor apartment to me?
To servant.
What did you want to bring me here for?

GLOUMOV, *pushing forward a chair and again busying himself with his writing*. Do sit down.

MAMAEV, *sitting down without looking at him*. Thanks. . . .
What's the point of bringing me here?

SERVANT. Sorry, sir.

MAMAEV. You know perfectly well a bachelor apartment's no good to me. A place like this for a Minister of State! . . . You know quite well that Madame Mamaeva likes to keep open house.

SERVANT. Sorry, sir.

MAMAEV. Where's the drawing-room?

SERVANT. Sorry, sir.

MAMAEV. Don't "sorry sir" me! . . . Damn stupidity.
As though seeing GLOUMOV *for the first time.*
There you are, you see, there's a man sitting here writing. We're probably disturbing him only he's too polite to say so; and it's all your fault, you silly fool!

GLOUMOV. Please don't blame him! I happened to hear him inquiring about an apartment in this building and I suggested mine. I'm afraid I didn't realise you were a family man.

MAMAEV. Are you the owner of this apartment?

GLOUMOV. Yes.

MAMAEV. What do you want to let it for then?

GLOUMOV. It's beyond my means.

MAMAEV. Why take it then in the first place? Who forced you to? Were you dragged here by the scruff of your neck? That's right—take an expensive apartment with no money to pay for it. And now, of course, you don't know which way to turn! Oh, I know, I know . . . and after getting used to spacious surroundings you'll have to come down and live in one room with bare boards and an oil store. You'll enjoy that, won't you?

GLOUMOV. Well, as a matter of fact, I'm planning to move to a bigger apartment.

MAMAEV. A bigger one! You haven't got the means to keep up this and you want to take a bigger one. Are you quite right in the head? Is that the reason?

GLOUMOV. No, I don't think so. . . . It's just stupidity.

MAMAEV. Stupidity, what nonsense!

GLOUMOV. I wish it were, but I'm just plain stupid.

MAMAEV. Stupid, that's funny. In what way stupid?

GLOUMOV. I'm a bit simple . . . not enough brains. There's nothing funny in that, is there? It's quite usual.

MAMAEV. Now this is very interesting—a man accuses himself of being stupid.

GLOUMOV. Well, it comes better from me than other people. I mean I'd rather say it first. It's no use my trying to hide it.

MAMAEV. Yes, of course, it's rather difficult to hide a defect like that.

GLOUMOV. I never try to.

MAMAEV, *shaking his head.* Tch, tch, tch, very sad, most regrettable.
GLOUMOV *inclines his head.*
There's no one to teach you, to guide you, I suppose?

GLOUMOV. No one.

MAMAEV. But there *are* teachers. Very intelligent teachers, but nobody listens to them these days. Of course, you can't expect much from the old folks. Most of them imagine just because they're old, they must be intelligent and in no need of instruction—but when the youngsters won't listen to you either, well, what's the world coming to? Take one case for instance, I stopped a schoolboy who was rushing away from school. "Yes," I said, "you rush out of school fast enough, but it's a different story hen you're going to school in the morning. You creep along slowly enough then, I'll be bound." Well, you'd think any decent boy would be grateful that a man of my standing should bother to stop in the street and talk to him, but not a bit of it with this young puppy. Instead of kissing my hand as you'd expect, do you know what he said?

GLOUMOV. No.

MAMAEV. "Save your lectures for your fat wife," he said. Then he stuck out his tongue, called out a rude name and ran off.

GLOUMOV. Disgusting! . . . Well, poor lad, I suppose he'd got no one to set his footsteps on the right path.

MAMAEV. Exactly. Do you know why servants are so bad nowadays? Because they no longer have to look to their masters for instruction and guidance. In the old days I used to advise my employees on the conduct of every detail of their lives. I used to lecture them all—from the highest to the lowest. I used to spend about two hours on every one of them giving them instructions. I used to rise to the very highest spheres of thought and there he'd be standing in front of me—so overcome that by the time I'd finished he'd be worn out with sighing. It was good for him and a noble occupation for me. But all that's changed now—since the great calamity. You know what I'm referring to?

GLOUMOV. The freeing of the serfs?

MAMAEV, *shaking his head and drawing his breath between his teeth.* The worst thing that ever happened to this country. You try lecturing a servant these days. You give him one or two lectures on metaphysics or something exalted and he goes and gives notice. "What's this a punishment for?" he says. "I haven't done anything." Yes, a punishment he calls it—a punishment!

GLOUMOV. Oh, it's wicked, really wicked!

MAMAEV. You know, I'm not a stern man, I do it all with words. Not like some of these nouveau riche gentlemen. When they have to reprimand a servant they catch hold of him by the hair and pull it at every word. I've seen them. He understands it better that way, they say. Makes it more comprehensible. Well, that's not my method. Do it all with words, I say, but do you think they're grateful to me? Not a bit of it.

GLOUMOV. Yes, it must be heart-breaking for you.

MAMAEV. Heart-breaking? Every time I think about it it's like a knife going through me here.
Pressing his hand to his chest.

GLOUMOV. Where did you say a knife was going through you?
Indicating on his own chest.
Here?

MAMAEV. No, no, not there. Here.

GLOUMOV. What, here?

MAMAEV. No, higher up. Look . . . here.

GLOUMOV. Oh, I see. Here.

MAMAEV. No, no, not there at all. Higher up I tell you.

GLOUMOV. Do forgive me. I told you I was stupid.

MAMAEV. Yes, I'm afraid you are. . . . It's a very great disadvantage but it can be overcome if you've elderly, experienced friends or relations to advise you.

GLOUMOV. That's just the trouble. I haven't anyone like that. There's my mother, of course, but she's even more stupid than I am.

MAMAEV. Tch, tch, tch, it's a very bad position for a young man to be in.

GLOUMOV. I *have* got an uncle in Moscow, at least, he's really only a cousin but I think of him as my uncle——

MAMAEV. Well, can't you go to him?

GLOUMOV. I wish I could. I hear he can give invaluable advice out of his great fund of knowledge and experience. But he doesn't even know of my existence and nothing would induce me to scrape acquaintance with him.

MAMAEV. That's a most regrettable attitude to take.

GLOUMOV. Oh, you misunderstand me! If he were poor like myself I'd kneel in front of him, I'd kiss the hem of his garment. But he's rich, he's a great man in Moscow. If I were to go and ask for his advice he'd think I'd come for money. How could I explain that I didn't want a farthing from him, that all I wanted as the help and guidance that he alone could give me, that I'm thirsting and starving for those divine words of guidance, for some heavenly lecture that would drop from his lips like manna from heaven! . . . Oh, if he were only poor and I could meet him, I'd listen to him day and night!

MAMAEV. Mmm. . . . You don't appear to be as stupid as you say.

GLOUMOV. Yes, at times lucid moments come over me—a fog seems to clear from my brain, but only for a second; most of the time I feel as if I'm not quite all there. That's where I need someone to advise me.

MAMAEV. And who is this cousin—this uncle?

GLOUMOV. I hardly remember his name. I think it's, um . . . it's Mamaev, I think. Neel Fedoseitch Mamaev.

MAMAEV. Mamaev! . . . And may I ask what is your name?

GLOUMOV. Gloumov. Yegor Gloumov.

MAMAEV. Dmitri Gloumov's son?

GLOUMOV. Yes.

MAMAEV. Well, God bless my soul, what an extraordinary thing!

GLOUMOV. Did you know my father?

MAMAEV. Why I am that very Neel Fedoseitch Mamaev that you're speaking of.

GLOUMOV. *What?*

MAMAEV. Yes, it's me—it's I—it's me!

GLOUMOV. Oh good heavens! You're Uncle Mamaev! I can hardly believe it! Oh uncle, you *will* let me call you uncle, won't you?
Almost in tears.
Please let me take your hand, let me look at you. Oh, but uncle, I've heard you don't like your relations. I quite understand you must know so many wonderful people, but don't worry, I shall never intrude on you. It's quite enough for me that I've seen you in the flesh and talked to you. I shall never forget what you've said to me. The wonderful advice you've given me today.

MAMAEV. My dear boy, whenever you want advice about anything come to me.

GLOUMOV. But I *always* need it, uncle, always.

MAMAEV. Well, there you are. Come in tonight.

GLOUMOV. Oh, how can I ever thank you! But I must break the wonderful news to Mamma. Do you think I might present her to you?

MAMAEV. Well, why not? Fetch her in.

GLOUMOV, *calling out.* Mamma! She's not very brilliant I'm afraid, but she's got a heart of gold.

MADAME GLOUMOVA *comes in. Going to her.*

Mamma, darling, what *do* you think, only you must promise
me not to cry.

To MAMAEV.

It may be too much for her.

Turning to his mother again.

Who do you think has turned up? It's Papa's dear second
cousin, Mr. Mamaev—for years Mamma's been longing
to meet you.

To MADAME GLOUMOVA *again.*

Isn't it wonderful, Mamma, and he's going to let me call
him uncle.

MADAME G. Indeed, I've always longed to see him.

Coming down to MAMAEV.

I've heard so much about you from dear Dmitri, my sainted
husband, God rest his soul. Why you were almost the last
person he spoke of before he passed away, do you remember,
Yegor? . . . And to think God has sent you to us at last.
Weeps.

MAMAEV. } Come now, you mustn't take it like this.

GLOUMOV. } Mamma, darling, you promised not to cry.

MADAME G., *through her tears.* Oh no, I can't help it. I know it's
stupid of me. . . . But they say that uncle doesn't like his
relations. God has sent him to us and now he'll snatch himself away again.

MAMAEV. No need to get upset. After all, there are relations
and relations.

MADAME G., *wiping her nose and drying her eyes.* You must
forgive me, it's the shock coming so suddenly like this. . . .
But let me look at you, dear Neel Fedoseitch. Dmitri's own
second cousin! . . . But Yegor, he's not a bit like it.

During the ensuing scene, STYOPKA *enters and unobtrusively
lays the table for a meal.*

GLOUMOV, *in a hoarse whisper.* Mamma!

He nudges her violently.

MADAME G. What's the matter? He isn't like it, is he, you
can't say he is.

MAMAEV. What is all this? Who is it I'm not like?

GLOUMOV, *to* MADAME GLOUMOVA. Why must you blurt things out like this? Don't listen, uncle, she's only talking nonsense.

MAMAEV. Oh no, one must tell the whole story or nothing at all.

MADAME G. I'm simply saying that the portrait isn't a bit like you.

MAMAEV. What portrait? Where have you got a portrait from?

MADAME G. Well you see, Yegor Kourchaev comes to see us sometimes. He's a nephew of yours too, isn't he?

GLOUMOV. Such a charming fellow.

MAMAEV. Yes? well, and what?

MADAME G. He happened to draw a picture of you. Yegor, show it to uncle.

GLOUMOV. Oh, Mamma! I really don't know where I put it.

MADAME G. Oh well, do find it. He was drawing it just now, you remember, and who was that with him, that peculiar man, you know, who writes rude rhymes about people? Kourchaev said, "I'll draw a picture of my uncle for you and you write something underneath." I was in the room, I heard them.

MAMAEV. Show me this picture. Show it to me!

GLOUMOV, *handing it to him.* Mamma, you really ought to be more discreet!

MAMAEV. That's right, teach your mother to be a hypocrite.
Looks at the picture.
What's this, a—a hippopotamus? What's it say underneath?

GLOUMOV, *looking over his shoulder.* Uncle Mamaev, the talking hippopotamus.

MADAME G. Talking hippopotamus, that's it.
A pause.

MAMAEV, *suddenly crumpling the picture up in his fist.* If that young man dares to show his face in my house again, I—I'll teach him! So that's gratitude, after all I've done, young blackguard! I've advised him, I've lectured him, I've tried to put him on the right path. Well, thank the lord my eyes have been opened anyway. . . .

To GLOUMOV.

Do you draw libellous portraits of me, young man?

GLOUMOV. Oh uncle, please, what do you take me for?

MAMAEV. Well, you must come round this evening without fail. I shall expect you, and you too, Madame Gloumova.

MADAME G. Oh no, let Yegor go alone. I'm sure you don't want me to come, boring you with my nonsense.

MAMAEV. Not at all, my wife will be delighted.

He makes for the door, GLOUMOV *following.* MAMAEV's *servant holds the door open for them.*

GLOUMOV. Mamma and I will look forward to it. What time will you expect us then?

MAMAEV. Any time after eight o'clock.

GLOUMOV. What a wonderful chance your coming here today.

At door.

Good-bye, uncle.

MAMAEV. Good-bye. Don't come before eight or we shan't have finished supper.

Calling out to servant as he goes toward the stairs.

Come on, hurry up. Don't stand there gaping like a half-wit!

Servant hurries after him.

GLOUMOV. Good-bye, Uncle.

He half closes the door and turns to the others. STYOPKA *bursts into peals of long-suppressed laughter.* GLOUMOV *comes back into the room. He speaks jubilantly, signing to* STYOPKA *to be quiet.*

It's working, it's working—everything's working according to plan!

STYOPKA, *doubled up with merriment.* Oh! . . . the old codger's face when he saw the hippopotamus! I thought I'd burst, I really did.

MADAME G. Be quiet, can't you? He'll hear you on the stairs. Dolt!

STYOPKA. I said he'd soon have us all on our feet in a fine mansion again, didn't I?

MADAME G. Don't put the smoked herring on the table like that. Put it on a plate properly.

GLOUMOV. Mamma, you were very helpful indeed about the picture. Thank you.
Embraces her.

MADAME G., *modestly.* Oh well, I was only doing my best.

GLOUMOV. Come on, let's begin, I'm hungry.
All three seat themselves at the table.

MADAME G. This must have cost a few roubles.

GLOUMOV. It's all right. He got it on Kourchaev's account.

MADAME G. Good. Open the wine, Styopka.

GLOUMOV. Better call Madame Maniefa in.

MADAME G. She's asleep, let's leave her. She'd put me off my food.

STYOPKA. The old gentleman's face when he saw the hippopotamus!
Imitating him.
"If that young man dares to show his face in my house again!"
They all choke with laughter.
KOURCHAEV *bursts in at the front door. He is pale and trembling with fury.*

KOURCHAEV. Has my uncle been here?
They stop laughing abruptly. All three turn and look at him, then STYOPKA *jumps up and pretends to be waiting at table.*

GLOUMOV. Yes, why? And do you mind knocking before you come in?

KOURCHAEV. Have you been discussing me with him?

GLOUMOV. Discussing you? Why should I be? He just came in to see the apartment.

KOURCHAEV, *advancing into the room.* I don't believe it, do you
hear me? It's a plot, that's what it is. It's some devilish plot
against me.

MADAME G. Don't raise your voice in front of me, please.

KOURCHAEV. I'm sorry but I can't control myself. I ran into my
uncle in the street just now and he told me he never wanted
to see my face again. Can you imagine that?

GLOUMOV. I'm imagining it. Can you imagine it, Mamma?

KOURCHAEV. I go to Madame Tourousina's and she refuses to
see me—sends up one of her so-called companions, one of
those disgusting hangers-on of hers to forbid me the house!
Do you hear what I'm saying?

GLOUMOV. Yes, I hear.

KOURCHAEV. I demand an explanation of it!

GLOUMOV. Why come to me for an explanation? If you want to
know I should think the explanation's in the sort of life
you lead.

KOURCHAEV. It's no different from any other fellow's Whatever
I may have done, it's no reason to—break off a fellow's engagement to a girl, to take a fellow's legacy away.

GLOUMOV. And what about your friends? Golutvin for instance.

KOURCHAEV. Golutvin?

GLOUMOV. Yes, Golutvin!
Springing to his feet.
How dare you bring that creature to this house?! How dare
you introduce him to my mother!

MADAME G. Yes, how dare you!

GLOUMOV. I happen to be particular about the people I mix
with. I must protect Mamma and myself against the re-
currence of such an incident, therefore I ask you kindly
not to visit us again.

MADAME G. I should think not!

KOURCHAEV, *to* GLOUMOV. Have you gone mad?

GLOUMOV. Mr. Mamaev's thought it fit to turn you out and I wish to follow his example, that's all. Styopka, show this gentleman the door.

KOURCHAEV. All right, all right, I'm going. But let me tell you this, if this is your work, my fine fellow, if my suspicions prove correct, you'd better look out. I'm warning you, take care, that's all.

GLOUMOV. I shall take care when it's necessary, but at the moment I see no serious danger.

STYOPKA. This way, sir.

Holding the door open.

KOURCHAEV *glares at* GLOUMOV *for a second, then turns on his heel and marches out.* STYOPKA *closes the door, bursting into raucous laughter again.* GLOUMOV *and his mother join in, then still laughing start to pile into the food.* STYOPKA *sits at the table again and helps himself.* MANIEFA *appears, the empty vodka bottle in her hand and a tipsy smile on her face. She moves unsteadily to the table.*

Curtain.

ACT ONE

SCENE 2

The MAMAEVS' *house. A conservatory. At the back is a door leading to the ballroom, which is obscured by palms, ferns and trellis-work. A ball is in progress and gay music can be heard throughout the scene. Two elderly gentlemen are heard.*

MAMAEV, *off.* Yes, we are going somewhere, we're being led towards something or other;

Entering, followed by KROUTITZKY.

but neither we nor those who are leading us know whither we're going, or what we're going to do when we get there.

KROUTITZKY *is as tall, thin, pallid and distinguished, as* MAMAEV *is short, red-faced, fat and commonplace.* MAMAEV *has a plate of "refreshments" which he is eating with his fingers.*

KROUTITZKY. The younger generation can't settle down. They want to alter everything: let's try this, let's try that, I'll alter this, I'll change that. It's easy enough to change anything. The furniture in this conservatory for instance, I can take it and I can stand it upside down— there's change for you: but what of the centuries of wisdom, of experience, which lie behind the making of a table with four legs to stand on? There stands a table on four legs and does it stand firmly?

MAMAEV. Firm as a rock.

Places his hand on it. It wobbles.

Oh, something's wrong with the leg.

Bending down and peering at the leg.

It needs a wedge underneath.

KROUTITZKY. That's beside the point. Now we'll take the table and we'll turn it upside down.

They do so.

There you are, you see, we've done it.

MAMAEV, *proudly surveying their handiwork.* That's it, we've done it.

KROUTITZKY. So much for change.

Sitting down, they contemplate the upturned table. KROUTITZKY *adds.*

Or we could lay it sideways.

MAMAEV *gets up.*

No, no, upside down is more telling. This should show the younger generation what their passion for change will lead to.

MAMAEV. But will they see?

KROUTITZKY. Well, if they don't they must be taught to see. There are people capable of teaching after all!

MAMAEV. Yes, I know there are, but the tragedy of it is they won't listen. They don't want to listen to men of intelligence and wisdom.

KROUTITZKY. It's our own fault. We may know how to express our opinions in words but that's not enough. We should write them. Only the young people write nowadays. That's the answer to the problem. One must write more, write, write.

MAMAEV. It's all very well to say write, but you've got to have the knack of it. One may be the most intelligent man in Moscow and yet not have that particular knack. Take myself for instance: I can express myself in words. If you asked me to I could start talking now and continue till this time tomorrow, but if you asked me to write—I couldn't do it, merely because I haven't got the knack. . . . Have you got the knack?

KROUTITZKY. Oh yes, I write a great deal.

MAMAEV. Ah well, I suppose some people are born with it.

KROUTITZKY. The time has gone when a command of language is sufficient to make oneself felt. In these days one must have command over the pen.

MAMAEV. Yes, but suppose one lacks the knack. It's not a question of intelligence.

KROUTITZKY. Oh no, no, I wasn't suggesting such a thing. . . . By the way, do you happen to know of a young man, fairly well-educated, of fairly good family, who could express on paper ideas, thoughts, plans for the improvement of the Russian people, for instance?

MAMAEV. Yes. I know exactly the young fellow you want.

KROUTITZKY. He mustn't be one of these frivolous, free-thinking young men one finds today, always gossiping and turning everything to ridicule.

MAMAEV. Not in the least! But I'll present him to you later.

KROUTITZKY. Is he here now—in the ballroom?

MAMAEV. He's not turned up yet.

KROUTITZKY. The truth is I've worked out a very important Plan for the Improvement of the Russian Peoples. Well, as you know, I'm a man who's been educated in the old school.

MAMAEV. And a far, far better one, too.

KROUTITZKY. So naturally I express myself in the old style, the—how shall I describe it—well, if I may say so, in the style of the great Lomonosoff.

MAMAEV. Ah, Lomonosoff, yes, the Russian Shakespeare!

KROUTITZKY. Not at all. Shakespeare was the English Lomonosoff. But as I was saying, if one writes nowadays in the style of Lomonosoff or Sumarokoff one would only be laughed at; so do you think this young friend of ours might, well, slightly rewrite my work for me in the less eloquent language of today?

MAMAEV. I don't see why not.

KROUTITZKY. I should pay him adequately, of course.

MAMAEV. Even if you gave him too little, he'd consider it an honor.

KROUTITZKY. I wouldn't care to be under an obligation to him, er—what did you say his name was?

MAMAEV. My cousin, my dear cousin, Yegor Dimitrich Gloumov.

MADAME MAMAEV *hurries in from the ballroom followed by* MADAME GLOUMOVA. KLEOPATRA IVOVNA MAMAEVA *is a woman in her forties, over-dressed in a style too young for her, exceedingly vain and making much coy play with her fan.*

KLEOPATRA, *as she enters.* He has everything one hopes to find in a young man, charm good manners, looks.

Seeing MAMAEV *and* KROUTITZKY.

Oh, you two naughty men! Boring each other in here. You should be entertaining the guests. Yegor and dear cousin Glafira have arrived. Let me present you—Glafira Gloumova —Mr. Kroutitzky.

MADAME G., *as* KROUTITZKY *takes her hand.* I'm quite bewildered at so much splendour—so many distinguished gentlemen, but it's always the same at Cousin Kleopatra's.

Turning to MAMAEV.

I've a bone to pick with you, dear Neel Fedoseitch.

MAMAEV. What about?

MADAME G. You're taking my son away from me. He doesn't love his poor old mother any more. It's uncle this, uncle that, "nobody's as clever as uncle" he says.

MAMAEV. He's a good boy, a good boy.

KLEOPATRA. And so charming, so modest. He doesn't want to dance with any of the young girls in the ballroom. He's quite content just to sit and watch or to talk to his auntie.

KROUTITZKY *to* MAMAEV. Is this the young man you were speaking of?

MAMAEV, *leading the way to the ballroom.* Come in and meet him.

MADAME G., *following them, determined to get a few more words in.* He was always the same, even as a tiny boy. He'd never forget to kiss Papa and Mamma good night.

MAMAEV *and* KROUTITZKY *are forced to stop and listen to her. She continues.*

And he'd kiss all his grandmammas and grandpapas good night too, and even great aunt Eudoxia Gregorovna he'd kiss, although she had a big wart and quite a long moustache. I shall never forget one morning, he put his little head round the door, "Mamma," he said, "I dweamt about ve angels las' night. Two ever such booful angels flew wite up to my cot and vey said, Love papa and mamma and obey vem in everyfing and never forget when you gwow up always love your elders and betters and obey vem too. And I said fank you, fank you, booful angels and I'll always obey evwebody." I can see it as if it were yesterday, with his little head poking round the door and his lovely long ringlets hanging round his face.

KLEOPATRA. Oh, the darling pet!

MAMAEV. I'm very pleased with your son. You can tell him that. I'm very pleased with him.

He follows KROUTITZKY *who goes into the ballroom, then coming back to* MADAME GLOUMOVA *says, confidentially.*

I know your husband's death left you in a bad way. Tell you what, you come and see me one morning, and I'll give you some. . . .

MADAME G. Oh, it's too kind of you. I couldn't take it.

MAMAEV. Not money. Something much better. Advice. You bring your household accounts to me. I'll go through them and see what items you can cut out.

He goes into the ballroom.

MADAME G. Oh, you're too good to us, dear Kleopatra. If it hadn't been for you, poor Yegor would have lived out all his life in obscurity—never going anywhere or meeting anyone.

KLEOPATRA. Oh, but we'd have been bound to notice him some time or other.

MADAME G. I don't see why. You have to be clever for people to notice you.

KLEOPATRA. Not at all. There's no need for a great brain when you're as handsome as Yegor. What does he want a brain for, he's not going to be a professor. A good-looking young man can always find somebody who'll help him simply out of sympathy. Either to make a career or just with money so that he can live comfortably. With a clever man it's different. Nobody minds if they see a clever man shabbily dressed, living in a cheap apartment and dining off a cold sausage and a piece of bread—that doesn't bring a lump to your throat and make you feel you must do something for him. You expect a clever man to live like that. But when you see a poor boy who's young and handsome, shabbily dressed, then it's unbearable. It mustn't be allowed, no, and it won't be, never. I'll see that it isn't!

MADAME G. What an angel you are. An angel!

KLEOPATRA. The women of Moscow must band together! We must insist that our friends, our husbands, all the authorities rise to their feet to help him. We simply cannot allow a handsome young man to be spoilt by poverty. There are so few of them nowadays. Of course, we should sympathise with all poor people, it's our duty, that goes without saying —but to see a handsome young man with sleeves too short, or frayed shirt collars, that's what touches the heart! And besides a man can't be bold and dashing when he's poor, he can't have that conquering expression, that air of jauntiness which is so pardonable in a handsome young man.

MADAME G. Yegor's so grateful to you, dear Kleopatra. And no one knows how to be grateful better than he does.

KLEOPATRA. That's very pleasant to hear.

MADAME G. It's more than gratitude even. He positively adores you both.

KLEOPATRA. Adores? . . . Aren't you exaggerating?

MADAME G. Not a bit. It's part of his character, his beautiful soul. Of course, it's not for me to praise my own son and he hates my talking about him, but——

KLEOPATRA. Oh, please go on. I promise not to tell.

MADAME G. Well, there's no one in the world like you two, he thinks. Neel Fedoseitch's brain, well you know what he thinks about that, but your beauty—well, he says it's indescribable. It should be immortalised on canvas.

KLEOPATRA. Oh, really! . . . Did he really say that?

MADAME G. And shall I tell you something else he said to me —no, perhaps I hadn't better.

KLEOPATRA. *Do* go on, please. What was it he said?

MADAME G. Well, promise not to be angry with me.

KLEOPATRA. No, no, of course not.

MADAME G. I'm so stupid, I always blurt everything out.

KLEOPATRA, *eagerly.* Yes, yes, what was it he said?

MADAME G. Well, "Auntie's an angel," he said to me one day. "An angel," and all at once he put his head on my bosom and burst into tears.

KLEOPATRA. Oh! . . . Whatever made him do that? . . . How strange. . . . What else did he say?

MADAME G., *hesitantly.* It's . . . it's not so much what Yegor said in words, but dear Kleopatra, do forgive him, he's only a young man and you know what young men are. I'm afraid he has a passionate nature—how can I explain? . . . He's like a volcano underneath, and ever since he's met you, well, I'm frightened all the time that any moment he might erupt.

KLEOPATRA, *faintly.* Oh! . . . Do you think he might?

MADAME G. Oh dear, I'm afraid I've said too much and spoilt everything, but . . . whatever he feels for you it's purely as a relation. . . . And yet, one has to admit at his age the proximity of a beautiful woman—well he never sleeps a wink at night after seeing you . . . I can hear him tossing and turning.

KLEOPATRA. Tell me. . . . Does he confide in you? . . . Or does he hide his very deepest feelings?

MADAME G. From his mamma? Never! He's just like a little boy, he tells me everything.

KLEOPATRA. Yes . . . a little boy . . . but like a volcano, too. What he wants is an experienced woman to guide him.

MADAME G., *fervently.* Oh, couldn't it be you!

KLEOPATRA, *laughs delightedly.* You're very fond of him, I can see that.

MADAME G. Fond? He's my only child.
As though carried away.
I love him, I love him!

KLEOPATRA, *taking her hand.* We must love him together.

MADAME G. We must! We will!
They embrace. MADAME GLOUMOVA *apparently recovering from overwhelming emotion, blows her nose.*
I don't know what Yegor would say if he knew I'd told you all this. You'll never let him know, will you? Promise?

KLEOPATRA. Darling, never, never.
Clasping her hands.

MADAME G. Only, you see, he feels quite ashamed of his poor old mother sometimes because she's so stupid. I know he does.

GLOUMOV, *entering from the ballroom.* Oh!
As though taken aback at seeing KLEOPATRA.
I was looking for Mamma. I didn't know you were with her, auntie.

KLEOPATRA. Come in, come in. There's nothing to be afraid of. Why so shy still?

GLOUMOV. If you and Mamma are talking. . . .

MADAME G. Auntie's had quite enough of my foolish nonsense,

I'm sure. Kleopatra, dear, let me get you some refreshments. You've been so busy with your guests you've had nothing.
She makes for the door.

KLEOPATRA. No, no thank you. How thoughtful you are. Get yourself something, darling.

MADAME G. Don't you worry about silly old mother.
To GLOUMOV.
You mustn't be so bashful, dear. Stay and talk to auntie. You must learn how to behave with young, beautiful ladies, mustn't he, Kleopatra? . . . But you'll soon learn; auntie will teach you. . . .
She goes out.
A pause. KLEOPATRA *waits for him to speak but he stands bashfully in front of her like a schoolboy.*

KLEOPATRA. Come. Sit down next to me.
He does so awkwardly.
You must be more free and easy in your manner. After all, I'm only a human being like everybody else, am I not?

GLOUMOV. Yes, Auntie.

KLEOPATRA, *tapping with her fan.* And don't call me auntie all the time.

GLOUMOV. May I really call you—Kleopatra?

KLEOPATRA. Of course, silly boy—and why aren't you more open with me?

GLOUMOV. Open?

KLEOPATRA. Yes. I feel that something's worrying you. I see a wild look in your eyes sometimes. Couldn't you tell me what it is? I might be able to help you.

GLOUMOV. Oh, if only I could! If only you were——

KLEOPATRA. Were what?

GLOUMOV. A middle-aged woman.

KLEOPATRA. But I don't want to be a middle-aged woman.

GLOUMOV, *with sudden passion.* The very thought of it's unbearable! What I mean is if you weren't so young and beautiful I wouldn't feel so shy.

KLEOPATRA. Now sit closer and tell me everything frankly. Why wouldn't you be so shy if I were a middle-aged woman?

GLOUMOV. A young woman has her own affairs, her own interests, she's no time for bothering about her poor relations! Whereas a middle-aged woman has nothing else to do.

KLEOPATRA. And why can't a young woman take an interest in her relations?

GLOUMOV. She can, but one wouldn't like to ask her. One's afraid of boring her. Her life's full of gaiety and amusement. The last thing in the world she wants to see is some dull nephew or cousin with a long face, always importuning her with tedious requests. With a middle-aged woman, it would be different. She'd have a new interest in life. She'd enjoy bustling about Moscow using her influence for him, and letting all her friends know what a kind heart she had.

KLEOPATRA. Well, suppose I were a middle-aged woman, what would you ask me to do for you?

GLOUMOV. But you're not, you're a very young woman. You're trying to catch me.

KLEOPATRA. Well, it's all the same. Go on—suppose I were middle-aged just for the sake of argument.

GLOUMOV. It's not all the same but—well, for instance, I know you'd only have to say one word to Ivan Gorodoulin and I should get a good post in the Civil Service.

KLEOPATRA. Yes, one word to Gorodoulin would be enough.

GLOUMOV. But I wouldn't bother you with such a tedious request.

KLEOPATRA. Why not?

GLOUMOV. To begin with, it wouldn't be fair to ask him.

KLEOPATRA. Not fair, why?

GLOUMOV. Because he's in love with you.

KLEOPATRA. What makes you think that?

GLOUMOV. I'm certain of it.

KLEOPATRA. What a lot you know! And can you tell me what I feel towards him?

GLOUMOV. Only you know that.

KLEOPATRA. Aren't you . . . interested in what I feel?

GLOUMOV. It's not for me to pry into your secret feelings.

KLEOPATRA. Well, what would *you* feel if you thought that I returned his passion?

GLOUMOV, *after hesitating.* I only know this, there's nothing Gorodoulin dare refuse you. He'd be delighted if you asked a favor of him so to make you ask him for something for me would be like giving him a bribe.

KLEOPATRA. Sheer imagination! So you don't want me to speak about you?

GLOUMOV. Positively not. I couldn't let myself be indebted to you. What could I do to repay you?

KLEOPATRA. How would you repay—a middle-aged woman?

GLOUMOV. Oh, that would be simple! I should pander to her, indulge her whims, carry her dog, push the footstool towards her, keep kissing her hand and telling her she didn't look a day over twenty-five. But unless she were middle-aged, there'd be no point in all that.

KLEOPATRA. No, of course not.

GLOUMOV. And I daresay I'd soon become very attached to her if she were kind and charming. Really fond of her, in fact.

KLEOPATRA. But couldn't you become fond of a young woman?

GLOUMOV. I could, but I wouldn't dare to!

KLEOPATRA, *behind her fan.* At last! . . .

GORODOULIN *appears in the door of the ballroom. He is a man of thirty-five or so, consciously sophisticated.*

GORODOULIN. Am I intruding?

KLEOPATRA, *starting but quickly recovering herself.* Come in,

Ivan. I was thinking of you only a moment ago. Let me present my cousin, Yegor Dimitrich Gloumov—Ivan Ivanovitch Gorodoulin.

The two men bow.

Yegor, be a dear boy and fetch me a glass of wine.

Fanning herself.

It's insufferably hot tonight.

As YEGOR *reaches the door, his mother appears carrying some refreshments and peering into the conservatory with an eager, crafty expression. Unseen by the others, he intercepts her, pushing her back into the ballroom in front of him.*

KLEOPATRA. Why pursue me in here when there are so many eligible young ladies to dance with?

GORODOULIN. I can't even see them. I may appear calm, Kleopatra, but there's a tumult in my brain and a storm of passion in my heart.

KLEOPATRA. That's very nice of you. I'm very glad I'm not entirely forgotten—poor, lonely, neglected me.

GORODOULIN. Who is this man who dares to neglect you? Is he here? Point him out to me, that's all. I'm in a particularly pugnacious mood today.

KLEOPATRA. You're the principal culprit. It's you who deserve to be shot—or at least punished in some way.

GORODOULIN. At your fair hands, lady, I don't mind which.

KLEOPATRA. I've already thought of a punishment for you.

GORODOULIN. What is it? To be strangled in your embrace?

KLEOPATRA. No, I'm going to ask a favour of you.

GORODOULIN. Oh, I see, you wish to reverse our roles.

KLEOPATRA. What do you mean?

GORODOULIN. You wish to come to me in the humble role of a petitioner.

KLEOPATRA. Are you a petitioner? I thought you were a judge or likely to become one, one day.

GORODOULIN. Yes, but with women I'm always——

KLEOPATRA. Do stop being fatuous. I've serious business to discuss.

GORODOULIN. I'm all attention.

KLEOPATRA. My nephew is badly in need of a——

GORODOULIN. Of a what? A new school uniform, some white mice?

KLEOPATRA. Oh, don't be tiresome. Listen to me and don't interrupt. He's not really my nephew, he's my cousin—the young man you've just met and he's very charming, intelligent, and good-looking.

GORODOULIN. So much the worse for me.

KLEOPATRA. He wants a job.

GORODOULIN. What do you fancy for him?

KLEOPATRA. An important job in the Civil Service. He's extremely capable.

GORODOULIN. In that case they wouldn't want him.

KLEOPATRA. I shall become very bored with you in a moment and we shall quarrel. Do you know of a post for him?

GORODOULIN. Well, I might know of something for an ordinary young man: for a paragon of intelligence, I should find it difficult. Let's have a look at this phenomenon, and I'll tell you what I could recommend him for.

KLEOPATRA, *as* GLOUMOV *comes in.* Thank you, Yegor.
Getting up and going towards him.
How kind of you.
Taking the wine he's brought her.
Now I shall leave you two men together. I'm neglecting my guests.
Raising her glass.
Here's to your friendship. . . . I shall come back in a little while and see how you've got on.

GLOUMOV, *opening the door for her.* Allow me.

*She gives him a languishing glance and goes out. He turns
to* GORODOULIN.

What a charming woman my cousin is.

GORODOULIN, *without enthusiasm.* Yes, charming, charming.
A pause.
Ever been in the Civil Service?

GLOUMOV, *jauntily.* I was once but I gave it up.

GORODOULIN. Why?

GLOUMOV. I hadn't the qualifications for the job. Whatever
qualities I may have, they're not much use there.

GORODOULIN. Surely all one needs is an average brain and the
ability to work a few hours a day.

GLOUMOV. I wouldn't say I was lacking in either of those qualities, but are they likely to get one anywhere? They might
be enough if one's content to finish one's life as a petty
government official. If you're to go on without influence
some very different qualities are necessary.

GORODOULIN. What, for instance?

GLOUMOV. One must be able to keep one's reasoning powers
in abeyance unless specifically ordered to use them, to
laugh loudly but not too loudly, when one's boss unbends
enough to make a joke, to do all the thinking for one's su-
periors as well as all the work for them, at the same time
giving the impression that you're unutterably stupid and
that they've thought of everything themselves. Besides
this, you must have several sycophantic qualities which
at the same time mustn't be too obvious; for instance, as
soon as your boss enters the office you must jump to your
feet and spring to attention in a way that's both obsequious
and yet not obsequious, cringing and yet at the same time
noble and trustworthy. Then when he sends you for something you must tear off to get it but without giving the impression of an undignified rush. Something between a
mazurka, a gallop, and a goose step.

GORODOULIN, *laughing.* You put it most amusingly. But it
doesn't hold good still. Things have changed in the last
few years.

GLOUMOV. I don't see any difference. It's all papers and forms, the entire Civil Service is like a fortress made of papers, forms, and red tape. The unfortunate ciitzens of Moscow have to cower before it under an incessant bombardment of circulars, orders, forms, and certificates.

GORODOULIN. Do you realise that you've a considerable talent for expressing things?

GLOUMOV. I'm so glad you sympathise with my ideas. There aren't many people who would.

GORODOULIN. It's not the ideas! Anyone can have ideas. It's the wording, the phrasing that's good. Would you do me a very great favour?

GLOUMOV. Of course. What?

GORODOULIN. Write all that down on paper.

GLOUMOV. Of course, if you want it—but what for?

GORODOULIN. I'll be quite frank with you. I wouldn't dream of telling this to anybody else, but you and I understand each other. We are both men of principle, we can be completely open. The trouble is I've got to make an after-dinner speech tomorrow and I simply haven't had the time to think.

GLOUMOV. Well, of course I'll help you.

GORODOULIN, *patting his hand.* Do this for me as a friend.

GLOUMOV. Don't say another word about it. No, you give me a job where I can be of some use to my fellow men, where I can study them—study their daily needs and see that they're satisfied promptly and sympathetically.

GORODOULIN. That's wonderful, really wonderful! Would you mind writing that down too. . . . Now I think the best post for an honest, idealistic man like yourself would be as head of some State philanthropical institution.

GLOUMOV. I don't mind what work I do as long as it would be useful and constructive, would augment the quantity of good necessary for the well-being of the masses.

GORODOULIN. I say, would you write that down too? "To augment the quantity of good——" that's very fine indeed.

GLOUMOV. Would you like me to write the whole speech for you?

GORODOULIN. Would you really? There you are, you see, we've only spoken a few words and we're friends in no time. Simply because we share the same principles and ideas.

Glancing at his watch.

I'd better go back and have a word with Kleopatra. Poor soul, she will give these insufferable receptions; she's the only one who enjoys them and one spends the evening waiting on and flattering her because one can't afford to fall out with the old man. . . .

Going towards the ballroom.

Are you coming?

GLOUMOV. Not for a moment.

GORODOULIN. But you talk so well, my dear fellow! We need men like you in Moscow! A pity there aren't more like you. *He goes.*

Left to himself GLOUMOV *produces a notebook and writes in it.*

MADAME G., *putting her head round the door, then coming into the conservatory carrying a plate of caviar with which she is stuffing herself. She says conspiratorially.* Oh, you're alone. How did everything go? What did she say?

GLOUMOV. I can't tell you now, Mamma. Don't interrupt me.

MADAME G. What are you doing?

GLOUMOV. Making notes for my diary. I must put everything down while it's fresh in my mind.

MADAME G., *peering over his shoulder.* Have you put down everything she said to you? This caviar's delicious. I've got four pots in my bag to take home.

GLOUMOV. Do leave me alone, Mamma.

MAMAEVA *comes in.*

MAMAEV. Just the man I'm looking for.

MADAME G. Oh, I won't disturb you if you two want to talk. *Scuttling out.*

Go on, go on, don't take any notice of me. Silly old mother, always in the way.

GLOUMOV. Yes, Uncle?

MAMAEV. Here, come here.

Mysteriously.

I've been talking to Kroutitzky; he wanted my advice on a certain matter. Very decent old fellow—he's written a treatise, an article or something, and wants it polished up a bit. I mentioned your name. He's not particularly bright, poor fellow. It's probably all a lot of drivel, but when you see him just flatter him a bit.

GLOUMOV, *in a shocked voice*. Oh, Uncle! You're asking me to do a thing like that!

MAMAEV. I'm not suggesting one should flatter people all the time, but there's no harm in just buttering him up a bit. Just one or two compliments on his style or something will give pleasure to the poor old fellow. He can be useful to you at the moment. Later on, we can abuse him as much as we like, but not for the moment. He's gone now, but I'll take you to see him tomorrow. Then there's another rather delicate matter. . . . What exactly are your relations with your aunt?

GLOUMOV. I beg your pardon, Uncle?

MAMAEV. How are you behaving to her?

GLOUMOV. Correctly, I hope, Uncle.

MAMAEV. Never mind correctness! If you don't understand what I'm driving at, you must listen and learn. And be grateful you have someone to teach you! Women aren't interested in correctness of behaviour. All they want is their beauty to be recognised.

GLOUMOV. Oh yes, yes, uncle, of course, how stupid of me! It simply never entered my head!

MAMAEV. Well, there you are, my boy. I know of course you're really only a second cousin of ours, or something, but still you are related. You can be much freer with my wife than if you were just a mere acquaintance; there's no reason why you shouldn't sometimes, say . . . absentmindedly kiss

her hand—then having kissed it once, kiss it again, or . . .
do something with your eyes. I suppose you know how to
do it?

GLOUMOV. I'm afraid I don't.

MAMAEV. Good heavens, you've a lot to learn! Well, like this.
Rolls up his eyes.

GLOUMOV. Don't, don't, Uncle. What on earth are you doing?

MAMAEV. You just practise it properly in front of a mirror. Then
you must sigh sometimes. That always goes down very well
with them.

GLOUMOV. What sort of sigh should I give, Uncle?

MAMAEV. You know the sort of thing. Very languid, as if you
couldn't stand it any longer. Like this.
Heaves deep sigh.
But it needs practice, mind. You must practise it.

GLOUMOV. I will, indeed, I will, uncle, and thank you very, very
much for your advice.

MAMAEV. Not at all, my boy. I feel much easier in my mind now
I've spoken to you. Do you understand?

GLOUMOV. No—I'm afraid I don't.

MAMAEV. Bless the boy! Well, she's a woman of very—ah—passionate temperament. She gets very easily heated. It's quite
on the cards that she might become infatuated with some
young scoundrel, one of these dandies, you know the sort of
type. You never can tell, she might even fall in love with
an escaped convict. Whereas here you are, a decent young
fellow, one that I can heartily approve of—in the words of
the old proverb: the wolf will be satisfied and the sheep
will remain untouched.
Laughs loudly.
Now do you understand?

GLOUMOV. I can hardly speak, uncle.

MAMAEV. Hardly speak, why?

GLOUMOV. It takes my breath away, the amazing power of your
brain!

MAMAEV. Well, it's always at your service, my boy, as long as you come to me for advice.

GLOUMOV. Uncle . . . I've had an idea. I don't suppose it's much good but——

MAMAEV. Come on, let's hear it.

GLOUMOV. Well, you know how careful one has to be in Moscow society—there's so much whispering and scandalmongering. Now suppose you were to introduce me to Madame Tourousina, for instance, I could openly pay court to her niece and even propose to her if you approved. All eyes would be fixed on that and no one would notice what Aunt Kleopatra and I were doing. Then indeed the wolves really would be satisfied and the sheep remain untouched.

MAMAEV. Good, my boy, good! A very sound idea.

GLOUMOV. Of course, it wouldn't do to let Auntie know anything about it. Not that she'd be jealous but—it's always best to use a little tact with women.

MAMAEV. Don't I know it! We won't say a word to her then—not a word!

GLOUMOV. Er—when did you say you were taking me to Madame Tourousina's, Uncle?

MAMAEV. Any time you like. Tomorrow evening? And don't forget to do everything I've told you. As soon as we get there, start on the niece.

KLEOPATRA, *entering from the ballroom, followed by* GORODOULIN. No, no, no, not tonight. I'm grateful for your help, Ivan, but not tonight.

To MAMAEV.

Ivan's going now.

MAMAEV. So early?

Shaking hands with him.

Well, glad you could come.

GORODOULIN. It's been enchanting.

To GLOUMOV.

Goodby. Let me know when you've completed that little matter we spoke of.

GLOUMOV. I shall send it to you in the morning.

MAMAEV. Er—Gorodoulin, I want a word with you in connection with the club. I want to give you some advice.

GORODOULIN, *hastily*. I—I haven't time, if you'll excuse me.
Looking at his watch.
I'm in a great hurry, I really haven't a minute. Goodnight, Kleopatra.
Kisses her hand. To GLOUMOV.
Au revoir.

MAMAEV, *following him out*. That's all right, I'll walk part of the way with you. I can give you some advice on the way.

KLEOPATRA, *sinking into a chair*. Well, I've settled it.
She holds out her hand for him to kiss.
A job for you. And a very good one too, in the Civil Service.

GLOUMOV. Oh, Kleopatra!
Kisses her hand.
Why did you do it? I'd never have asked you to do a thing like this for me.

KLEOPATRA. You'd no need to. I guessed.

GLOUMOV, *impulsively, kissing her hand again*. Thank you! Thank you!
Suddenly he dashes off in the direction of the ballroom.

KLEOPATRA, *sharply*. Where are you going?

GLOUMOV. To find Mamma. I'm so happy. I must share my happiness with her.

KLEOPATRA. Are you sure you're happy, Yegor?

GLOUMOV. As happy as I can ever hope to be.

KLEOPATRA. Do you mean—there's something lacking to make your happiness complete?

GLOUMOV, *after a pause*. There's nothing more I dare hope for.

KLEOPATRA. Now come, be frank with me. What do you want more than anything in the world?

GLOUMOV. I've a job in the Civil Service. What more could a man ask?

KLEOPATRA. I don't believe it—not for a moment! You expect me to believe that you, Yegor, with your eyes, your brow— are a common materialist who wants nothing more from life than a weekly salary and a job in the Civil Service.

GLOUMOV. Kleopatra! . . .

KLEOPATRA. You expect me to believe that your heart never beats, that you never dream, never cry, never lie awake at nights, that you love no one?

GLOUMOV. No, no, Kleopatra, I didn't say that.

KLEOPATRA. Then you do love someone?
He hangs his head.
I knew it, I knew it, and she doesn't love you in return. Who is she, tell me, who is this cruel woman?

GLOUMOV. Oh my God, Kleopatra, this is agony!

KLEOPATRA. Tell me, tell me, Yegor, I insist. I know it all, I can see it in your eyes. Poor darling boy, are you suffering very much?

GLOUMOV. Don't, I can't bear it! In a minute I shall have to tell you! It's not fair to try and trick me like this.

KLEOPATRA. Who is she, who is it you love?

GLOUMOV. Have pity on me, for the love of heaven!

KLEOPATRA. Is she worthy of you?

GLOUMOV. Oh, my God, what are you doing to me!

KLEOPATRA. Is she capable of responding to your passion? Could she understand your noble suffering heart?

GLOUMOV. Kill me, kill me with your own hands, Kleopatra, but I dare not tell you!

KLEOPATRA, *faintly.* Whisper, only whisper the name.

GLOUMOV. The name of the woman I love?

KLEOPATRA. Yes. . . .

GLOUMOV, *falling on his knees.* You.

KLEOPATRA. Ah. . . .

GLOUMOV. Beat me, kill me, punish me in any way you will,
only don't send me away from you! Force me to be silent,
forbid me even to look at you any more, tell me I'm to be
cold and distant to you, but don't, don't I beg of you, be
angry with me! It's all your own fault! Why were you so
kind, so enchanting, so gracious to me? If you'd been harsh
and cruel, then I might have kept my passion within the
bounds of decency! But you heavenly adorable woman,
angel of goodness that you are, you've turned me, a sane,
reasonable man, into a crazy madman!

Springing to his feet.

Yes, I am mad! I'm not responsible for my actions any more.
One moment longer with you and I don't know what I
might do! . . . Oh my God, what have I said? Forgive me,
forgive me.

*Flinging himself on his knees again and trying to kiss the
hem of her garment.*

KLEOPATRA. I forgive you, Yegor.

*Springing up again he clasps her in his arms. They kiss.
He gives her a wild look and dashes back to the ballroom.
The band strikes up a furious gallop, and* KLEOPATRA *sinks
on to a chair in a swoon of delight.*

Curtain

ACT TWO

SCENE 1

*The drawing-room of a country house a few miles outside
Moscow. Two elderly women,* MADAME TOUROUSINA'S *"companions," are enjoying a siesta.* MATRIOSHA, *round and
plump, warms herself before the stove, her skirts pulled
over her knees.* LUBINKA, *an untidy, witch-like creature,
nods over a bottle of vodka and some playing cards. At
the sound of raised voices in the passage, both open their*

eyes with a start and busy themselves, MATRIOSHA—*after pulling her skirts down—with some sewing snatched up from the floor,* LUBINKA, *hastily concealing the vodka bottle, with laying out the cards.*

MADAME T., *off.* No, no! I won't set foot outside the house again today!

MATRIOSHA *and* LUBINKA *exchange glances.*

MASHENKA, *off.* Oh, Auntie, *please,* Auntie!

MADAME TOUROUSINA, *a woman in her late forties, still beautiful in spite of her unhealthy pallor, enters, followed by her niece,* MASHENKA.

MADAME T. Not for anything in the world. It would be sheer madness. Besides I've had the horses unharnessed.

Sinking into a chair, a hand to her brow.

Oh, I'm quite exhausted. Matriosha—the footstool.

MATRIOSHA *heaves herself up and brings the stool over.*

MATRIOSHA. Aren't you going for your drive, dear?

LUBINKA, *coming down from card table.* I told you she'd be ill today. I saw it in the cards.

MATRIOSHA. Yes, she told me.

MASHENKA. Auntie's not ill. What *is* the matter, auntie darling? It's the first time for months we've been for a drive, we hardly get ten yards from the gates and we have to turn back again!

Flinging herself disconsolately into a chair.

MADAME T. Why run into danger when it's not necessary?

MASHENKA. But what danger? I didn't see any.

MADAME T. I really wonder sometimes, darling, whether you're quite right in the head. You must have seen that white cat cross the path in front of us as we came out of the gates.

MATRIOSHA, *in a tone of alarm.* It crossed the path in front of you?

LUBINKA. From the right or the left, was it?

MADAME T., *dramatically.* From the *left.*

LUBINKA
MATRIOSHA }*gasping and shaking their heads.* Tch, tch, tch.

MATRIOSHA. You poor dear. It must have given you a shock.

MADAME T. I wanted to give orders to stop but I thought, no, no, I must be brave, it's no good giving in.
Gasps of admiration from the companions.

LUBINKA. She's always the same. She will carry on whatever happens.

MATRIOSHA. Never thinks of herself. She must be more careful.

MADAME T. It was Mashenka I was thinking of. My heart was right up in my throat. But I wouldn't say anything, so we drove on and we hadn't gone more than a few yards when suddenly I saw, coming down the road towards us, a man in a brown hat.
MATRIOSHA *and* LUBINKA *draw in their breaths with horror.*

MASHENKA, *dryly.* On the left or the right side of the road?

MADAME T. I've told you before, I will not have you making fun of these things.

MASHENKA. Well, as if it could make any difference!

MADAME T. You know quite well it's a sign of terrible misfortune. I will not have this free-thinking in my house, Mashenka. You can go to your room if you persist. There's quite enough blasphemy from the guests who come here. I have to put up with that, but I will not put up with it from you.
While she is talking the two companions move back to their seats and resume their occupations.
Surely, Mashenka, it's our duty to preserve our lives. What's the purpose of signs and warnings if we're merely to ignore them. Look at the dreadful accidents one hears about nowadays. The horses bolt, the carriage overturns, the coachman gets drunk and lands in a ditch! If God takes the trouble to send us a sign—two signs in fact—telling us not to go out today, the least we can do is to take notice of them.

MASHENKA. But God didn't tell us not to go out today.

MADAME T., *wearily closing her eyes.* Please darling, this dreadful free-thinking in a child of your age. . . . If there were a vital necessity to go out it would be a different matter, but to risk one's life merely to spend an evening in empty conversation, or discussing one's neighbours! No, I don't think so! . . .

Pulling herself together.

Matriosha and Lubinka, go into the morning room.

MATRIOSHA *takes up her sewing,* LUBINKA *her cards and they hurry out. Turning to her niece,* MADAME TOUROUSINA *addresses her in more practical tones.*

I know quite well why you're so keen on going there today. You're hoping to meet Yegor Kourchaev who's nothing but an atheist and whom I will not allow to enter my house. And so you try to drag your aunt there, not giving a thought to the fact that I may break an arm or a leg just so that you can enjoy yourself.

MASHENKA. I don't understand why you dislike Yegor so much.

MADAME T. Because he laughs at the most sacred things in my presence.

MASHENKA. But when, Auntie, when?

MADAME T. Continually. He's always laughing at the holy pilgrims who come here. He even laughs at my having poor Lubinka and Matriosha as companions.

MASHENKA. But you said he laughed at sacred things.

MADAME T. Well, of course he does. Only the other day I was saying, "Look, my Matriosha's face is beginning to shine with saintliness," and do you know what he dared to say to me? "It's not with saintliness," he said, "its with grease." And I won't forgive that sort of remark. That's what free-thinking leads to! No, I seldom make a mistake in people and you see what sort of man he's turned out to be. I got two more of those letters about him yesterday. You can read them if you like.

MASHENKA. I know auntie, but surely you don't take any notice of anonymous letters?

MADAME T. If there'd only been one I might not, but several! . . . And from different people.

GRIGORI, *the servant, comes in with a letter which he hands to her.*

GRIGORI, *sourly*. Those tramps are downstairs again.

MADAME T. Tramps? I don't know whom you're referring to. You don't mean my holy pilgrims, do you?

GRIGORI. Tramps I call them, madam.

MADAME T. That's quite enough, Grigori. You know my orders. Any pilgrims that come to my house are to be taken to the kitchen and given a good meal.

GRIGORI *goes out.* MADAME TOUROUSINA *opens the letter.* Here you are, here's another one! Obviously written by a most trustworthy woman.
Reads aloud.
"Dear Madam, though I have not the pleasure of . . ."
Reads to herself.
Here you are, listen! "I am filled with horror at your choice of a creature like Yegor Kourchaev and I tremble to think of what will happen to poor Mashenka. Do you realise that he is a well-known liberal . . ." and so on and so on.

MASHENKA. May I see?
Taking the letter and looking at it.
Isn't it extraordinary? I just don't know what to think about it.

MADAME T. Well, Mashenka dear, if you persist in going your own way I shall do nothing to stop you.
Sniffing at her smelling salts.
Nobody shall say I've treated you like a tyrant, but you know what very deep distress you're causing me and you can hardly complain if I . . .

MASHENKA. Don't give me a dowry?

MADAME T. And more important still, dear, my blessing!

MASHENKA. Oh, don't worry, Auntie. I wouldn't dream of marrying without a dowry. I like Yegor Kourchaev very much, but if you won't give me one there's no more to be said. I shan't pine away or go into a decline. But, Auntie darling, try to understand what I feel. I'm quite well off, thanks to you, but I want to enjoy myself, to get something out of life.

MADAME T. I know, I know, dear.

MASHENKA. I'll marry anybody you find for me, as long as he's not too boring. I want to go about in society. After all, I'm quite pretty, I want to be admired. But the tedium of living as we do, Auntie! It's too much, you must admit.

MADAME T. Oh well, one can't be cross with you at your age.

MASHENKA. I've no doubt I shall live exactly your sort of life when I'm older. It's in the family.

MADAME T. I only pray that you do, darling. I pray with all my soul! It's the right road, the straight road.

MASHENKA. I know, Auntie. But I must have a gay time first. Please, can't you arrange a marriage for me?

MADAME T. It's so difficult nowadays. The young men are so spoiled.

MASHENKA. Oh dear! Surely there must be someone in Moscow! Couldn't you ask some of your friends, Mr. Kroutitzky, for instance, Mr. Mamaev, or Mr. Gorodoulin? They'd be delighted to help you find a husband for me.

MADAME T., *with a tired laugh*. They're only human beings. They can be misled and they can mislead other people.

MASHENKA. Well then, what are we to do?

MADAME T. We must wait for a sign. I shan't make any decision until we receive some special sign.

MASHENKA. And where's this sign to come from?

MADAME T. You'll know soon enough when the time comes; today perhaps.

MASHENKA. Auntie, don't forbid him the house. Do let him come here.

MADAME T. Who?

MASHENKA. Yegor Kourchaev.

MADAME T. As long as you realise he's not the man for you.

MASHENKA. Whatever you say, auntie. I'm your obedient, dutiful little niece.

MADAME T., *kissing her.* You're a dear child.

MASHENKA. I'm determined to be rich and lead a gay life. Auntie, you used to lead a gay life, usen't you?

MADAME T. I—I can't remember.

MASHENKA. Oh, auntie, you did! A very, very gay life.

MADAME T. Oh—you know quite a lot, I see. But whatever you know, dear, I'd much rather you didn't know any more.

MASHENKA. I think you're the very best woman in the world, and I'm going to base my life on yours. I shall have the gayest of gay times and then repent. Sin and repent, just like you.

MADAME T. I don't know what you're talking about, Mashenka!

GRIGORI, *entering.* Mr. Kroutitzky, madam.

MADAME T. Show him in.
Sniffing her smelling salts.
My head's aching with all your prattle, Mashenka dear. Go and amuse yourself in the garden or the library, I'll see Mr. Kroutitzky alone.

MASHENKA, *going towards the garden.* All right, Auntie. Don't forget to ask him, will you?

MADAME T. Ask him what?

MASHENKA. If he knows of a young man for me.

MADAME T. All right, my pet. Run away, run away.

GRIGORI, *entering.* Mr. Kroutitzky.
MASHENKA *runs out.* KROUTITZKY, *enters and* GRIGORI *goes out.*

MADAME T., *smiling wanly at him.* What a pleasant surprise!

KROUTITZKY, *taking her hand.* You're very pale, my dear. Nerves bad again?

MADAME T. My nerves are in a dreadful state.

KROUTITZKY. Your hands are cold, too. I wish you'd give up all this——

MADAME T., *defensively*. Give up what?

KROUTITZKY. Too much religion's bad for the nerves.

MADAME T. I've told you before. I won't discuss it with you.

KROUTITZKY. I'm only saying that in the old days when you went about and enjoyed yourself you were a different woman. Why, I remember one night when——

MADAME T. Oh don't, don't remind me of it!

KROUTITZKY. Why not? There was a great deal that was very good in your old life and if there happened to have been a few things that you'd—er—rather not think about now, well I'm sure you've amply atoned for them. Personally, I look back on some of them with a great deal of pleasure. Far from repenting, I like to recall every detail and enjoy them again.
Chuckling reminiscently.
Do you remember that occasion when we——

MADAME T. Stop! Stop!
As GRIGORI *enters.*
Yes, what is it, Grigori?

GRIGORI. That dirty old tramp's downstairs again.

MADAME T. How dare you refer to a holy pilgrim like that? You should be ashamed of yourself! Take him to the kitchen and see that he's given a good meal.
GRIGORI *goes, muttering under his breath.*
The ignorance of these servants!

KROUTITZKY. Well, to return to what I was saying, when you lived a different kind of life you were much healthier.

MADAME T. Physically I may have been, not spiritually.

KROUTITZKY. At any rate you looked healthier then. But you're still young. You've plenty of time to enjoy yourself.

MADAME T. I've no desire for that sort of enjoyment.

KROUTITZKY. If I were you I should postpone repenting till your looks start to go.

MADAME T. I've already asked you not to——

KROUTITZKY. Sorry, sorry, I won't.

GRIGORI, *entering*. There's another of those dirty tramps come now.

MADAME T. I've told you once already. You're not to refer to them like that. Take him into the kitchen with the others. See that he's given a good meal.

GRIGORI. I won't go into the kitchen, madam, not with them there. I can't stand the stench.

MADAME T. Do as I tell you at once!

GRIGORI *goes out, grumbling under his breath.*

KROUTITZKY. You ought to be more careful whom you ask into your house.

MADAME T. I'm quite capable of looking after myself.

KROUTITZKY. Well, be careful, my dear, that's all. It's a well-known fact that a woman who takes up religion is fair game for all kinds of charlatans and swindlers. It's very easy to make a fool of her.

MADAME T. Do you think I wouldn't know if someone were trying to deceive me? Do you think God wouldn't send some sign? Why, only today I was saved from the most dreadful accident. If it hadn't been for God warning me not to go out, the carriage would have overturned and I should be lying in the road, a mangled corpse with broken arms and legs.

KROUTITZKY. Well, as you didn't go out, how do you know the carriage would have overturned?

MADAME T., *with an exasperated sigh.* There are some things one can't discuss with you. Let's not talk of it. . . . Will you give me your advice on a very important matter?

KROUTITZKY. With pleasure. I'm always delighted to be of service to you. What is it?

Moving closer to her.

MADAME T., *moving away from him.* You know Mashenka's reached the age when she——

KROUTITZKY. Yes, yes, I know.

MADAME T. Do you know of a young man for her?

KROUTITZKY. None whom you'd approve of, I'm afraid.

MADAME T. *with a sigh.* That's the trouble.
   A pause.

KROUTITZKY. Wait a minute! . . . I know exactly the right
   young fellow for you.

MADAME T. Really?

KROUTITZKY. Yes. He's extremely charming, rather shy and
   diffident, has the right ideas and comes of a good family.
   He was recommended to me for a small job I wanted done,
   so I put him through his paces and I can tell you he's a
   most exceptional fellow.

MADAME T. But who is he?

KROUTITZKY. What's his name? Oh lord, what a memory! Wait
   a minute though, he gave me his address.
   *Takes out some papers from his pocket and goes through
   them.*
   Ah, here it is! Yegor Dimitrich Gloumov. A very beautiful
   hand, too: even lettering—that means he's methodical, no
   flourishes—that means he's not a free-thinker. . . . Here,
   keep it. It may be useful to you.

MADAME T., *taking it.* Thank you.

KROUTITZKY. Well, I hope it comes to something. One likes
   to help on the young people.
   Looking at his watch.
   I must be getting along.
   Taking the hand which she extends to him.
   Good-bye, Sophia. May I come again or are you angry
   with me?

MADAME T. You know I'm always glad to see you.

KROUTITZKY. If I weren't fond of you I wouldn't speak so
   frankly.

MADAME T., Do come again.

KROUTITZKY. For old time's sake?

Laughs knowingly. MADAME TOUROUSINA *closes her eyes, wrinkling her brow with displeasure.*

Well, I'd better go before you're cross with me again. . . . Au revoir.

He goes out.

MADAME T., *to herself.* At his age too! . . .

She takes out the piece of paper and studies it. MASHENKA *appears from the garden.*

MASHENKA. Has he gone?

MADAME T. Mashenka, you've not been eavesdropping?

MASHENKA, *coming into the room.* Of course not, Auntie. Did he think of anyone for me?

GRIGORI, *entering.* Mr. Gorodoulin, madam.

MADAME T. Show him in.

MASHENKA. I'm sure *he'll* know of someone. Don't forget to ask, will you? Anybody you like, but he mustn't be too tedious.

She runs out.

GRIGORI, *appearing at the door again.* Mr. Gorodoulin.

GORODOULIN *comes in and* GRIGORI *goes out.*

MADAME T. Well, aren't you ashamed of yourself? Where have you been hiding all these weeks?

GORODOULIN. I haven't had a moment. Business appointments, official dinners, then there was the opening of the railway.

MADAME T. I don't believe a word of it. I think you just find it dull here. . . . Anyway, it's nice of you to call and see me sometimes. Sit down. . . . I've been hoping for some news from you.

GORODOULIN. News? Of what?

MADAME T. You don't mean to tell me you've forgotten! Well, that's charming, that's very kind of you. I'm sorry, I should have realised that a person who has such important matters to attend to, could hardly find time to worry about the poor and oppressed. Such trivialities are beneath your notice, of course.

GORODOULIN. This is the first I've heard about the poor and oppressed. I remember you asked me to make some enquiries about some fortuneteller.

MADAME T. Nothing of the sort! A clairvoyante! There's a great difference. I would never have gone to a fortuneteller.

GORODOULIN. Sorry. I confess my ignorance of these subtle distinctions. Well, anyway, it was about Oulita Schmigaeva, widow of an old clothes dealer.

MADAME T. Her social status has nothing to do with it. She's a most remarkable woman and I'm proud, yes proud, that she's granted her special favors to me.

GORODOULIN. She's granted most of those to a discharged sailor.

MADAME T. That's the most disgusting slander! Why, she's been received in the best houses in Moscow. It's envy, it's jealousy, that's all it is, because she's been successful. Oh—the world's too evil to live in! . . . But she'll be acquitted. You'll see, God will vindicate her.

GORODOULIN. I'm afraid she'll have to tell fortunes in Siberia now.

MADAME T., *springing to her feet.* So that's your famous court of justice! To send an innocent woman to Siberia! For what? For doing good to others!

GORODOULIN. But she's been convicted of fortunetelling.

MADAME T. I'll tell you what it is. It's all part of a plot to turn us into atheists. Oh, yes, you can laugh at me but mark my words, she was convicted because she was believed! As *I* would be convicted if some people had their way.

GORODOULIN. Quite apart from fortunetelling, she was accused of receiving stolen goods, keeping a brothel and poisoning a commercial traveller.

MADAME T. I don't believe a word of it! Who—who said so?

GORODOULIN. It's the solemn truth. The commercial traveller's wife went to her to have her fortune told and came away with a recipe that was guaranteed to reawaken her husband's passion. Well, she brewed this concoction according to the instructions and gave it to him in a glass of port. But she'd forgotten one thing—to ask permission of the Ministry of Health.

MADAME T. What happened to the commercial traveller?

GORODOULIN. It worked. He died. But not from love.

MADAME T. I suppose you find that funny. There were plenty of people to plot against this poor woman it seems, but no one to defend her.

GORODOULIN. Not at all. She had the best lawyer in Moscow. A positive torrent of eloquence flowed through the court, overflowed the banks and finally quieted down to a scarcely audible whisper. All to no purpose—because she confessed —after the discharged sailor had given her away.

MADAME T. I'd never have believed it! . . . It only shows how easily one can be mistaken in people. It's impossible to live in this world.

GORODOULIN. It's not impossible, but it's difficult unless one can see it clearly as it is. There've been great strides in the studies of mental diseases and hallucinations lately and——

MADAME T. I've told you before I don't want to discuss the subject.

GORODOULIN. Sorry. I forgot.

MADAME T. Let me be mistaken in people, let me be deceived. My only happiness is in helping the poor and oppressed.

GRIGORI, *entering.* There's *another* dirty old tramp downstairs.

GORODOULIN. What, another?

MADAME T. I don't understand what you're referring to.

GRIGORI. Sorry, madam, a holy pilgrim.

MADAME T. That's better. What is he like?

GRIGORI. Well, he scared me. He gave me a terrible turn. It gives you a turn just to look at him even.

MADAME T. What do you mean "gives you a turn"? What nonsense!

GRIGORI. He's so fierce-looking, madam. All covered in hair. You can only see his eyes.

MADAME T. He must be an Italian.

GRIGORI. No, I don't think he's an Italian, madam. He's not quite the right color. If you ask me he's a proper Hungarian.

MADAME T. A Hungarian?

GRIGORI. That's it, madam. The kind that sells mousetraps.

MADAME T. Well, take him into the kitchen, see that he gets a good meal and ask him if there's anything he needs.

GRIGORI. They're getting very noisy in there, madam. One of them's got a bottle of——

MADAME T. Don't talk so much, Grigori. Do as I say at once.

GRIGORI. Yes, madam.
He goes.

MADAME T., *seeing the smirk on* GORODOULIN's *face.* Spare me your humorous comments, Ivan. . . . Listen, I want to ask you something. It's about Mashenka. Do you know of a nice young man for her?

GORODOULIN. I hardly think I'm the right person to come to. You can't say that I look like a matchmaker. I'm against any form of chains, even matrimonial ones.

MADAME T. But you wear them yourself.

GORODOULIN. That's why I wouldn't condemn my worst enemy to wear them.

MADAME T. Seriously though, can you think of anyone?

GORODOULIN. Wait a minute! I did meet someone the other day who had "ideal husband" written in large letters across his forehead.

MADAME T. Who was it? Do try and remember.

GORODOULIN. Oh yes . . . Gloumov.

MADAME T. Is he a *good* young man?

GORODOULIN. He's thoroughly trustworthy, I'm sure. I think he's a very nice fellow.

MADAME T. Wait a minute. What did you say his name was? *Taking out the paper which* KROUTITZKY *gave her.*

GORODOULIN. Gloumov.

MADAME T. Yegor Dimitrich?

GORODOULIN. Yes.

MADAME T. How extraordinary. Anton Kroutitzky only mentioned him to me just now.

GORODOULIN. Well, that must mean he's the right man. He can't escape his fate. Or perhaps destiny would be more tactful. . . . I must go.

MADAME T. Well, good-bye. I won't keep you from all your important appointments.

GORODOULIN. Let me know if my matchmaking proves successful.

MADAME T. I will, of course. And thank you for the advice. Good-bye.

He goes out. MADAME TOUROUSINA *rises and begins to pace the room, glancing occasionally at the paper in her hand.*

MADAME T. Yegor Gloumov. . . . Yegor Gloumov. . . .
Going to the door, she calls.
Matriosha, Lubinka.

After a second or two they come in, LUBINKA *holding her pack of cards,* MATRIOSHA *carrying a small poodle in her arms.* MADAME TOUROUSINA *sinks into the chair again.* I don't know what to think. Both Mr. Kroutitzky and Mr. Gorodoulin have suggested the same young man for Mashenka but I haven't confidence in either of them. Still, there must be something in it if they both think highly of him. Oh . . . what a loss for Moscow when Ivan Yakovlevitch died. He was the last of the Russian saints in my opinion. Life was so easy, so simple, when he was here. I can't sleep at night now for wondering what I'm going to do with Mashenka; and if I make a mistake, the sin will be on my own head. If he were alive still, I'd have nothing to think about even. I'd go and ask him what to do and there'd be nothing more to worry about. I wonder if this Madame Maniefa will take his place? I think there's something very supernatural about her, don't you?

MATRIOSHA, *bringing the footstool.* Oh, yes. They say Peter the Great appeared to her in a cloud and she just gave one look at a lady with toothache and the tooth stopped aching.

MADAME T. Don't drop the poodle, Matriosha.

LUBINKA, *who has seated herself at the table.* Shall I lay the cards out?

MADAME T. In a minute.

The sound of wild music accompanied by shouts and cries, which for the last few minutes has been increasing in volume, is now loud enough to force itself on MADAME TOUROUSINA'S *attention.*

Listen, what's that? It sounds like gypsies.

LUBINKA. It's those pilgrims, dear.

MASHENKA, *running in from the garden.* Auntie, those pilgrims are having a party in the yard. Varya and Masha and the new cook are all dancing with them.

MADAME T. Oh, the world's too evil for me. . . .

MASHENKA. May I go and watch?

MADAME T. No, no, Mashenka, stay here. I want to talk to you.

MASHENKA. What did Mr. Gorodoulin say?

MADAME T. Well, it's very strange but he and Mr. Kroutitzky both suggested the same young man.

MASHENKA. Auntie, how wonderful! He's bound to be nice then.

MADAME T. Well, I don't entirely trust them.

LUBINKA. Shall I start, dear?

MADAME T. Yes, tell my fortune. See if they spoke the truth.
To MASHENKA.
No, I don't trust them. They could easily be mistaken.

MASHENKA. But why, Auntie darling?

MADAME T. Because they're ordinary human beings.

MASHENKA, *disconsolately.* Who will you ever believe then? Nothing will ever get settled. It quite frightens me.

MADAME T. Of course it does, darling. You *should* feel frightened. How can we raise even a corner of the veil which hides our future without feeling afraid? Behind that veil lie your happiness, your unhappiness, your life and your death. Matriosha, don't drop the poodle.

MASHENKA. But who's going to raise it for us?

MADAME T. There is someone in Moscow, darling. One living being who has the power.

GRIGORI, *entering*. There's a person to see you, madam.

MADAME T. *eagerly*. Who is it?

GRIGORI. She says her name's Madame Maniefa.

MADAME T., *getting to her feet*. Show her in at once. It's she, it's she, Mashenka.

To the two companions who have also got to their feet. How extraordinary her coming just at this moment, as if she knew what was happening, could read our thoughts! . . .

MADAME MANIEFA *appears at the door. As usual, she is slightly drunk.*

Come in, please come in, we didn't expect such an honour. Matriosha, Lubinka, lead Madame Maniefa to a chair. Never mind the poodle.

They hurry to support her on either side. The barbaric music from the yard adds to the impression that a ritual is taking place.

MANIEFA. There's holiness in the house when she who's holy brings her holiness to the holy ones.

MATRIOSHA. O, did you hear that, Lubinka?

MADAME T. Be quiet, can't you. Mashenka, take that dog outside.

MASHENKA *does so.*

MANIEFA, *as she is lowered into the chair*. She came like a bird and went like another bird.

LUBINKA. Oh Matriosha, did you hear that?

MATRIOSHA. Isn't she wonderful?

To MADAME TOUROUSINA.

Did you hear that, dear?

MANIEFA, *suddenly.* Who do you think you're staring at?

MADAME T. We're all so happy that you've come to visit us. God grant we're not too unworthy.

MATRIOSHA. Yes, God grant we're not!

LUBINKA, *to* MADAME TOUROUSINA. *You're* not, dear.
To MADAME MANIEFA.
She's a saint if ever there was one.

MADAME T., *to* MANIEFA. May we humbly ask you to speak to us? Have you a message for us?
MADAME MANIEFA *appears to go into a trance.*

LUBINKA. Oh, my God, it's the spirits descending into her.

MATRIOSHA. Oh, my holy fathers!

MADAME T. Ssh, listen! Support her, hold her hands. If she gets a shock she might die.
They do so.

MANIEFA, *in a voice like a little girl.* They expected her in slippers and she came in boots.

LUBINKA, *in a hoarse whisper.* Remember that, don't forget what she said! . . .

MADAME T. Memorise it somebody! Ssh, she's going to speak again.
Nothing happens. MADAME TOUROUSINA *ventures in an awestruck voice.*
I wanted to ask you. . . .

MANIEFA. The one who knows runs, the one who doesn't lies down. One girl less—one woman more.

MATRIOSHA. Oh, my God, isn't it wonderful!

LUBINKA. It's a spirit speaking! . . .
Whispering to MADAME TOUROUSINA.
Ask her who it is, dear!

MADAME T. No, no, no! Do stop.
Then humbly to MADAME MANIEFA.
Have you something to tell us about a young man? Won't

you say something to your servant Sophia? Don't you see a young man in your vision?

MANIEFA. I see a cloud, the cloud is shifting. In the centre of the cloud is Yegor.

MATRIOSHA. Yegor!

LUBINKA. Did you hear that, dear?

MASHENKA, *whispering in her aunt's ear.* But, Auntie, that's Mr. Kourchaev's name.

MADAME T. Ssh. . . . May we humbly ask, who is Yegor?

MANIEFA. When you see, you'll know.

MADAME T. When shall we see him?

MANIEFA. A guest who is wanted, need not be invited.

LUBINKA, *in a whisper to* MADAME TOUROUSINA. There you are, dear.

MADAME T. Please tell us, how can we recognise him?

MATRIOSHA, *To* MADAME TOUROUSINA *in a whisper.* Ask what colour his hair is!

MADAME T. Oh, be quiet.
Then resuming her humble, awestruck tone.
Is he dark or fair?

MANIEFA. To some he is dark, to you he is fair.

MASHENKA, *in a whisper.* Mr. Kourchaev's fair, auntie.

MADAME T. Don't be so silly. As if a Hussar could appear in a vision.

LUBINKA. It's wonderful, even the cards said Yegor.

MADAME T. What are you talking about? How can you see a name in the cards?

LUBINKA. I'm sorry, dear. I didn't mean that. I meant I saw a fair man in the cards.

MADAME T. Ssh, she's going to speak again.

MANIEFA. The stranger is far away but the one who is coming is at the gate.

MADAME T.
MATRIOSHA. } At the gate?
MASHENKA.

MANIEFA. Get ready, prepare the banquet, visitors are coming.

MADAME T. When? When?

MATRIOSHA. } When?
LUBINKA.

MANIEFA. Now . . . they are here.
Her head falls forward.

GRIGORI, *entering.* Mr. Mamaev to see you, madam.
All except MADAME MANIEFA, *turn and look at him.*

MADAME T. Alone?

GRIGORI. There's a young gentleman with him, madam.

MADAME T. A—fair young gentleman?

GRIGORI. That's right, madam.

LUBINKA. Oh, isn't it wonderful!

MATRIOSHA. I can't believe it! It's like a dream!

MADAME T., *flinging her arms round* MASHENKA. Mashenka, darling, my prayers have been answered.

MASHENKA. It's all so peculiar, Auntie. I—I'm trembling all over.
MADAME MANIEFA, forgotten for the moment, draws attention to herself by a groan. MADAME TOUROUSINA *flies to her.*

MADAME T. Madame Maniefa, are you all right?

MANIEFA. Where am I?

MADAME T. You're amongst friends. You've had a vision.

MANIEFA. I'll be all right when I've had a drop of something.

MADAME T. Lead her into the dining-room and give her tea, tea.

MANIEFA. Tea's no good after a vision.

MADAME T., *as they start to lead her off*. Vodka, then, wine, anything.

LUBINKA. Wait, wait, we must have a glimpse of him, just one glimpse.

MATRIOSHA. It's a miracle, that's what it is, dear, a miracle!
MAMAEV *and* GLOUMOV *appear at the door*.

MAMAEV. Sophia Ignatieva—allow me to present my nephew, Yegor Dimitrich Gloumov.

LUBINKA. Exactly as she described!

MATRIOSHA. Fair hair and all!

MAMAEV. He's a good lad, you'll like him.

MADAME T., *holding out her hand for* GLOUMOV *to kiss*. I shall love him as my own son.

Curtain

ACT TWO

SCENE 2

The same as Act One, Scene 1. STYOPKA *as usual, is lolling in his shirtsleeves, picking his teeth.*

GLOUMOV, *calling through the door to his mother's bedroom*. Mamma, aren't you going to Madame Tourousina's?

MADAME G. *off*. All right, I'm coming. What's the hurry?

GLOUMOV. You're late!
Coming back into the room followed by his mother who is putting on her bonnet.
You should be there first thing in the morning, every day. You ought practically to live there.

MADAME G. I can't do more. I do my best. I'm worn out with it.
Giving STYOPKA *a push*.

For the love of God, go out and do the shopping. Nothing to eat in the house as usual. The whole place'll go to rack and ruin with me out all day!

GLOUMOV has seated himself at the table and is writing in his diary.

What are you putting in that diary now?

GLOUMOV. Another stupid conversation with Mr. Kroutitzky. Heaven knows how I remember it all.

MADAME G. Heaven knows what Kleopatra's going to say when she finds out you're engaged. *Has* she found out?

GLOUMOV. I don't know. I wish I did, then I'd know how to handle her.

MADAME G. Yes, it's very worrying.

STYOPKA, *who has been moving lazily about the room, pulling on his jacket.* We don't want her upsetting everything just when you're getting us on our feet.

MADAME G., *to* STYOPKA. You get on your feet down to Smirnoff's and get some provisions in.
To herself.
Lazy dolt!

STYOPKA, *ignoring her and talking to* GLOUMOV. Anything particular you fancy, sir?

GLOUMOV. No, no, get another bottle of vodka in case Madame Maniefa comes in.

STYOPKA. You couldn't let me have something off that 400 roubles, could you?

GLOUMOV. Put down a tip for yourself on the account.

STYOPKA. Thanks very much, sir.
Going to a mirror on the wall he combs his hair, fixes it in a becoming manner with the aid of saliva, and, while GLOUMOV *and his mother continue talking, ambles out.*

MADAME G. Well, I'm going.
Making for the door.

GLOUMOV. Mamma, just a minute, come here. Are you bosom friends with Madame Tourousina's "companions"?

MADAME G. More or less.

GLOUMOV. And the servants and pilgrims, the whole of the ménage?

MADAME G. Oh yes, they tell me anything.

GLOUMOV. Well, don't leave anything to chance. On your way there you'd better buy two snuff boxes for Matriosha and Lubinka.

MADAME G., *starting to go.* All right, I will.

GLOUMOV. And don't forget to keep an eye on everybody who comes into the house. Watch for any suspicious characters from our point of view.

MADAME G. All right. Good-bye.

GLOUMOV. Good-bye. And for heaven's sake get them to hurry up with the reception.

MADAME G. Which reception?

GLOUMOV. Don't be stupid, Mamma. For the formal announcement of the engagement.

MADAME G. They say it can't be for another two weeks at least.
She goes. GLOUMOV *reads through his diary, chuckling wryly to himself once or twice. Then he says to himself.*

GLOUMOV. Let's see, what was I going to put in? Oh yes, the expenses.
Writing.
Two snuff boxes for Matriosha and Lubinka.
There is a knock at the front door. GLOUMOV *answers it and* KROUTITZKY *appears.*
Oh! . . . come in, Mr. Kroutitzky. This is an honour.

KROUTITZKY, *entering.* The paper's waiting for my article. They must have it this morning.

GLOUMOV, *getting some papers from a drawer.* It's all ready. I hope you'll find it satisfactory.
Indicating the room.
We live very humbly, I'm afraid.
Handing him the papers.
Here.

KROUTITZKY, *studying the first page*. Excellent, bravo! A good round hand, thoroughly legible. "Treatise" though, I don't like that. It should be "plan".

GLOUMOV. Well, I thought the word "plan" gave the impression that you were suggesting something new. Whereas the whole point of the article is that you're opposed to anything new.
With ingratiating smile.
And quite rightly so.

KROUTITZKY. So you think "treatise" is better?

GLOUMOV. Much.

KROUTITZKY. Very well.
Reads.
"A Treatise on the Betterment of the Russian Peoples by the Immediate Abolition of all Progressive Ideas." Don't you think that "all" is perhaps a little strong?

GLOUMOV. But that's the theme of your article, isn't it, Mr. Kroutitzky? That all reforms, all progressive ideas are harmful?

KROUTITZKY. I'm not against infinitesimal changes here and there.

GLOUMOV. In that case they wouldn't be reforms, they'd be modifications.

KROUTITZKY. True, true, most penetrating. I'm very pleased with you, young man. You should go far.

GLOUMOV. Thank you, Mr. Kroutitzky.

KROUTITZKY, *putting on his spectacles*. Well, to continue, I'm most interested to see how you've commenced the exposition of my principle thesis.
Reads.
"Every progressive idea is harmful. What is a progressive idea? It is a poisoned arrow aimed at the vitals of the state. How is a progressive idea translated into action? (*a*) By the abolition of something old. (*b*) By the introduction of something new. Which of these two actions is harmful? Both are equally harmful. By sweeping away the old we

create an opportunity for the dangerous keenness of the human brain to penetrate the reasons why this or that is being swept away and to come to the following conclusions: only useless things are swept away; if a certain institution has been abolished, it must have been useless. Such conclusions inevitably lead to dissatisfaction with the existing state of affairs and would bring about discussions in which the government of the country might be criticised. It is clear, therefore, that progressive ideas can only be viewed with abhorrence by anyone who has the welfare of his country at heart."

GLOUMOV. And quite true, Mr. Kroutitzky.

KROUTITZKY, *reading again.* "In admitting a new idea we are making an unnecessary concession to the so-called spirit of the times, which is nothing but the invention of idle brains." Very well expressed.

GLOUMOV. I take no credit for that. It's your fundamental truths which create my style.

KROUTITZKY. You think these are fundamental truths?

GLOUMOV. But there's no question of it.

KROUTITZKY. Yes, I think this should prove very popular.

GLOUMOV. I have to apologise for something—there are several words and expressions which I've left exactly as you wrote them.

KROUTITZKY. Oh, yes?

GLOUMOV. I thought our modern way of writing too weak to express the full splendour of your thoughts.

KROUTITZKY. For instance? . . . Give me an example.

GLOUMOV. Well . . . the passage about the position of minor officials in the Civil Service.

KROUTITZKY. Yes?

GLOUMOV. You most forcibly express the excellent idea that on no account should minor officials have their salaries raised, nor their living conditions improved. That, on the contrary, it's the heads of the departments and ministers who should have their salaries raised.

KROUTITZKY, *turning over the papers*. I don't recall saying that.

GLOUMOV. You *did*, Mr. Kroutitzky. I know the paragraph by heart and not only that but the whole article.

KROUTITZKY. Excellent. Well, tell me what I said in this paragraph.

GLOUMOV. "The raising of Civil Servants' salaries should be carried out with the greatest care and must only be granted to heads of departments and ministers, in no case to minor officials and clerks. The salaries of important officials should be raised so that the power of the state may be upheld with all due pomp and majesty. No subordinate Civil Servant must be contented or well-fed, as this might lead to his acquiring a dignity and self-respect wholly out of keeping with the station to which God has called him. This applies equally to workers of all classes."

KROUTITZKY. Quite right, quite right.

GLOUMOV. I thought the expression "pomp and majesty" most felicitous.

KROUTITZKY, *now engrossed in the article*. Have you shown this to your cousin, your uncle as you call him?

GLOUMOV. Mr. Mamaev?

KROUTITZKY. Yes.

GLOUMOV. Good heavens, no!

KROUTITZKY. Well, look out. He pretends to be intelligent but the man's a complete idiot.

GLOUMOV. I wouldn't argue with you on that point, Mr. Kroutitzky.

KROUTITZKY. He's always telling people how to do things but let him try to write something—we'd soon see. And I wouldn't say his wife was remarkable for her brains.

GLOUMOV. I wouldn't argue on that point either.

KROUTITZKY. How you manage to get on with them I can't understand!

GLOUMOV. It's simply a case of necessity.

KROUTITZKY. Are you in the Civil Service?

GLOUMOV. Not yet, but my aunt spoke to Ivan Gorodoulin about me.

KROUTITZKY. What a man to go to! A fine sort of post you'll get from him. Surely you want something permanent. All these Gorodoulin posts won't last long—you'll soon see. We consider him extremely dangerous.

GLOUMOV. It's not a newly created post though. Nothing progressive about it.

KROUTITZKY. In that case it's not so bad. You should accept it for the time being. Later, you must get transferred to St. Petersburg—things are much better there—I'll give you some letters of introduction. I suppose you've a perfectly clean record?

GLOUMOV, *round-eyed*. A clean record, Mr. Kroutitzky?

KROUTITZKY. I must be able to recommend you in all good faith. Is there anything in your past that——

GLOUMOV. I was very lazy at the University, I'm afraid.

KROUTITZKY. That's all to the good. Far worse if you'd learnt too much. Isn't there anything more important?

GLOUMOV. I—I hardly like to tell you, Mr. Kroutitzky.

KROUTITZKY, *sternly*. Come on, better make a clean breast of it.

GLOUMOV. I was very young at the time—I was easily infatuated, sometimes indiscreet.

KROUTITZKY. Don't be afraid to tell me.

GLOUMOV. I didn't behave like these—these progressively minded students nowadays.

KROUTITZKY. What do you mean?

GLOUMOV. I—I confess I spent some rather riotous evenings. I sowed one or two wild oats. I've sometimes even been in scraps with the police.

KROUTITZKY. Is that all?

GLOUMOV. All, Mr. Kroutitzky? I sincerely hope so.

KROUTITZKY. Well, I like the sound of this. Any young fellow at a university is expected to get drunk and smash up a few things occasionally and get in trouble with the police. It's not as if you came from the lower classes. Now I can be quite easy in my mind about you. Frankly, you have made a good impression on me from the start and I can tell you now I've spoken very highly of you in a certain quarter.

GLOUMOV. Yes, Madame Tourousina told me. I—I can hardly find words to tell you how grateful I am.

KROUTITZKY. Have you proposed yet? There's a lot of money attached to the niece.

GLOUMOV. I'm so stupid about money, Mr. Kroutitzky. But I'm quite enchanted with Mashenka.

KROUTITZKY. Well, I couldn't tell you about that. They're all the same to me. I know the aunt's a terrible humbug.

GLOUMOV. Nobody believes in true love nowadays, but I do. I know it exists, Mr. Kroutitzky. I've felt it in my own heart.

KROUTITZKY. You mustn't give way to it. That's a fatal mistake. I was foolish enough to give way once. It happened about forty years ago. I nearly died of love. I was staying in Omsk at the time. . . . Why are you looking at me like that?

GLOUMOV. I was feeling for you, Mr. Kroutitzky. I know what you must have suffered.

KROUTITZKY. Yes, I was in a terrible state. They thought I had scarlet fever. Well . . . a young man like you deserves the best out of life. We'll soon find you an important position. We need men of your sort. Although you're a youngster I consider that you're one of us. Your support will be invaluable in combating this new wave of dangerous thinking. Anyway, my dear fellow, how much do I owe you for your work?

GLOUMOV. Please, Mr. Kroutitzky, I shall be offended.

KROUTITZKY. No, no, tell me or *I* shall be offended.

GLOUMOV. Well, I wouldn't dream of taking money from you but if you insist there is something you could do for me.

KROUTITZKY. What's that?

GLOUMOV. Marriage is such a tremendous step for a man to take . . . I beg you not to refuse me. The blessing of a person like yourself would be a—a kind of guarantee of happiness. . . . Even to know you, Mr. Kroutitzky, is a happiness in itself and the idea of a relationship, even though it were only spiritual, would mean such a tremendous lot to . . . to any children Mashenka and I may have.

KROUTITZKY. You want me to be godfather to your children, is that the idea?

GLOUMOV. Oh, Mr. Kroutitzky, if you only would!

KROUTITZKY. Of course, why not? There's nothing so wonderful in that. You should have asked me straight out.

GLOUMOV. Oh, but it *is* wonderful, too wonderful. May I tell Madame Tourousina?

KROUTITZKY. Tell her by all means.
Looking at his watch.
We've been sitting here talking and the articles should have been at the Moscow Gazette half an hour ago.

GLOUMOV. My servant's out I'm afraid. Let me get a cab and take it down myself.

KROUTITZKY, *handing it to him.* There's a good fellow. And, look here, as you know, it's to be published anonymously, so don't say a word about it to anyone. If there's any discussion as to who wrote it you pretend you don't know.

GLOUMOV. I promise you I shan't breathe a word.

KROUTITZKY. Hurry up then, I'll make my own way down. I haven't got young legs like you.

GLOUMOV. Very well.
Fervently.
I can never thank you enough for what you've done for me.

KROUTITZKY. I'm indebted to you, too. Goodby.

GLOUMOV *bows and taking the papers hurries out. Left to himself* KROUTITZKY *has a good look round the room, then taking his hat, adjusts his tie in the mirror preparatory to*

going out. There is a light tap on the door and KLEOPATRA
MAMAEVA *roguishly puts her head round. On seeing* KROU-
TITZKY *her face falls.*

KLEOPATRA. Oh! . . . What are you doing here?
She comes into the room.

KROUTITZKY. I called to see your young cousin.
Kissing the hand which she extends to him.
How are you, my dear lady?

KLEOPATRA. Where's Yegor?

KROUTITZKY. He'll be back presently . . . if you'll excuse me I
was just on my way out.

KLEOPATRA, *seating herself. Coyly.* No, you must stay and
talk to me. You are an unchivalrous old gentleman! Aren't
you interested in young ladies any more?

KROUTITZKY, *laughing waggishly.* No, no, my day's over, I'm
afraid. Though in my time I had the reputation for—
stops short.
well, I think it's time I made way for the young men.

KLEOPATRA. But they're worse than the old ones nowadays.

KROUTITZKY. Now come, a charming woman like you. . .

KLEOPATRA. They're very disappointing.

KROUTITZKY, *seating himself.* Yes, there are no noble feelings,
no poetic flights of passion nowadays. Shall I tell you the reason? They don't give enough tragedies in the theatres. If
only they'd revive the plays of Ozeroff. Young people of
today would assimilate those fine, delicate feelings. Yes,
they should give tragedies much oftener, every other night
say. I've been working on a plan for spiritually uplifting
the younger generation. I prescribe Ozeroff's tragedies for
the upper classes and for the lower classes, cheaper beer. In
my time we knew all the tragedies by heart, but nowadays!
They don't even know how to read them. That's why we
had chivalry and fine feelings in our time and today they're
only interested in money.
He recites.
"Must I wait for fate to cut short my days, when those days
are so lacking in laughter?" Do you remember?

KLEOPATRA, *acidly.* Yes, of couse I remember. Fifty years ago. I would remember, wouldn't I?

KROUTITZKY. I'm so sorry. Do forgive me. I always look upon you as my contemporary. . . . Oh, I was going to say, I'm very taken with your young cousin. A most delightful young fellow.

KLEOPATRA. I think so, too.

KROUTITZKY. But you musn't spoil him.

KLEOPATRA. Spoil him?

KROUTITZKY. Wait a minute, I think I've remembered some more.
Recites.
"Oh, Gods! 'Tis not the gift of oratory I crave, but for the language of the heart and soul."

KLEOPATRA. How do I spoil him?

KROUTITZKY. Well, arranging such a fine marriage. What a charming girl she is, too.

KLEOPATRA. Charming girl? What . . .
She is unable to go on but sits gaping at him, while he continues to recite.

KROUTITZKY.
Oh Mother, dry your flow of tears,
And sister hide your signs of grief.

KLEOPATRA. What girl? What are you talking about? Whom do you mean?

KROUTITZKY. Good heavens! Mashenka, of course. Sophia Tourousina's niece. As if you didn't know! Twenty thousand dowry.

KLEOPATRA, *getting to her feet.* Oh, my God, I can't believe it! It's not true. . . .

KROUTITZKY, *intent on remembering lines from his favourite tragedy.*
Your soul was sick when you heard the news
And you hid in your breast your sighs,
But gloomy grief is upon your brow,
And . . .

KLEOPATRA. Oh, stop, stop! I shall go mad with this awful re-citing!

KROUTITZKY. Yes, the boy seems to have a heart, too. "Don't think it's for money, Mr. Kroutitzky," he said. He asked me to become godfather to his children. "It would be such an honour for them," he said. Well, why not? "It's not because of her dowry," he said, "I really love the girl. She's an angel, an angel." And he said it with such feeling. It did my heart good. Do you remember those marvellous lines in Donskey, "When a Russian gives his word, only death can break his pledge"?

KLEOPATRA, *groaning*. Oh! . . .

KROUTITZKY. What? What's the matter?

KLEOPATRA. Oh, I'm ill. It's migraine. It's . . .

KROUTITZKY. Oh, you'll soon get over that. Do you remember that beautiful line, "Thou accusest me, my rival, of betrayal of thy woman"?

KLEOPATRA, *screaming*. Oh, go away, go away! I shall go mad, I can't stand it!

KROUTITZKY. My dear lady, I——

KLEOPATRA. Go away! Leave me alone, go, go!

KROUTITZKY *takes one look at her and runs, with a frightened glance over his shoulder.* KLEOPATRA *collapses on the nearest chair.*

Oh, my God, I can't believe it! Oh . . . Oh! . . .

After a minute or two she pulls herself together.

Perhaps it's a mistake. . . . Oh, if only I knew.

Looking round the room.

I wonder if there's something here, some love letters per-haps.

She starts to search, muttering between her sobs.

I'll do something dreadful to him if it's true. I will, I will! Oh God, pray that it's not! It's that wicked Old Kroutitzky making mischief!

Opening the drawer.

What's this? . . . His diary? . . .

Hearing footsteps she quickly replaces the diary, shuts the

drawer and wiping away her tears, forces herself to appear
composed. GLOUMOV *comes in. He stops short on seeing her.*

GLOUMOV. Kleopatra! What a wonderful surprise! Is it really
you sitting here in my poor little humble home like a goddess descended from the skies?

KLEOPATRA. I came to call on your mother.

GLOUMOV. You've just missed her. She went out a few moments
ago.

KLEOPATRA. What a pity.

GLOUMOV, *bringing forward a chair for her.* Do sit down. You're
going to stay and talk to me, aren't you? Kleopatra, you
look unhappy. Are you worried about something?

KLEOPATRA, *sitting down.* About someone.

GLOUMOV. Who is it? Anyone who could make you unhappy
must be a black-hearted wretch!

KLEOPATRA. Yes he is, that's what he is, a black-hearted wretch.

GLOUMOV. Well, as I'm neither black-hearted nor a wretch,
it means that——

KLEOPATRA. That what?

GLOUMOV. That at least it can't be me.

KLEOPATRA. Can I really believe that?

GLOUMOV. You must believe it.

KLEOPATRA. Oh, I want to, I want to! . . .

GLOUMOV. Look into my eyes. Can't you see there that I'd
rather die than cause you a moment's pain? Until I met you
I was a shy, timid boy, uncertain of myself, always troubled
with longings and desires which you, and you alone, have
taught me to understand. I was so lonely that I thought I'd
lose my reason sometimes and always I was searching,
searching for the one woman in the world on whom I could
pin my dreams and hopes. But I was poor, insignificant and
women turned away from me. And then I met you. I shall
never forget the first time I saw you—you were wearing
that beautiful pink dress with brown bows on. My heart
missed a beat and then started to pound so violently that I

thought I should faint. You were so young, so beautiful, so far, far above me! . . . When we were introduced I hardly dared to speak. But you didn't turn away, you weren't cold and cruel like the other great society ladies of today, you were sweet and gracious and when I told you I loved you, Kleopatra, you listened. Oh, if you only knew how many times your sweet, gentle smile has stopped me on the very brink of impropriety. But even that day when I forgot myself, you didn't turn me from the house! Oh, my God, what happiness you've given me.

Feverishly kissing her hands.

What happiness, what happiness!

KLEOPATRA. When are you going to be married?

GLOUMOV, *sitting up with a start.* Married? . . . I . . . er . . . what do you mean?

KLEOPATRA. I understand you're getting married.

GLOUMOV, *after a pause.* I—I must explain it to you, Kleopatra. I was going to tell you today. . . . I'm in a terrible dilemma. Your husband wants me to marry. It was his idea. But I loathe the very thought of it.

KLEOPATRA. He must be fond of you, to want to make you happy against your will!

GLOUMOV. It's simply a question of money. He hates the idea of my being poor. He wants to see me independent and comfortably situated instead of just a poor nobody. It all comes from the goodness of his heart, but unfortunately he didn't consult my feelings.

KLEOPATRA. Do you like the young woman he's chosen for you?

GLOUMOV. She's repugnant to me. Any woman is, but you!

KLEOPATRA. So you don't love her?

GLOUMOV. How could I? But I daren't show her, of course. Whom should I deceive, her or you?

KLEOPATRA. Both, perhaps.

GLOUMOV. You're torturing me with your suspicions! I can't bear it. I shall stop the whole thing.

KLEOPATRA. Stop it? How?

GLOUMOV. Let Uncle be angry with me! I will not marry that girl! I shall tell him so!

KLEOPATRA. Do you mean that?

GLOUMOV. I shall tell him today.

KLEOPATRA. Oh, you must! . . . Without love, whatever sort of marriage would it be?

GLOUMOV. And to think you thought so badly of me! . . . Aren't you ashamed of yourself?

KLEOPATRA. Yes, I've misunderstood you. I'm ashamed.

GLOUMOV, *passionately*. I'm yours, yours, you know that, Kleopatra! Only don't breathe a word to uncle or anyone, or you might give yourself away. Just leave everything to me.

KLEOPATRA. Of course, of course.

GLOUMOV. It's all come about through my cursed shyness. I was afraid to tell uncle straight out that I wouldn't marry. I just went on saying, "Well, let's see . . . there's no hurry," and so on. And this is what's come of it.
The front door bell rings.
Who's that? I expect it's someone to see me. Kleopatra, you must be exhausted with all these fearful emotions. Would you like to go and lie down in Mother's room? I'll get rid of the visitors as quickly as I can.
Leading the way, KLEOPATRA *following him.*

KLEOPATRA. Thank you, Yegor. I couldn't bear to face anybody now.

GLOUMOV *opens the front door disclosing* GOLUTVIN.

GLOUMOV, *rudely*. Well?

GOLUTVIN. Firstly, this is hardly the way to receive a guest. And, secondly, I'm tired because I walked here.
He pushes his way past GLOUMOV *into the room.*

GLOUMOV. What do you want?

GOLUTVIN. Twenty-five roubles minimum. You can make it more if you like. I shan't be offended.

GLOUMOV. Look here, who gave you the idea I was a charitable institution?

GOLUTVIN. I'm not asking for charity. I've done a lot of work on your account and I expect to be paid for it.

GLOUMOV. What work?

GOLUTVIN. Writing your biography.

GLOUMOV. What are you talking about?

GOLUTVIN. I've followed you, watched you, collected information about you and your past history, I've described your latest activities with a wealth of interesting detail and unless you care to buy the manuscript from me I shall send it to the Moscow Weekly Chatterbox with your portrait enclosed. You see, I'm not asking much for it. I don't put a high value on my literary work.

GLOUMOV. Very well, publish it! Don't think you can intimidate *me*. Do you think anyone will want to read what *you* write!

GOLUTVIN. But it's not as if I was asking a thousand roubles. I know I can't do you very much harm but it might be quite unpleasant, so why not pay?

GLOUMOV. There's a very ugly word for what you're trying to do.

GOLUTVIN. Do you consider it less honest than sending anonymous letters?

GLOUMOV. What letters? How can you prove it?

GOLUTVIN. No need to get excited. All I'm asking for is twenty-five roubles.

GLOUMOV. Not one kopeck.

GOLUTVIN. You're marrying a rich young woman. Suppose she were to read your biography and say, oh! . . . much simpler to pay up instead of quarrelling with me. I'd be able to eat for a week and you could have peace of mind. Really, I'm asking very little.

GLOUMOV. And suppose I do pay? That wouldn't be the end of it.

GOLUTVIN. I give you my word it would. What do you take me for?

GLOUMOV, *going to the door and opening it.* Get out, go on.

GOLUTVIN. Very well, in the very next issue——

GLOUMOV. Whichever issue you like!

GOLUTVIN, *after a pause.* Well, look here, what about making it twenty roubles? That's not much.

GLOUMOV. Not one kopeck.

GOLUTVIN. All right then, have it your own way. . . . Haven't got a cigarette, have you?

GLOUMOV. No. Do you mind getting out of here?

GOLUTVIN. When I feel like it. I'll have a rest first.
Sits.

GLOUMOV. Who sent you here? Kourchaev?

GOLUTVIN. Oh no, we've quarrelled. I've finished with him.

GLOUMOV. I asked you to get out.
  GOLUTVIN *gets up, goes to the door leading into the bedroom and peers in.*

GOLUTVIN. What have you got in there?

KLEOPATRA, *from inside.* Who's that? What is it?

GLOUMOV, *pushing* GOLUTVIN *away and pulling the door to.* I give you one minute.

GOLUTVIN. Mm. Madame Mamaeva. Most interesting.

GLOUMOV, *threateningly.* Are you going?

GOLUTVIN, *sauntering out.* You're such a rotten character yourself that you can't recognise decent feelings in other people. . . .
  By this time he is in the hall.

GLOUMOV. Just a minute, I want a word with you.
  He hurries after him, closing the living-room door. KLEOPATRA *puts her head round the other door.*

KLEOPATRA. That's funny. Who was that, I wonder?
  Suddenly recollecting.
  The diary!

Running to the desk, she pulls open the drawer and takes the diary out.

Perhaps there's something about me—or Mashenka. . . .

Turns the pages.

Here's something. "Mashenka is enchanting. What a relief after poor old Auntie Kleo who looks exactly like a horse." Oh! . . . Oh my God! Oh, I feel ill, I'm going to faint! Oh, how low, how low of him! I'll never forgive him, never. I'll make him pay for it. Oh, to think he should have done this to me.

Tearfully.

But he can't mean it. I don't look like a horse, I know I don't! Neel Fedoseitch doesn't think I look like a horse. . . . There's no humiliation bad enough for him. . . . I'll have him crawling back to me on his knees and begging forgiveness, that's what I'll do.

Looking down at the diary.

Yes, and I can, too, with this.

Hides the diary in her bag, then, as she hears the outer door closing.

Oh my God, I mustn't let him see anything. I must keep calm.

GLOUMOV, *coming in.* A most impossible person.

KLEOPATRA. Who was it?

GLOUMOV. I'll throw him down the stairs next time. He's written an abusive article about me and he had the cheek to come here demanding money. Says he'll have it published otherwise.

KLEOPATRA. How horrible. What horrible people there are in the world. Who is this man?

GLOUMOV. Why do you want to know?

KLEOPATRA. Well, it's best to be warned about people like that.

GLOUMOV. Alexander Golutvin his name is.

KLEOPATRA. Where does he live?

GLOUMOV. I don't know; but one could easily find out. Why?

KLEOPATRA. Well, suppose someone were to affront me—it

would be a way of revenging myself. What else can a woman do? We can't fight duels.

GLOUMOV. You're joking, aren't you?

KLEOPATRA. Yes, of course. Did you give him any money?

GLOUMOV. Only a few roubles. Still, I feel easier in my mind now.

KLEOPATRA. But suppose one of your enemies were to give him more?

GLOUMOV. Enemies? I haven't any.

KLEOPATRA. Then you've nothing to worry about. Poor dear boy, has he upset you?

GLOUMOV. Oh, I'm not worried about him.

KLEOPATRA. What is it then?

GLOUMOV. I'm still miserable at the thought of your mistrusting me.

KLEOPATRA. Have you quite made up your mind not to marry Mashenka?

GLOUMOV. You know I have.

KLEOPATRA. You realise fully what you're giving up?

GLOUMOV. Money. I can do without that if it means losing you.

KLEOPATRA. It's a lot of money though. Twenty thousand, don't forget.

GLOUMOV. Do you think I'd change you for all the wealth in the world?

KLEOPATRA. You really mean it?

GLOUMOV. With all my heart.

KLEOPATRA. You're a truly noble character, Yegor, there's no doubt about that. Come here and let me kiss you.

GLOUMOV *obediently comes over and kneels before her. She puts her hands on his neck as if she would like to strangle him, then kisses him violently as though inflicting a punishment. Suddenly she stops, leaving* GLOUMOV *gasping.*

I must go now. Your uncle will wonder what has happened to me. . . . Goodby, dear Yegor.

GLOUMOV. Kleopatra! . . . When shall I see you again?

KLEOPATRA. I shall expect you this evening.

GLOUMOV, *following her.* Don't think any more of Mashenka. By that time it will all be arranged.

KLEOPATRA, *turning to the door.* Goodby.

GLOUMOV. Until this evening. . . .

She holds out her hand to be kissed; as he kisses it she lowers it abruptly so that he has to bow almost to the ground. Pulling it away, she hurries out.

GLOUMOV, *when her footstps have died away.* Phew! . . . Thank God that's over. . . . Oh well, I'd better get off to see Mashenka.

On his way to the table, he stops short and says.

Let's see, Golutvin's paid off . . . Kleopatra's all right for the moment.

His spirits beginning to rise.

Things aren't going too badly. I'll be able to bring it off with a bit of luck. . . .

Looking round the room.

Now let's see, what am I looking for? I'm becoming quite absent-minded with all these worries. Hat and gloves, that's it . . . now I wonder if I've got everything . . . er . . . wallet in this pocket, diary in that. . . . Oh! . . .

Discovering it's not there.

Where did I put it? . . . the desk of course.

Pulls open the drawer and stops dead.

That's funny, I swear I put it in there. My God, this is terrible! . . .

Starts to search frantically.

I know I put it in the desk, I remember now . . . if she's stolen it, this'll finish everything.

Then a sudden thought strikes him.

I wonder if Golutvin took it.

He continues to search again.

What a fool, what a fool to have left it lying about like that. Why didn't I lock the drawer? Oh my God, it *has* gone, it *has*.

Collapsing on a chair, he holds his head in his hands, then after a moment.

What on earth did I keep it for? It's not as if I had any heroic deeds to record . . . simply out of foolish, childish spite—The Memoirs of a Scoundrel written by himself. . . . *Pause.*

Well, it's no good reproaching myself now. I've got enough reproaches coming from everybody else.

Clutching his head.

God, let me think! There must be some way out.

After a moment.

If it's Golutvin I can always get it back with money. . . . Yes, I'll have to buy it back. But suppose it's Kleopatra? "—no fury like a woman scorned." Oh good God, and I said she looked like a horse!

Another pause, during which he takes in the full horror of the situation.

I mustn't be defeated. I won't be. I won't be! Not at this stage. . . . I wonder if she's planning some horrible revenge?

Suddenly making up his mind.

There's only one thing to do.

Gets up resolutely, takes his hat and gloves and adjusts his hat at a becoming angle in the mirror.

Yes, Kleopatra Mamaeva, I'm not going to be defeated by you, or Mr. Golutvin . . . so here we go, straight into the lioness's jaws! And heaven help me to explain that bit about the horse!

He squares his shoulders and hurries out.

Curtain

ACT THREE

The same as Act two, Scene 1. It is late afternoon. The French windows on to the garden are flung open. KOUR-CHAEV *and* MASHENKA *are talking, he seated, she pacing the room restlessly.*

KOURCHAEV. Well, I can't understand the thing at all.

MASHENKA. Neither can I. . . . It all happened so suddenly. . . . Do you think it could possibly be some deep-laid plot?

KOURCHAEV. Perhaps there is something in these queer superstitions of your aunt's.

MASHENKA. I've given up trying to understand. I feel dazed by it all.

KOURCHAEV. I've known him for years. I never noticed anything very special about him. I lost my temper with him once recently, when I thought he'd been running me down to my uncle, but it was just my hot-headedness. He's much too decent to have done a thing like that.

MASHENKA. One moment we weren't aware of his existence and the next he'd become the most important thing in our lives. Ever since then auntie's companions invariably see him in their dreams; whenever they tell fortunes he comes out in the cards; even the professional fortunetellers who come here keep seeing visions of a fair young man named Yegor, and those horrid old pilgrims do, too. And then as the finishing touch, Madame Maniefa, whom I don't like a bit because she always smells of rum, but whom auntie looks upon practically as a saint, described his appearance in detail although she'd never set eyes on him, and foretold the exact moment when he'd arrive at the house. And I've no answer to it all. I can't go against auntie's wishes and she's become absolutely devoted to him.

KOURCHAEV, *gloomily.* It all comes of my not leading a better life. Now Gloumov will get you—and the money too. Virtue will be rewarded and vice punished—vice being me. All I can do is quietly to disappear. If it were some bounder who was getting you I'd put up a fight, but when it's a decent chap like Gloumov I don't see how I can.

MASHENKA. Ssh, they're coming. Oh, I don't want to see him now.

She runs out and KOURCHAEV *jumps to his feet as* GLOUMOV *and* MADAME TOUROUSINA *enter from the garden.*

GLOUMOV. You see, as soon as I realised what a deep longing I had for a settled family life, I took the matter very seriously. Nothing is more abhorrent to me than the idea of marrying for money. Turning what should be a sacred institution into a business transaction. The alternative is to marry for love—but even love is too much of this world. No, I believe a true marriage must come from something higher than all this. It must be dictated by some mystic decree of fate——

MADAME T. Yes, Yes, that's what I always say!

GLOUMOV. By the mysterious powers lurking in the air, with whom we can make contact if we only have intelligence enough to try.

MADAME T. Yes, we can, we can! I entirely agree with you.

GLOUMOV. All my life I've fought against this horrible, radical free-thinking that decries everything mystic or occult—to me, the only things that matter in the world.

MADAME T. Yes, yes, exactly! That's just what I say!

GLOUMOV. I've always believed in miracles——

MADAME T. So have I, always! How right you are.

GLOUMOV. —and I realised that the only way to discover the one woman who'd been waiting for me since the beginning of time, was through a miracle. I prayed for one—and it happened.

MADAME T. It was! It *was* a miracle, your coming here that day! I've always said so. Do you know Yegor, you're the only young man in Moscow who thinks as I do? Everywhere one looks one sees nothing but hideously-minded liberals.

Glancing at KOURCHAEV *who bows. She turns to* GLOUMOV *again.*

But do go on, Yegor. This miracle, tell me about it.

GLOUMOV. Well, I went to a wonderful clairvoyante I know of.

MADAME T. Madame Maniefa?

GLOUMOV. Who? No, I've never heard of her. It was someone quite different. Anyway, as soon as I entered the room, before I'd uttered a word, before she'd even had time to glance at me—she was sitting with her back to me, as a matter of fact—she said, "It's you who are looking for a wife. It's they who are looking for you. Go forward with your eyes closed and you will find her."

MADAME T, *gasping.* How extraordinary! What did you say?

GLOUMOV. Well, a most peculiar feeling came over me. I felt just as if I were enveloped in a cloud.

MADAME T. In a cloud? How extraordinary! Madame Maniefa *saw* you in it. You were in this cloud, slowly descending. . . .

GLOUMOV. That's it, as though in a balloon. But I pulled myself together and managed to say, "Where shall I go, show me?" So she said, "You'll enter a strange house. You must search and you will find. They're waiting for you." Well, the very same evening my cousin brought me to you. And you *were* waiting for me.

MADAME T. It's undoubtedly a miracle. If only everyone could know of this. We could start a religious revival.

KOURCHAEV. I remember a case like that in Kiev once. It happened to a ginger-haired fellow. . . .

MADAME T. Why don't you go for a little walk in the garden? KOURCHAEV *bows, hesitates a minute or two, while they continue talking, then goes out.*

GLOUMOV. It's so clearly a case of predestination that I've never even asked you about Mashenka's feelings. It seemed quite enough that she'd given her consent.

MADAME T. That's all that's needed.

GLOUMOV. She may not be in love with me at the moment, but she will be later on.

MADAME T. Of course she will be.

GLOUMOV. It's written in the stars that Mashenka will love me or we'd never have been brought together in this way.

MADAME T. That's exactly what I was going to say.

GLOUMOV. A marriage like ours has nothing to do with ordinary human motives, so it cannot go wrong.

MADAME T. If only everyone in Moscow could hear you speak. You could be a great teacher, we've all something to learn from you, everyone of us, even I.

GRIGORI, *entering.* Mr. Gorodoulin, madam.

MADAME T. Oh, entertain him for a little, will you, Yegor? I feel too exalted to make idle conversation. All right, Grigori, show him in.
   GRIGORI *goes, she continues.*
   I think I'll go down into the summerhouse and look into the crystal. Perhaps we shall see something today. I thought I saw something yesterday, but when I looked closer it was only an earwig crawling on the other side.
   She goes into the garden. GRIGORI *shows in* GORODOULIN.

GORODOULIN. Oh hello, Gloumov.

GLOUMOV. How are you?

GORODOULIN. How much money are you getting?

GLOUMOV. Twenty thousand, I believe.

GORODOULIN. How did you manage it?

GLOUMOV. But you yourself suggested me. Madame Tourousina told me so.

GORODOULIN. What? Oh yes, I remember. . . . But how do you get on with her—an agnostic like you?

GLOUMOV. I just don't argue.

GORODOULIN. Well, what do you say to all her unutterable bosh?

GLOUMOV. Nothing will cure her of it, so why try?

GORODOULIN. Well, you'll be a rich man soon. I'll put you up for membership of my club.

GLOUMOV. Thanks. . . .

Lowering his voice.

Did you know that Kroutitzky's treatise is to be published in a week or two?

GORODOULIN. Good God! Well, I only hope it gets torn to pieces by the press.

GLOUMOV. Nothing could be easier, anyway.

GORODOULIN. You could do it superbly. You're just the man, with your talents. The only thing is that it might do you a lot of harm. Tell you what, why don't you write it and I'll sacrifice myself for you. I'll make out it's by me, purely out of friendship of course. They need showing up, these intolerable old bores.

GLOUMOV. One's only to look at the trash they write.

GORODOULIN. They're figures of fun, and they should be exposed as such. I'd do it myself, only I haven't the time. You know, we need men like you. We've plenty of good business men, of course, but no one who can write or speak well— so when we're attacked by the old gentlemen of Kroutitzky's sort, it's most unfortunate. One or two of the younger men aren't unintelligent but they're too young. If we allowed them to speak they'd get above themselves. No, you can start the chorus and we'll all join in. Where's your fiancée by the way?

GLOUMOV. I think she's in the garden.

GORODOULIN. I'll go and have a chat with her.

GLOUMOV. I'll come out directly. Aunt Kleopatra's coming to see me here and she's perfectly reconciled to my marriage. Don't you think that's charming of her?

GORODOULIN *goes out. There is the sound of voices in the hall.*

GLOUMOV, *going to the door.* Kleopatra! I'm in here.

After a moment, MADAME MAMAEVA *enters.*

KLEOPATRA. Well, have you found it?

GLOUMOV. No. Golutvin vows on the sacred memory of his mother that he didn't take it. He was in tears almost. "I'd rather starve," he said, "than do a dishonest thing like that."

KLEOPATRA. Who could have taken it then? Are you sure you haven't left it somewhere?

GLOUMOV. Absolutely certain.

KLEOPATRA. Perhaps your servant threw it away by mistake.

GLOUMOV. I wish to God he had.

KLEOPATRA. Why? What are you so afraid of people reading?

GLOUMOV. Nothing particular. Only my intimate thoughts. A few love poems. Some tender lines about women's faces. I'm embarrassed at the idea of a stranger reading them.

KLEOPATRA. Well, you needn't worry. Nobody's going to take any notice of love poems and tender lines. Everyone writes diaries like that. But why are you alone? Where's your fiancée?

GLOUMOV. Somewhere about. I'm not interested. . . . There's proof for you, that I'm only marrying for money and position. I can't always rely on my youth to get along. I've got to become a man whom people look up to and respect. Wait till I have my own carriage with a really spanking pair of horses! Nobody notices me now, but then it'll be, "Who's this striking-looking man who's suddenly appeared in Moscow? He must be an American," and everyone will be jealous of you.

KLEOPATRA. Why of me?

GLOUMOV. Because I belong to you.

KLEOPATRA. It'd be much nicer if you could get the money without Mashenka. But at any rate, you'll have a charming young wife.

GLOUMOV. That won't make any difference to me. I've offered my hand to the bride, my pocket for the money, and my heart remains with you.

KLEOPATRA. You're a dangerous person. One listens and listens and in the end one almost believes you.

GLOUMOV. Think how proud you'll feel when I drive up to your house in my beautiful carriage.

KLEOPATRA. You'll often drive up, won't you? . . . Well, go on, you'd better go to your fiancée. You must be with her as much as possible, if only for appearances sake.

GLOUMOV. You see, you're sending me to her yourself.

KLEOPATRA. Yes, go, go.

GLOUMOV goes out into the garden.

Yes, my friend, you're rejoicing a little too soon. You won't be so pleased with yourself, when I've finished with you.

KOURCHAEV strolls in, looking gloomy.

Where are you going, Yegor?

KOURCHAEV. Home.

KLEOPATRA. Home? You do look sad. Wait a minute! I think I can guess why.

KOURCHAEV bows and makes for the door.

No, wait!

He bows and makes for the door again.

Oh, you are a horrid creature! Stay here, I want to talk to you.

KOURCHAEV waits, but it is quite clear that he is longing to get away. KLEOPATRA continues.

There are a lot of things that you are not aware of.

KOURCHAEV. Please let me go, Auntie Kleopatra.

KLEOPATRA. *I'm* going quite soon. You can see me home.

KOURCHAEV bows.

Have you lost your tongue, or something? Listen. Be frank with me. I'm your aunt and I order you to obey me. I know you're in love with Mashenka. Does she love you?

KOURCHAEV bows.

I'm sure she does. Well, don't give up hope. Life's full of surprises.

KOURCHAEV. If only she'd had ordinary parents, instead of——

KLEOPATRA. And what's the matter with her aunt?

KOURCHAEV. She's got such queer ideas.

KLEOPATRA. What do you mean?

KOURCHAEV. Well, an ordinary fellow can't live up to them. Particularly if he's in the army.

KLEOPATRA. What can't he live up to?

KOURCHAEV. My education hasn't fitted me for it.

KLEOPATRA. What *are* you talking about?

KOURCHAEV. What Madame Tourousina was trying to find for her niece was a . . .

KLEOPATRA. Well?

KOURCHAEV. I mean, I'd never have thought of it. I wouldn't have known there was such a thing.

KLEOPATRA. As what, what?

KOURCHAEV. I've never heard of . . .

KLEOPATRA. Do explain yourself!

KOURCHAEV. She was looking for a thoroughly chaste and virtuous man.

KLEOPATRA. Well, go on.

KOURCHAEV. I haven't any virtues.

KLEOPATRA. None? So you only have vices.

KOURCHAEV. No more than any other fellow, I mean, not to speak of. I'm just an ordinary fellow. But the idea of looking for an absolutely virtuous fellow. Where could she have found one if it hadn't been for Yegor? He's the only one in the whole of Moscow. Miracles happen to him, he appears in cards, he sees visions. How can a fellow compete with that?

KLEOPATRA. Well, don't go yet. Do what I tell you, wait.
As MASHENKA *comes in.*
My dear, congratulations. You look prettier each time I see you. I'm so glad to hear you're so happy.

MASHENKA. Mr. Gloumov's such a noble character that I feel quite frightened. I don't feel I'm worthy of him.

KLEOPATRA. I'm sure you are dear—with your upbringing—
your aunt's example always before you.

MASHENKA. I'm very grateful to auntie. But the only virtue
I've learned is to do what she tells me.

MADAME TOUROUSINA *and* KROUTITZKY *come in from the
garden, deep in conversation.*

MADAME T. But why must it be tragedies? Why not comedies?
To the others.
We're discussing how to bring spirituality to the younger
generation.

KROUTITZKY. For the reason that a comedy depicts lowness
whereas a tragedy depicts sentiments of the highest order,
and that's what they need.

KOURCHAEV *and* KROUTITZKY *bow to each other.* KROU-
TITZKY *kisses* MADAME MAMAEVA'S *hand as* MADAME TOUR-
OUSINA *continues.*

MADAME T. Nobody believes in anything today. All I hear is,
"Madame Maniefa's a charlatan. Why do you allow her in
your house?" I'd only like some of them to hear her. They'd
see what a charlatan she was! Well, I'm delighted for her.
Now I've taken her up, she'll become the most fashionable
clairvoyante in Moscow, and I hope Moscow will be grateful to me. . . . I consider myself a public benefactress.

KLEOPATRA. Where's your niece's fiancé? I don't see him.

MADAME T. *to* MASHENKA. Where is Yegor?

MASHENKA. He's in the garden with Gorodoulin.

MADAME T. You know, I expected him to be a very exemplary
young man, after I'd heard such glowing accounts from my
friends, and for other reasons, too, but now that I've come
to know Yegor I find he's much more wonderful than anything I dared to hope for.

MAMAEV, *coming in.* Who's this who's so wonderful?

MADAME T. Yegor Gloumov.

MAMAEV. I knew you'd thank me for him. I didn't offer him
any other fiancée, I brought him straight to you. I always
know the right man for the right job.

MADAME T. It would have been a sin to take him anywhere else.

KROUTITZKY. Yes, Gloumov should go a long way.

KLEOPATRA. With our help, of course.
GRIGORI *comes in.*

MADAME T. I don't know why so much happiness has been granted to me. Perhaps for my—
to GRIGORI
what do you want? Perhaps for my good deeds.
He hands her an envelope.
What's this?
Opens it.
A newspaper? It must be for someone else.

KLEOPATRA, *taking the envelope.* No, it's for you. Here's the address.

MADAME T. Surely it is a mistake. Who brought it?

GRIGORI. A postman.

MADAME T. Where is he?

GRIGORI. He's gone long ago.
He goes out.

MAMAEV. Here. Give it here. I'll read it and explain it to you.
He takes the envelope and extracts a printed sheet.
What is it? It's a newspaper and yet not a newspaper. It's a page of a newspaper, an article.

MADAME T. But who sent it to me? The editor?

MAMAEV. From some friend I expect.

MADAME T. Well, what's the article about?

MAMAEV. That we shall see. The article's called "How to Become a Success."

MADAME T. That's of no interest to any of us. Leave it.

MAMAEV. We might as well have a look. There's a portrait in the middle. What's it say underneath? . . .
Reads out.

"Portrait of an Ideal Husband." What's this? It's—it's a picture of Yegor! Yegor Gloumov!

KLEOPATRA. May I see? This is most interesting.
She takes the paper from her husband.

MADAME T. Oh, there must be some vile intrigue against him! He's too good for Moscow. The liberals and freethinkers must be plotting against him!
She glares at KOURCHAEV. MAMAEV *also glares at him.*

KOURCHAEV. Are you suggesting it's me? I can't draw portraits.
To MAMAEV.
You're the only person I've ever drawn.

MAMAEV. Yes, yes, I know that.

KLEOPATRA. Whoever wrote this article must know Yegor very well: here are all the most intimate details of his life, if they're not inventions.

MAMAEV, *taking* GLOUMOV'S *diary from the envelope.* There's something else here.
He opens it.

KROUTITZKY, *peering over his shoulder.* That's Gloumov's handwriting. I know it. I swear it's his.

MAMAEV. Yes, this is his handwriting; but it's someone else's signature on the article. Which shall we read, the article or this?

KROUTITZKY. Let's have the original first.

MAMAEV. Here you are, there's a book-mark in it. We'll start here then. Seems to be a bill. "To Madame Maniefa: twenty-five roubles. To Madame Maniefa: another twenty-five roubles. She's always half-pickled with rum yet takes upon herself to foretell the future. I've spent hours trying to teach her what to say, but it was with the greatest difficulty that I got an ounce of sense out of her. I've also sent her a bottle of rum and given her another twenty-five roubles at least. What a pity that such a profitable profession should be practised by such stupid people. I am curious to know how much she gets from poor Madame T. A great deal I should think, as Madame T. is slightly cracked."

MADAME T., *falling on the couch and feeling for the smelling salts.* Oh! Oh! I can't bear it! I can't bear it!

MASHENKA, *running to her.* It's all right, Auntie. It's best to know now. Mr. Mamaev, please go on.

KLEOPATRA. Yes, go on. It's better for Sophia to know the truth.
MAMAEV *takes a deep breath and continues.*

MAMAEV. "The two nauseating companions have had seven roubles fifty kopecks each, as well as a couple of silver snuff boxes costing ten roubles, in return for which they guarantee to see me in the cards, as well as in their dreams each night."

MADAME T., *suddenly screaming.* They must go at once! I won't have them in the house another minute! Oh my God, this world's too evil to live in. Oh, Mashenka darling, what can one think after this? If one's wicked, one's a sinner, if one's good, one's a fool.

KLEOPATRA. You needn't complain. You're not the only one to be made a fool of.

MAMAEV, *continuing doggedly.* "Six anonymous letters to Madame Tourousina—thirty kopecks."

MASHENKA. So that's where they came from!

MADAME T. Forgive me, forgive me, darling. I should never have attempted to arrange your life. I see now, I've neither the brain nor the strength. Do as you like from now on. Make your own choice. I shall do nothing to stop you.

MASHENKA, *softly.* I've made my choice, Auntie.

MADAME T., *weakly.* At least, darling, you won't be deceived by him; he doesn't pretend to be anything wonderful.
KOURCHAEV *bows.* MADAME TOUROUSINA *suddenly screaming.*
Matriosha and Lubinka must leave the house at once!

KROUTITZKY. To make way for other companions?

MADAME T. I don't know.

MAMAEV. Do you want me to go on?

MADAME T. Yes, go on. Nothing matters now.

MAMAEV. "Mr. Mamaev's servant who brought his master to me, deceitfully taking advantage of the old fellow's weakness for looking over apartments, has received three roubles. A sum well spent, for I hope to get a great deal more than that from the poor old hippopotamus."
Controlling himself with difficulty.
There's no necessity to read any more of this.

KROUTITZKY. Here. Give it to me. I'll read it out.

MAMAEV. That's all right, thanks. I can do it. There's a—a conversation with me here, of no interest to anybody. Ah, this is better. "First visit to the doddering old Kroutitzky."

KROUTITZKY. What? What's that? What?

MAMAEV. "Let's sing the praises of this great old man and his awe-inspiring projects! One cannot admire you enough, venerable aged gentleman. Tell us, only tell us, how you've reached the age of sixty and managed to preserve intact the brain of a six-year-old child."

KROUTITZKY. Enough! Stop! It's a libel! Hand me that book. Give it to me at once.
GORODOULIN comes in from the garden. Nobody notices him.

MAMAEV, *struggling for the diary with* KROUTITZKY. Allow me. Please!
Gets it away from him.
Thank you. I see there are a few words about Gorodoulin here. "Gorodoulin was taking part in some idiotic discussion about housing problems the other day, and someone, in a moment of passion, accused him of being a liberal; he was so delighted that for three whole days he drove about Moscow telling everybody he was a liberal. So now he's accepted as one." Well, there you are, that's just like him.

KROUTITZKY. Why don't you read the part about *yourself?* "The poor old hippopotamus," that's you.

GORODOULIN, *coming down to* MAMAEV *and taking the diary from him.* So you think this is just like me?

MAMAEV. Oh . . . er . . . hallo, Ivan. I didn't notice you. Well, so you see what a study's been made of us all?

GORODOULIN. Who is this youthful Juvenal?

MAMAEV. Yegor Gloumov.

MADAME T., *faintly*. Ivan. Take that diary back to its owner and ask him to leave as quietly and quickly as he can.

GLOUMOV *comes in from the garden;* GORODOULIN *hands him the diary.*

GLOUMOV. Don't alarm yourself, Madame Tourousina. I'm not going to make a fuss, to explain anything, or attempt to justify myself in any way. I should only like to point out that in dismissing me from your society you're making a very big mistake.

KROUTITZKY. We have no use for you, young man. We're decent, honest people here.

General chorus of agreement.

GLOUMOV. Oh. And who has decided that I am dishonest? Was it you, Mr. Kroutitzky? Perhaps your piercing brain became convinced of my dishonesty when I undertook to rewrite your treatise for you? Did you decide that no decent person would agree to do such nauseating work, or did you realise my dishonesty that day in my apartment when I expressed delighted admiration at your most pompously puerile phrases, and fawned upon you so much that I practically licked your boots? Oh no, you were ready to kiss me then, weren't you? What's more, if you'd never got hold of my diary, you'd have looked upon me as a decent honest man until your dying day.

KROUTITZKY. If I hadn't read the diary, yes, but . . .

GLOUMOV. And what about *you*, uncle? When did you decide I wasn't a fit person for your society? When you were teaching me how to flatter Mr. Kroutitzky? Or was it when you gave me a lesson in how to make love to your wife, so as to keep away other admirers, and I blushed and stammered, pretending I didn't know how, and saying I felt ashamed? You knew perfectly well I was pretending, but what did you care, so long as you could fancy yourself as an experienced man of the world teaching an inexperienced youngster how to handle women and get on in life? I'm twenty times more intelligent than you and you know it, but when I pretend to be a fool and ask for your advice you're delighted and prepared to swear that I'm the most honest and decent fellow in the world.

MAMAEV. Well—it's no good bringing up these things now. Better keep quiet about them. We all belong to the same family.

GLOUMOV, *turning to* MADAME TOUROUSINA. I admit I made a fool of you, Madame Tourousina, but I'm not ashamed of that. I'm only sorry for Mashenka. You ask to be made a fool of every day of your life. In fact, you enjoy it. You let a rum-sodden old woman from the streets enter your house and you obediently choose a husband for your niece on that woman's advice. Who does your Madame Maniefa know? Whom can she recommend? The one who gives her the most money, of course. You were lucky it happened to be me and not an escaped convict she saw descending in a cloud. You'd have accepted him in just the same way.

MADAME T. I only know one thing, the world's too evil to live in.

GLOUMOV, *turning to* GORODOULIN. Well, and what about you, Ivan?

GORODOULIN. Not a word. I've the greatest admiration for you. Here's my hand. Every word you've said about us—at least about me, I don't know about the others—is the complete truth.

GLOUMOV. You see, ladies and gentlemen, you all need me. You can't live without a person like me. People much worse than I will come along, and you'll say, "This fellow's worse than Gloumov—but still I can't help liking him. . . ." You're a very staid old gentleman, Mr. Kroutitzky, but when you're with a young man who treats you deferentially and humbly agrees with every word you say—a feeling of rapture goes right through you. You'd do anything to help a man like that. But if he is honest, if he dares to give his true opinion of your futile plans and projects, you'd see him starve before you'd lift a finger for him.

KROUTITZKY. You're taking too great an advantage of our leniency, Mr. Gloumov. You can go too far.

GLOUMOV, *politely*. Don't be offended, please. You can't get on without me, uncle. Even the servants won't listen to your interminable lectures, however much you pay them; whereas I listen to them for nothing.

MAMAEV. That's quite enough. If you haven't understood yet that it's indecent for you to remain here any longer, I must explain it to you.

GLOUMOV. It's quite unnecessary.
Turning to GORODOULIN.
And you're another. You can't get on without me either.

GORODOULIN. I admit it.

GLOUMOV. Where will you get the epigrams for your after-dinner speeches, without me?

GORODOULIN. I've no idea.

GLOUMOV. And how will you write those scathing criticisms without my help?

GORODOULIN. I don't know.

GLOUMOV. And you have need of me too, auntie.

KLEOPATRA. I've nothing to say. There's only one thing I can't forgive you and I'll try to forget that.

KROUTITZKY, *to* MAMAEV. You know, I thought there was something fishy about him from the beginning——

MAMAEV. So did I, something about his eyes.

GLOUMOV. You thought nothing of the sort. You're furious about my diary, that's all. I don't know how it got into your hands, but even the cleverest man makes a slip sometimes. I'd like you to know, ladies and gentlemen, that all the time I was moving in your august society, I was only honest when I was writing in that diary. And any decent person would have the same attitude towards you. Frankly, you make me sick! What's offended you in it, anyway? Surely there's nothing new here. You yourselves constantly say the same things behind each other's backs. If I'd read out to each of you separately what I'd written about the others, you'd have roared with laughter and patted me on the back. I'm the one who should feel offended and furious, not you! I don't know who it was, but it was one of your decent honest members of society who stole my diary. Well, you've ruined everything for me. You're kicking me out, and you think that'll be the end of it. But you're mistaken. You've not heard the end of it, not by any means.

Looking round at them all.

I consider that you've behaved abominably, that your conduct is indefensible and you're not fit to enjoy the society of a decent, honest man like myself.

Turns suddenly, and goes out through the garden. Silence.

MAMAEV. Well . . . er . . . perhaps we oughtn't to let him go like this.

KROUTITZKY. It might be making a mistake.

KLEOPATRA. No, I don't think we ought to let him go.

MADAME T. I'd like to talk to him again. I'm beginning to see things in quite a different light.

GORODOULIN. Let's get him back.

Running to the French windows, he calls.

Yegor! Yegor! Come back!

MAMAEV, *following him.* That's right, call him. He'll hear you.

Yelling.

Come back, Yegor, come back!

MADAME T. *to* KOURCHAEV. Run after him, stop him before he gets to the gates.

KOURCHAEV *runs out.*

KLEOPATRA, *who has joined the others.* Yegor, come back!

MADAME T., *also joining them, followed by* MASHENKA. I feel I'd like to have a talk with him. He's such an interesting person.

MASHENKA. I don't want to marry him, Auntie, but I agree with everything he said.

MAMAEV. There he is. Kourchaev's catching him up!

ALL, *including* KROUTITZKY, *who has hobbled up in the rear.*
Come back! Yegor, come back, come back!

GRIGORI, *appearing.* Madame Maniefa to see you, madam. . . .
He stands back deferentially to allow her to pass.

Curtain

LA RONDE

Ten Dialogues
by

ARTHUR SCHNITZLER

English version by
Eric Bentley

Characters

THE WHORE
THE SOLDIER
THE PARLOR MAID
THE YOUNG GENTLEMAN
THE YOUNG WIFE
THE HUSBAND
THE LITTLE MISS
THE POET
THE ACTRESS
THE COUNT

THE TIME: *The eighteen-nineties.*

THE PLACE: *Vienna.*

1 THE WHORE AND THE SOLDIER

Late in the evening. On the Augarten Bridge.

SOLDIER, *on his way home, whistling.*

WHORE. Want to come with me, Angel Face?

SOLDIER *turns round, then walks on.*

WHORE. Wouldn't you like to come with me?

SOLDIER. You mean me? Angel Face?!

WHORE. Who do you think? Come on. Come with me. I live near here.

SOLDIER. I got no time. Have to get back to the barracks.

WHORE. You'll get back to the barracks all right. But it's nicer with me.

SOLDIER, *near her now.* Yeah. Could be.

WHORE. Uh, uh! A cop might come.

SOLDIER. Nonsense! What's a cop? I got my sword on.

WHORE. Come on with me!

SOLDIER. Leave me alone. I got no money anyhow.

WHORE. I don't need no money.

SOLDIER *stops. They are under a street lamp.* You don't need no money? Who are you for God's sake?

WHORE. Civilians have to pay, sure. A guy like you can get it from me for nothing.

SOLDIER. So you're the one Huber told me about. . . .

WHORE. I don't know any Huber.

SOLDIER. You'd be it. That's right. The cafe in the Schiff Gasse. Then he went home with you.

147

WHORE. The cafe in the Schiff Gasse! I've taken plenty of guys home from there. Eh!
Her eyes tell how many.

SOLDIER. Let's go then, let's go.

WHORE. What? You're in a hurry now?

SOLDIER. Well, what are we waiting for? I gotta be back in the barracks at ten.

WHORE. How long you been in the army?

SOLDIER. What business is that of yours? Live far from here?

WHORE. Ten minutes' walk.

SOLDIER. Too far. How about a kiss?

WHORE *kisses him.* I figure that's the best part of it. When I like a guy.

SOLDIER. I don't. No. I can't go with you. Too far.

WHORE. Tell you what. Come tomorrow. In the afternoon.

SOLDIER. Okay. Give me the address.

WHORE. Only—I bet you won't come.

SOLDIER. I told you I would, didn't I?

WHORE. Tell you what—if it's too far tonight—how about over there?
She points toward the Danube.

SOLDIER. What's over there?

WHORE. Lovely and quiet there too. No one around this late.

SOLDIER. Aw, that's no good.

WHORE. It's always good—with me. Come on, stick around with me. How long do we have to live?

SOLDIER. Okay, then. But let's make it snappy.

WHORE. Easy. It's so dark there. One slip, and you're in the Danube.

SOLDIER. Might be the best thing.

WHORE. Pst! Hey, wait a second. We're just coming to a bench.

SOLDIER. You know your way around.

WHORE. Wish I had a guy like you for a boy friend.

SOLDIER. I'd make you jealous too much.

WHORE. I'd know how to take care of that.

SOLDIER. Think so?

WHORE. Not so loud. Could be a cop around at that—he might
be lost. You wouldn't think we were right in the middle of
Vienna, would you?

SOLDIER. Over here. Come on over here!

WHORE. What's eating you? If we slip, we're in the river!

SOLDIER *has grabbed hold of her.* Ah! now . . .

WHORE. Hold on tight now.

SOLDIER. Don't worry . . .

    *   *   *   *   *

WHORE. It'd have been a lot better on the bench.

SOLDIER. On the bench, off the bench . . . Well, you getting up?

WHORE. Where are you rushing off—

SOLDIER. Got to get back to the barracks. I'm late anyhow.

WHORE. Tell me, soldier—what's your name?

SOLDIER. What's my name got to do with you?

WHORE. Mine's—Leocadia.

SOLDIER. Ha! That's a new one!

WHORE. Soldier . . .

SOLDIER. Well, what do you want?

WHORE. How about a dime for the janitor?

SOLDIER. Ha! . . . What do you think *I* am? Goodby! Leocadia . . .

WHORE. You crook! You son of a bitch!
    He is gone.

2 THE SOLDIER AND THE PARLOR MAID

The Prater. Sunday evening. A path leading from the
WURSTELPRATER—*or amusement park—out into dark avenues*
of trees. The din of the amusement park is audible. So is the
sound of the FÜNFKREUZERTANZ—*a banal polka—played by*
a brass band. The Soldier. The Parlor Maid.

PARLOR MAID. Yes, but now you must tell me. What were you
wanting to leave for all the time?

SOLDIER *laughs stupidly; he is embarrassed.*

PARLOR MAID. I thought it was marvellous. I love dancing.

SOLDIER *takes her by the waist.*

PARLOR MAID, *letting him.* But we're not dancing *now.* Why
are you holding me so tight?

SOLDIER. What's your name? Kathi?

PARLOR MAID. You've got a Kathi on your mind.

SOLDIER. I know. I've got it: Marie.

PARLOR MAID. Look, it's dark here. I get so scared.

SOLDIER. Nothing to be afraid of with me around. Just leave it
to uncle.

PARLOR MAID. But where are we going to, through? There's no
one around at all. Let's go back, come on! How *dark* it is!

SOLDIER, *pulling at his Virginia cigar till the tip glows.* See it
get lighter? Ha! My little treasure!

PARLOR MAID. Ooh! What are you doing? If I'd known *this*. . .

SOLDIER. Nice and soft! Damned if you're not the nicest and
softest one in the whole bunch, Fräulein!

PARLOR MAID. What whole bunch?

SOLDIER. In there—in the Swoboda.

PARLOR MAID. You tried all of them?

SOLDIER. Oh, you notice. Dancing. You notice a lot of things. Ha!

PARLOR MAID. You danced with that blonde more than with me. The one with the face.

SOLDIER. Friend of a buddy of mine. An old friend of his.

PARLOR MAID. The corporal with the turned-up mustache?

SOLDIER. Nah. The civilian. You know—the one at the table with me before. With the hoarse voice?

PARLOR MAID. Oh, yes. I know. He's pretty fresh.

SOLDIER. Did *he* try something with you? I'll show the bastard. What did he try?

PARLOR MAID. Oh, nothing. I just saw how he was with the other girls.

SOLDIER. Now, Fräulein, tell me . . .

PARLOR MAID. Ooh! You'll burn me with that cigar.

SOLDIER. Oh, pardon me, Fräulein—or can I call you . . . Marie?

PARLOR MAID. We haven't known each other very long.

SOLDIER. Hell, there's lots of people use first names and don't even like each other.

PARLOR MAID. Let's make it next time, when . . . You see, Herr Franz . . .

SOLDIER. You got my name!

PARLOR MAID. You see, Herr Franz . . .

SOLDIER. Make it just—Franz, Fräulein.

PARLOR MAID. *You* mustn't be so fresh. Sh! What if somebody comes!

SOLDIER. What if they do? You can't see six feet in front of you.

PARLOR MAID. But, heavens, where are we getting to?

SOLDIER. Look! There's two just like us.

PARLOR MAID. Where? I can't see a thing.

SOLDIER. There. Right up there.

PARLOR MAID. What do you say like *us* for?

SOLDIER. Oh, I only mean—they kinda like each other.

PARLOR MAID. Hey, watch out! What was that? I nearly fell.

SOLDIER. It's these railings they put round the grass.

PARLOR MAID. Don't push so hard. I'll fall right over.

SOLDIER. Sh! Not so loud!

PARLOR MAID. Look now I'm *really* going to scream! What are you doing . . . hey . . .

SOLDIER. There's no one for miles around.

PARLOR MAID. Let's go back with the rest of them.

SOLDIER. But we don't need them, Marie, what we need is . . . uh, huh . . .

PARLOR MAID. Herr Franz, please! For Heaven's sake!! Now listen, if I'd had . . . any idea . . . oh! . . . oh!! . . . yes . . .

❋   ❋   ❋   ❋   ❋

SOLDIER (*blissfully*). Jesus Christ Almighty! . . . Ah-h! . . .

PARLOR MAID. . . . I can't see your face at all.

SOLDIER. My face? . . . Hell!

❋   ❋   ❋   ❋   ❋

SOLDIER. Now look, Fräulein, you can't stay in the grass all night.

PARLOR MAID. Oh, come on, Franz, help me up!

SOLDIER. Okay.
He grabs her.
Oops!

PARLOR MAID. Oh dear, Franz!

SOLDIER. Yes, yes? What's the matter with Franz?

PARLOR MAID. You're a bad man, Franz.

SOLDIER. Oh, so that's it? Hey, wait for me!

PARLOR MAID. What do you let me go for?

SOLDIER. Can't I get this cigar lit for God's sake?

PARLOR MAID. It's so dark.

SOLDIER. Well, tomorrow it'll be light again.

PARLOR MAID. Tell me something—do you like me?

SOLDIER. I thought you might have noticed!
   He laughs.

PARLOR MAID. Where are we going?

SOLDIER. Why, back!

PARLOR MAID. Oh, please, Franz, not so quick!

SOLDIER. What's the matter? I don't like running around in the
   dark.

PARLOR MAID. Tell me, Franz, do you . . . like me?

SOLDIER. I just told you I liked you.

PARLOR MAID. Come on then, give me little kiss.

SOLDIER, *condescending.* Here . . . listen! You can hear that
   music again.

SOLDIER. Sure. What's wrong with that?

PARLOR MAID. Well, Franz, look, I must be getting back. They'll
   gripe anyhow, the lady of the house is such a . . . she'd like it
   best if we never went out at all.

SOLDIER. Sure. You go home then.

PARLOR MAID. Herr Franz! I thought . . . you might take me.

SOLDIER. Home? Eh!
   The open vowel indicating disgust.

PARLOR MAID. Oh, please, it's so dreary—going home alone!

SOLDIER. Where do you live?

PARLOR MAID. It's not far—Porzellan Gasse.

SOLDIER. Oh! Then we go the same way . . . But it's too early
   for me! I want some fun. I got a late pass tonight. Don't have
   to be back in the barracks till twelve. I'm going dancing.

PARLOR MAID. *I* see how it is. It's that blonde. The one with the face.

SOLDIER. Ha! . . . Her face ain't so bad.

PARLOR MAID. Heavens, you men are wicked! I bet you do this to every girl.

SOLDIER. That might be *too* many.

PARLOR MAID. Franz, do me a favor. Not tonight—stay just with me tonight, look. . . .

SOLDIER. Okay, okay. But I can dance for a while first, I suppose?

PARLOR MAID. Tonight I'm not dancing with anyone but you.

SOLDIER. Here it is.

PARLOR MAID. What?

SOLDIER. The Swoboda, quick work, huh? And they're still playing *that* thing.
Singing with the band.
Tatatatum, tatatatum! . . . All right, if you want to wait, I'll take you home. If you don't, I'll be saying good night . .

PARLOR MAID. I think I'll wait.

SOLDIER. Why don't you get yourself a glass of beer?
Turning to a blonde, dancing by with her boy, putting on a "refined" accent.
May I have the pleasure?

3 THE PARLOR MAID AND THE YOUNG GENTLEMAN

A hot summer afternoon. His parents are off in the country. The cook is having her half-day. In the kitchen, the Parlor Maid is writing the Soldier a letter; he is her lover. There is a ring from the Young Gentleman's room. She gets up and goes into the Young Gentleman's room. The Young Gentleman is lying on the sofa with cigarette and French novel.

PARLOR MAID. You rang, Herr Alfred?

YOUNG GENTLEMAN. Oh, Yes . . . Marie . . . yes, I did ring as a matter of fact. . . . Now what was it? . . . Oh, I know, let the blinds down, Marie, will you? . . . It's cooler with the blinds down . . . don't you think? . . .

PARLOR MAID goes to the window and lets the Venetian blinds down.

YOUNG GENTLEMAN, *going on reading.* What are you doing, Marie? That's right. Oh, but now I can't see to read.

PARLOR MAID. The way you always study so, Herr Alfred!

YOUNG GENTLEMAN, *passing over this loftily.* That'll be all, thanks.

The PARLOR MAID goes out.

The YOUNG GENTLEMAN tries to go on reading; soon lets the book fall; rings again.

The PARLOR MAID is in the doorway.

YOUNG GENTLEMAN. Look, Marie . . . now, um, what I was going to say . . . well . . . yes, is there any cognac in the house?

PARLOR MAID. Yes, Herr Alfred. But it's locked up.

YOUNG GENTLEMAN. Oh. Well, who has the key?

PARLOR MAID. Lini has the key.

YOUNG GENTLEMAN. Who's Lini?

PARLOR MAID. The cook, Herr Alfred.

YOUNG GENTLEMAN. Oh. Then go and tell Lini.

PARLOR MAID. Well . . . Lini's having her half-day.

YOUNG GENTLEMAN. Oh.

PARLOR MAID. Shall I run over to the cafe for you, Herr Alfred?

YOUNG GENTLEMAN. Oh, no . . . hot enough as it is. I don't need cognac anyway. Listen, Marie, just bring me a glass of water. Wait, Marie—let it run, hm? Till it's quite cold?

The PARLOR MAID goes.

The YOUNG GENTLEMAN is watching her go when the PARLOR

MAID *turns round at the door. The* YOUNG GENTLEMAN *stares into space. The* PARLOR MAID *turns the faucet on and lets the water run. Meanwhile, she goes to her little room, washes her hands, and arranges her curls in the mirror. Then she brings the* YOUNG GENTLEMAN *the glass of water. She walks to the sofa.*

The YOUNG GENTLEMAN *raises himself part way. The* PARLOR MAID *puts the glass in his hand. Their fingers touch.*

YOUNG GENTLEMAN. Oh. Thanks. . . . Well, what is it? Now be careful. Put the glass back on the tray. . . .

He lies back and stretches out.

What's the time?

PARLOR MAID. Five o'clock, Herr Alfred.

YOUNG GENTLEMAN. I see. Five. Thank you.

The PARLOR MAID *goes; at the door, she turns; the* YOUNG GENTLEMAN *is looking; she notices and smiles.*

The YOUNG GENTLEMAN *lies where he is for a while, then suddenly gets up. He walks to the door; then returns and lies down on the sofa. He tries to read again. In a couple of minutes, he again rings.*

The PARLOR MAID *enters with a smile which she makes no attempt to hide.*

YOUNG GENTLEMAN. Look, Marie, what I was going to ask you . . . didn't Dr. Schueller call by this morning?

PARLOR MAID. No. No one called this morning.

YOUNG GENTLEMAN. Well. that's strange. So Dr. Schueller didn't call? You know him—Dr. Schueller?

PARLOR MAID. Oh, yes. The tall gentleman with the big black beard.

YOUNG GENTLEMAN. Yes. Maybe he *did* call?

PARLOR MAID. No. No one called, Herr Alfred.

YOUNG GENTLEMAN, *taking the plunge.* Come here, Marie.

PARLOR MAID, *coming a little closer.* Yes, Herr Alfred?

YOUNG GENTLEMAN. Closer . . . yes . . . um . . . I only thought . . .

PARLOR MAID. Yes, Herr Alfred?

YOUNG GENTLEMAN. Thought . . . I thought . . . about that blouse. What kind is it? . . . Oh, come on, closer. I won't bite you.

PARLOR MAID *comes.* What's this about my blouse? You don't like it, Herr Alfred?

YOUNG GENTLEMAN *takes hold of the blouse and, in so doing, pulls the* PARLOR MAID *down on him.* Blue, is it? Yes, what a lovely blue!
Simply.
You're very nicely dressed, Marie.

PARLOR MAID. Oh, Herr Alfred!

YOUNG GENTLEMAN. Well, you are!
He's opened the blouse. Matter-of-fact.
You've got lovely white skin, Marie.

PARLOR MAID. I think you're flattering me, Herr Alfred.

YOUNG GENTLEMAN, *kissing her bosom.* This can't hurt you, can it?

PARLOR MAID. Oh no!

YOUNG GENTLEMAN. How you're sighing! Why do you sigh like that?

PARLOR MAID. Oh, Herr Alfred . . .

YOUNG GENTLEMAN. And what nice slippers you have on . . .

PARLOR MAID. . . . but . . . Herr Alfred . . . if the doorbell rings . . .

YOUNG GENTLEMAN. Who'd ring at this hour?

PARLOR MAID. But, Herr Alfred . . . you see, it's so light!

YOUNG GENTLEMAN. Oho, you needn't be embarrassed with me! *You* needn't be embarrassed with anybody . . . pretty as you are! I swear you *are,* Marie! You know, your hair has such a pleasant smell.

PARLOR MAID. Herr Alfred . . .

YOUNG GENTLEMAN. Don't make such a fuss, Marie. I've seen you . . . quite different. When I came in late the other night, and went for a glass of water, the door to your room was open . . . yes . . .

PARLOR MAID *hides her face.* Heavens, I'd no idea you could be so naughty, Herr Alfred.

YOUNG GENTLEMAN. I saw a great, great deal . . . this . . . and this . . . and this . . . and . . .

PARLOR MAID. Herr Alfred!!

YOUNG GENTLEMAN. Come on . . . here . . . that's right, yes . . .

PARLOR MAID. But if anyone rings . . .

YOUNG GENTLEMAN. Now stop it, for Heaven's sake. We won't go to the door. . . .

❋   ❋   ❋   ❋   ❋

The doorbell rings.

YOUNG GENTLEMAN. Christ Almighty! . . . What a racket the man makes! Maybe he rang before and we just didn't pay attention.

PARLOR MAID. Oh, I kept my ears open the whole time.

YOUNG GENTLEMAN. Well, now, go and see—through the peephole.

PARLOR MAID. Herr Alfred . . . You *are* . . . No! . . . a naughty man!

YOUNG GENTLEMAN. Now please, go take a look.
The PARLOR MAID *goes. The* YOUNG GENTLEMAN *quickly pulls up the Venetian blinds.*

PARLOR MAID *comes back.* Whoever it was, he's gone away again. There's no one there. Maybe it was Dr. Schueller.

YOUNG GENTLEMAN, *disagreeably affected.* That'll be all, thanks.
The PARLOR MAID *comes closer.*

YOUNG GENTLEMAN, *retreating.* Look, Marie, I'm going. To the café.

PARLOR MAID, *tenderly.* So soon . . . Herr Alfred?

YOUNG GENTLEMAN, *severely.* I'm going to the café. If Dr. Schueller should come here . . .

PARLOR MAID. He won't be here today.

YOUNG GENTLEMAN, *more severely.* If Dr. Schueller should come here, I . . . I . . . I'm—in the café.

He goes into the next room.

The PARLOR MAID takes a cigar from the smoking-table, slips it in her pocket, and goes out.

4 THE YOUNG GENTLEMAN AND THE YOUNG WIFE

Evening. A drawing-room in a house in the SCHWIND GASSE, *furnished with cheap elegance.*

The YOUNG GENTLEMAN *has just come in and, still in hat and overcoat, lights the candles. Then he opens the door into the next room and glances in. The glow of the candles in the drawing room falls on the parquet floor and makes its way to the four-poster against the rear wall; a reddish glow from the fireplace in a corner of the bedroom is thrown on the bed curtains.*

The YOUNG GENTLEMAN *also inspects the bedroom. He takes an atomizer from the dressing table and sprays the pillows with a fine stream of violet perfume. Then he goes with the spray through both rooms, squeezing the little bulb the whole time, so that soon the whole place smells of violets. He takes off hat and overcoat, sits down in a blue velvet armchair, lights a cigarette, and smokes. After a short while he gets up to make sure that the green shutters are drawn. Suddenly he goes back to the bedroom, opens the drawer of the bedside table, feels around till he finds a tortoise shell hairpin. He looks round for a place to hide it, and finally puts it in his overcoat pocket. Then he opens a cupboard in the drawing room, takes out a silver tray, a cognac bottle, and two liqueur glasses, and puts it all on the table. He goes back to his overcoat and fishes out a small white parcel, which he opens and puts next to the cognac bottle. He returns to the cupboard and takes out two dessert plates, knives, and forks. From the small parcel he extracts a mar-*

*ron glacé and eats it. Then he pours himself a glass of cognac
and quickly drinks it down. He looks at his watch. He paces
the room. In front of the large mirror on the wall he stops
for a while, smoothing his hair and little moustache with a
pocket comb. He goes to the door to the hall and listens—not
a sound. He draws the blue curtains screening the door to
the bedroom. The doorbell rings. The* YOUNG GENTLEMAN
*gives a start. He drops into an armchair and only rises when
the door opens and the* YOUNG WIFE *enters.
The* YOUNG WIFE *thickly veiled, shuts the door behind her
and stands for a moment with her left hand on her heart, as
though she had to master intense emotion.*

YOUNG GENTLEMAN *goes to her, takes her left hand, and im-
prints a kiss on the white, black-trimmed glove; softly.* I
thank you.

YOUNG WIFE. Alfred—Alfred!

YOUNG GENTLEMAN. Come in, dear lady . . . come in, Frau
Emma.

YOUNG WIFE. Let me alone for a moment, please—oh, please,
Alfred!
*She stays close by the door.
The* YOUNG GENTLEMAN *stands before her, holding her hand.*

YOUNG WIFE. But where am I, actually?

YOUNG GENTLEMAN. In my house.

YOUNG WIFE. This place is a horror, Alfred.

YOUNG GENTLEMAN. Why? It's very dignified.

YOUNG WIFE. I met two men on the stairs.

YOUNG GENTLEMAN. People you know?

YOUNG WIFE. They may be. I'm not sure.

YOUNG GENTLEMAN. Forgive me—you must know who you
know!

YOUNG WIFE. But I didn't see a thing.

YOUNG GENTLEMAN. Even if they'd been your best friends, they
couldn't have recognized you. Even I . . . if I didn't know
it was you . . . this veil . . .

YOUNG WIFE. There are two.

YOUNG GENTLEMAN. Won't you come a bit farther in? And anyway do take off your hat.

YOUNG WIFE. What are you thinking of, Alfred? I told you—five minutes. No, not a second more! I swear . . .

YOUNG GENTLEMAN. Then the veil!

YOUNG WIFE. There are two.

YOUNG GENTLEMAN. Oh, well, both veils then—at least I'm allowed to see you!

YOUNG WIFE. Do you really love me, Alfred?

YOUNG GENTLEMAN, *deeply hurt*. Emma, can you ask . . . ?

YOUNG WIFE. It's so hot in here.

YOUNG GENTLEMAN. But you still have your fur cape on—you're going to catch cold!

YOUNG WIFE *at last steps into the room, throwing herself into an armchair*. I'm dead tired.

YOUNG GENTLEMAN. Permit me.
He takes her veils off, takes out the hatpin, puts hat, pin, and veils down side by side on the sofa.
The YOUNG WIFE *lets it happen.*
The YOUNG GENTLEMAN *stands before her, shaking his head.*

YOUNG WIFE. What's the matter with you?

YOUNG GENTLEMAN. Never were you so beautiful!

YOUNG WIFE. How's that?

YOUNG GENTLEMAN. Alone . . . alone with you . . . Emma . . .
He sinks on one knee beside the armchair, takes both her hands and covers them with kisses.

YOUNG WIFE. And now . . . let me go. I have done what you asked.
The YOUNG GENTLEMAN *drops his head on to her lap.*

YOUNG WIFE. You promised me to be good.

YOUNG GENTLEMAN. Yes.

YOUNG WIFE. This room's stifling.

YOUNG GENTLEMAN *gets up.* You still have your cape on.

YOUNG WIFE. Put it with my hat.

The YOUNG GENTLEMAN *takes off her cape and puts it on the sofa along with the hat and the other things.*

YOUNG WIFE. And now—adieu——

YOUNG GENTLEMAN. Emma!

YOUNG WIFE. The five minutes are up.

YOUNG GENTLEMAN. No, no! You haven't been here one minute yet!

YOUNG WIFE. Alfred, please, tell me exactly what time it is.

YOUNG GENTLEMAN. Quarter past six, on the nose.

YOUNG WIFE. I should have been at my sister's long ago.

YOUNG GENTLEMAN. You can see your sister any time . . .

YOUNG WIFE. Oh God, Alfred, why did you get me to do this?

YOUNG GENTLEMAN. Because I . . . worship you, Emma.

YOUNG WIFE. How many women have you said that to?

YOUNG GENTLEMAN. Since I saw you, to none.

YOUNG WIFE. What a frivolous woman I am! If anyone had told me—a week ago . . . or even yesterday . . .

YOUNG GENTLEMAN. It was the day before yesterday you promised . . .

YOUNG WIFE. Because you kept tormenting me. But I didn't want to, God is my witness—I didn't want to. Yesterday I'd made up my mind. . . . Do you know I even wrote you a long letter last night?

YOUNG GENTLEMAN. I didn't get it.

YOUNG WIFE. I tore it up. I should have sent it after all!

YOUNG GENTLEMAN. It's better like this.

YOUNG WIFE. No, it's scandalous . . . of me. I can't understand myself. Good-bye, Alfred, let me go.

The YOUNG GENTLEMAN *takes her in his arms and covers her face with hot kisses.*

YOUNG WIFE. So this is . . . how you keep your promise?

YOUNG GENTLEMAN. One more kiss! Just one.

YOUNG WIFE. The last!
He kisses her, she reciprocates, and their lips stay together a long time.

YOUNG GENTLEMAN. May I tell you something, Emma? Now I know what happiness is.
The YOUNG WIFE *sinks back in an armchair.*

YOUNG GENTLEMAN *sits on the arm of the chair, putting his arm gently round her neck. . . . Or rather, now I know what happiness* might *be.*
The YOUNG WIFE *gives a profound sigh.*
The YOUNG GENTLEMAN *kisses her again.*

YOUNG WIFE. Alfred, Alfred, what are you making of me?

YOUNG GENTLEMAN. It's not really so uncomfortable here, is it? And we are so safe. It's a thousand times better than meeting in the open air.

YOUNG WIFE. Oh, don't remind me.

YOUNG GENTLEMAN. Even those meetings I shall think of with delight! Every minute I've had the privilege of spending at your side will linger forever in the memory.

YOUNG WIFE. You remember the Industrial Ball?

YOUNG GENTLEMAN. Do I remember? . . . But didn't I sit next to you during supper—right up close? The champagne your husband——
The YOUNG WIFE *gives him a look of protest.*

YOUNG GENTLEMAN. I was only going to mention the champagne! Tell me, Emma, wouldn't you like a glass of cognac?

YOUNG WIFE. Maybe just a drop. But first let me have a glass of water.

YOUNG GENTLEMAN. Yes . . . now, where is . . . Oh yes.

*He draws the curtains back from the door and goes into the
bedroom.*
The YOUNG WIFE *looks after him.*
The YOUNG GENTLEMAN *returns with a filled decanter and
two glasses.*

YOUNG WIFE. Where were you?

YOUNG GENTLEMAN. In the—next room.
He pours a glass of water for her.

YOUNG WIFE. Now I'm going to ask you something, Alfred, and
you must swear to tell the truth.

YOUNG GENTLEMAN. I swear . . .

YOUNG WIFE. Was there ever another woman in these rooms?

YOUNG GENTLEMAN. But, Emma, this house has been around
for twenty years!

YOUNG WIFE. You know what I mean, Alfred . . . with you . . .

YOUNG GENTLEMAN. With me, here? Emma! You couldn't think
such a thing!

YOUNG WIFE. Then you have . . . how shall I . . . ? But no, I'd
better not ask you. It's better if I don't ask. It's my own
fault. We pay for everything!

YOUNG GENTLEMAN. But what is it? What's the matter with
you? *What* do we pay for?

YOUNG WIFE. No, no, no, I mustn't return to consciousness—or
I'd sink into the ground for very shame.

YOUNG GENTLEMAN, *still with the decanter in his hand, sadly
shakes his head.* Emma, if only you had any idea how you
hurt me!
The YOUNG WIFE *pours herself a glass of cognac.*

YOUNG GENTLEMAN. I'll tell you something, Emma. If you're
ashamed to be here—that's to say, if I'm nothing to you—if
you don't feel that for me you're all the bliss in the world—
then leave. Leave.

YOUNG WIFE. That is just what I'll do.

YOUNG GENTLEMAN, *seizing her hand.* But if you realize that

I can't live without you, that to kiss your hand means more to me than all the caresses of all the women in the whole world. Emma, I'm not like the other young men who know how . . . this sort of thing is done . . . call me naïve if you wish . . . I . . .

YOUNG WIFE. But what if you *were* like the other young men?

YOUNG GENTLEMAN. Then you wouldn't be here now: you aren't like the other young women.

YOUNG WIFE. How do you know?

YOUNG GENTLEMAN *has drawn her on to the sofa and sits down close beside her.* I've thought a lot about you. I know you're unhappy.
The YOUNG WIFE *looks pleased.*

YOUNG GENTLEMAN. Life is so empty, so trivial. And so short. . . . Isn't life frightfully short, Emma? There is only one happiness: to find someone who loves you.
The YOUNG WIFE *has taken a candied pear from the table and puts it into her mouth.*

YOUNG GENTLEMAN. Give me half!
She offers it to him with her lips.

YOUNG WIFE *takes the* YOUNG GENTLEMAN's *hands, which threaten to go astray.* What are you doing, Alfred? Is this your promise?

YOUNG GENTLEMAN *swallows the candied fruit, then says more boldly.* Life is so short!

YOUNG WIFE, *feebly.* But that's no reason . . .

YOUNG GENTLEMAN, *mechanically.* Oh, but it is.

YOUNG WIFE, *more feebly.* Now look, Alfred, you promised to be good. . . . And it's so light . . .

YOUNG GENTLEMAN. Come, come, my only one, my only . . .
He lifts her off the sofa.

YOUNG WIFE. What are you doing?

YOUNG GENTLEMAN. It's not light in there.

YOUNG WIFE. Is there another room?

YOUNG GENTLEMAN, *taking her with him.* A lovely one . . . and quite dark.

YOUNG WIFE. I'd rather stay here.
The YOUNG GENTLEMAN *has already got her through the curtains and in the bedroom; he begins to unhook her dress at the waist.*

YOUNG WIFE. You're so . . . Oh God, what are you doing to me? . . . Alfred!

YOUNG GENTLEMAN. Emma, I worship you!

YOUNG WIFE. Wait, please, at least wait . . .
weakly
Go, I'll call for you . . .

YOUNG GENTLEMAN. Let me . . . let you help me . . . let . . . me . . . help . . . you . . .

YOUNG WIFE. But you're tearing everything!

YOUNG GENTLEMAN. Don't you wear a corset?

YOUNG WIFE. I never wear a corset. Neither does Duse, incidentally. You can unbutton my boots.
The YOUNG GENTLEMAN *unbuttons her boots, kisses her feet.*

YOUNG WIFE, *slipping into the bed.* Oooh, I'm cold.

YOUNG GENTLEMAN. It'll get warm.

YOUNG WIFE, *laughing softly.* You think so?

YOUNG GENTLEMAN, *not liking this, to himself.* She shouldn't have said that!
He undresses in the dark.

YOUNG WIFE, *tenderly.* Come, come, come.

YOUNG GENTLEMAN, *in a better mood at once.* At once . . .

YOUNG WIFE. It smells of violets here.

YOUNG GENTLEMAN. It's you . . . yes
Close by her.
. . . you.

YOUNG WIFE. Alfred . . . Alfred!!!!

YOUNG GENTLEMAN. Emma . . .

    ❀   ❀   ❀   ❀   ❀

YOUNG GENTLEMAN. I must be too much in love with you . . . that's why . . . I'm nearly out of my senses.

YOUNG WIFE. . . .

YOUNG GENTLEMAN. All these past days I've been going crazy. I felt it coming.

YOUNG WIFE. Don't worry your head about it.

YOUNG GENTLEMAN. Of course not, you can almost take it for granted when a man . . .

YOUNG WIFE. Don't . . . don't . . . You're nervous. Just relax . . .

YOUNG GENTLEMAN. You know Stendhal?

YOUNG WIFE. Stendhal?

YOUNG GENTLEMAN. His book *De l'amour.*

YOUNG WIFE. No. Why do you ask?

YOUNG GENTLEMAN. There's a story in it that's most significant.

YOUNG WIFE. What sort of story?

YOUNG GENTLEMAN. A bunch of officers have gotten together . . .

YOUNG WIFE. Oh.

YOUNG GENTLEMAN. And they talk about their love affairs. And every one says that with the woman he loved most . . . most passionately, you know . . . she made him . . . with her he . . . well, the fact is, it happened to every one of them . . . what happened to me with you.

YOUNG WIFE. I see.

YOUNG GENTLEMAN. This is very indicative.

YOUNG WIFE. Yes.

YOUNG GENTLEMAN. But that's not all. One of them claims . . . it has never happened to him in all his life. But—Stendhal adds—this man was a notorious show-off.

YOUNG WIFE. Oh.

YOUNG GENTLEMAN. All the same it kind of throws you, that's the stupid thing about it, even if it doesn't really matter.

YOUNG WIFE. Naturally. Anyway . . . you promised to be good.

YOUNG GENTLEMAN. Please don't laugh! That won't improve things.

YOUNG WIFE. I'm not laughing. This Stendhal story's very interesting. I'd always thought it happened only with older men . . . or with very . . . well, you know, men who've been too fast.

YOUNG GENTLEMAN. What an idea! That has nothing to do with it. By the way, I forgot the most charming story in the Stendhal. A lieutenant of hussars even says that he spent three nights—or was it six? I can't remember—with a woman he'd been wanting for weeks—*désiré* and all that—and all those nights they didn't do a thing but cry with happiness—both of them . . . *

YOUNG WIFE. Both of them?

YOUNG GENTLEMAN. Both of them. Does that surprise you? I find it so understandable. Specially when you're in love.

YOUNG WIFE. But there must be a lot who don't cry.

YOUNG GENTLEMAN, *nervously*. Surely . . . after all, it was an exceptional case.

YOUNG WIFE. Oh . . . I thought Stendhal says all hussars cry on these occasions.

YOUNG GENTLEMAN. There, you're just making fun . . .

YOUNG WIFE. Not in the least. Don't be so childish, Alfred.

YOUNG GENTLEMAN. I can't help it, it makes me nervous . . . and I have the feeling you're thinking of it the whole time. I'm embarrassed.

YOUNG WIFE. I am not thinking about it.

YOUNG GENTLEMAN. You are. If I could only be sure you love me!

YOUNG WIFE. Do you want better proof than . . . ?

* The Young Gentleman's stories are based on *De l'amour*, Chapter 60: "Failures."

YOUNG GENTLEMAN. You see! You're always making fun of me.

YOUNG WIFE. Not at all! Come, give me your sweet little head.

YOUNG GENTLEMAN. Oh, this is *good*.

YOUNG WIFE. Do you love me?

YOUNG GENTLEMAN. Oh, I'm so happy!

YOUNG WIFE. But you don't have to cry as well!

YOUNG GENTLEMAN *moves away, highly irritated.* Again, again! Didn't I beg you?

YOUNG WIFE. I said you shouldn't cry, that was all . . .

YOUNG GENTLEMAN. You said "Cry *as well*."

YOUNG WIFE. You're nervous, my dear.

YOUNG GENTLEMAN. I know that.

YOUNG WIFE. You shouldn't be. It's rather nice that . . . that we —that we—we're . . . comrades, as you might say . . .

YOUNG GENTLEMAN. Now you're starting over.

YOUNG WIFE. Don't you remember? It was one of our very first talks: we wanted to be . . . "just comrades. . . ." Oh, it was lovely that time . . . at my sister's, in January, at the great ball . . . during the quadrille. . . . For Heaven's sake, I should have left long ago! My sister will be waiting—what shall I tell her? Adieu, Alfred. . . .

YOUNG GENTLEMAN. Emma! You're going to leave me like this?

YOUNG WIFE. Yes. Like this!

YOUNG GENTLEMAN. Just another five minutes . . .

YOUNG WIFE. All right, five minutes. But you must promise me to keep quite still . . . Yes? . . . I'm going to give you a good-bye kiss . . . Ssh . . . keep still, as I told you, or I'll get right up. My sweet . . . sweet . . .

YOUNG GENTLEMAN. Emma . . . I worsh . . .

    *   *   *   *   *

YOUNG WIFE. Darling Alfred . . .

YOUNG GENTLEMAN. Oh, it's heaven with you!

YOUNG WIFE. But now I really must go.

YOUNG GENTLEMAN. Oh, let your sister wait.

YOUNG WIFE. I must go *home*. It's too late for my sister. What time is it now?

YOUNG GENTLEMAN. How'd I find *that* out?

YOUNG WIFE. By looking at your watch!

YOUNG GENTLEMAN. But it's in my waistcoat.

YOUNG WIFE. Well, get it.

YOUNG GENTLEMAN *get up with a mighty heave*. Eight.

YOUNG WIFE, *rising hastily*. For Heaven's sake! Quick, Alfred, my stockings—whatever shall I say? They'll be waiting for me . . . at home . . . eight o'clock!

YOUNG GENTLEMAN. When do I see you next?

YOUNG WIFE. Never.

YOUNG GENTLEMAN. Emma! Don't you still love me?

YOUNG WIFE. That's why. Give me my boots.

YOUNG GENTLEMAN. Never again? . . . Here are the boots.

YOUNG WIFE. There's a buttonhook in my pocket book. Please hurry . . .

YOUNG GENTLEMAN. Here's the buttonhook.

YOUNG WIFE. Alfred, this can cost us both our necks!

YOUNG GENTLEMAN, *not liking this at all*. Why?!

YOUNG WIFE. Well, what can I tell him when he asks me where I've been?

YOUNG GENTLEMAN. At your sister's.

YOUNG WIFE. Yes, if only I were a good liar.

YOUNG GENTLEMAN. You'll just have to be.

YOUNG WIFE. All this for a man like you . . . Come here. Let me give you another kiss.
She embraces him.

And now leave me alone, go in the other room, I can't dress with you around.

The YOUNG GENTLEMAN *goes to the drawing room and gets dressed. He eats a little of the pastry, drinks a glass of cognac.*

YOUNG WIFE, *after a while, calling out.* Alfred!

YOUNG GENTLEMAN. Yes, my treasure?

YOUNG WIFE. Maybe it's good we didn't just cry.

YOUNG GENTLEMAN *smiles, not without pride.* You're a very naughty girl.

YOUNG WIFE. What will it be like if we meet at a party one day —by chance?

YOUNG GENTLEMAN. One day? By chance? Surely you'll be at the Lobheimers' tomorrow?

YOUNG WIFE. Yes. Will you?

YOUNG GENTLEMAN. Of course. May I ask for the cotillion?

YOUNG WIFE. Oh, I won't go. How can you think . . . ? Why . . . *She enters the drawing room, fully dressed, and takes a chocolate pastry.*
. . . I'd sink into the ground!

YOUNG GENTLEMAN. Well, tomorrow at the Lobheimers'. That's lovely.

YOUNG WIFE. No, no, I'll send word I can't come. . . . Definitely. . . .

YOUNG GENTLEMAN. Then the day after tomorrow—here.

YOUNG WIFE. What an idea!

YOUNG GENTLEMAN. At six.

YOUNG WIFE. There are cabs at the corner, aren't there?

YOUNG GENTLEMAN. As many as you like. Then it's day after tomorrow, six o'clock, here. Say yes, my dearest treasure.

YOUNG WIFE. . . . We'll talk it over tomorrow—during the cotillion.

YOUNG GENTLEMAN, *embracing her.* Angel!

6

YOUNG WIFE. Don't spoil my hair-do again.

YOUNG GENTLEMAN. So it's tomorrow at the Lobheimers' and the day after—in my arms.

YOUNG WIFE. Good-bye . . .

YOUNG GENTLEMAN, *suddenly worried again*. And what are you going to tell *him* tonight?

YOUNG WIFE. Don't ask . . . don't ask . . . it's too dreadful. Why do I love you so? Good-bye. If I meet people on the stairs again I shall have a stroke.

The YOUNG GENTLEMAN *kisses her hand yet again.*

The YOUNG WIFE *goes.*

YOUNG GENTLEMAN *left alone. He sits down on the sofa. Then he smiles away to himself.* An affair with a respectable woman!

5   THE YOUNG WIFE AND THE HUSBAND

A comfortable bedroom. It is 10:30 *at night. The* YOUNG WIFE *is lying in bed, reading. The* HUSBAND *comes into the room in his bathrobe.*

YOUNG WIFE, *without looking up.* You've stopped working?

HUSBAND. Yes. I'm too tired. And besides . . .

YOUNG WIFE. Yes?

HUSBAND. I suddenly felt so lonely at my desk. I began longing for you.

YOUNG WIFE *looks up.* Really?

HUSBAND *sits by her on her bed.* Don't read any more tonight. You'll ruin your eyes.

YOUNG WIFE *closes the book.* What is it then?

HUSBAND. Nothing, my child. I'm in love with you. But you know that.

YOUNG WIFE. One might almost forget it sometimes.

HUSBAND. One even *has* to forget it sometimes.

YOUNG WIFE. Why?

HUSBAND. Marriage would be imperfect otherwise. It would—how shall I put it? it would lose its sanctity.

YOUNG WIFE. Oh . . .

HUSBAND. Believe me—it's true. . . . If in the course of the five years we've been married we hadn't sometimes forgotten we're in love with one another, we probably *wouldn't* be in love any more.

YOUNG WIFE. That's over my head.

HUSBAND. The fact is simply this: we've had something like ten or twelve different love affairs with one another . . . isn't that how it seems to you?

YOUNG WIFE. I haven't kept count.

HUSBAND. If we'd pushed our first affair to the limit, if I'd blindly surrendered myself to my passion for you from the beginning, we'd have gone the way of millions of others. We'd be through by now.

YOUNG WIFE. I see what you mean.

HUSBAND. Believe me—Emma—in the first days of our marriage I was afraid it would turn out that way.

YOUNG WIFE. So was I.

HUSBAND. You see? Wasn't I right? That's why it's best—from time to time—to live together just as friends.

YOUNG WIFE. Oh, I see.

HUSBAND. That way we can always keep having new honeymoons, because I never risk letting the weeks of the honeymoon . . .

YOUNG WIFE. . . . run into months.

HUSBAND. Exactly.

YOUNG WIFE. And now it seems . . . another of those periods of friendship has come to an end?

HUSBAND, *tenderly pressing her to him.* It could be so!

YOUNG WIFE. But suppose it was different—with me?

HUSBAND. It isn't different with you. You're the cleverest creature alive—*and* the most bewitching. I'm very happy to have found you.

YOUNG WIFE. So you do know how to court a woman—from time to time. I'm glad.

HUSBAND *has got into bed*. For a man who's seen the world a bit—come, put your head on my shoulder—seen the world a bit, marriage means something far more mysterious than to girls from good families like you. You come to us pure and—at least to a certain degree—ignorant, and so you have in reality a much clearer view of the true nature of love than we have.

YOUNG WIFE, *laughing*. Oh!

HUSBAND. Certainly. Because we're insecure—confused by the various experiences we have before marriage—unavoidably. You women hear a lot, and know too much, I'm afraid you read too much too, but you can never have an accurate conception of what we men have to go through. What's commonly called love is made utterly repellent to us—because, after all, what *are* the poor creatures we have to resort to?

YOUNG WIFE. Yes, what *are* the poor creatures you have to resort to?

HUSBAND *kisses her on the forehead*. Be glad, my child, that you never had a glimpse of their condition. Most of them are rather pitiable beings, incidentally. Let us not cast the first stone!

YOUNG WIFE. You pity them? That doesn't seem quite right . . .

HUSBAND, *with fine mildness*. They deserve it. You girls from good families, who can quietly wait beneath the parental roof till a decent man proposes to you—you don't know the misery that drives those poor creatures into the arms of sin.

YOUNG WIFE. They all sell themselves, then?

HUSBAND. I wouldn't quite say *that*. And I'm not thinking merely of material misery. There is also—one might say—a moral misery: an insufficient grasp of what is . . . proper, and especially of what is noble.

YOUNG WIFE. But why should we pity them? Don't they have rather a nice time of it?

HUSBAND. You have peculiar opinions, my child. Don't forget that these creatures are destined by nature to sink forever lower and lower and lower. There is no stopping it.

YOUNG WIFE, *snuggles up to him.* Sinking sounds rather nice!

HUSBAND *pained.* How can you say such a thing, Emma? I should have thought there could be nothing more repellent to a decent woman than the thought of . . .

YOUNG WIFE. Yes, that's true, Karl, of course. I said it without thinking. Tell me more. It's so nice when you talk like this. Tell me more.

HUSBAND. What about?

YOUNG WIFE. About—those creatures!

HUSBAND. But what an idea!

YOUNG WIFE. Look, I asked you before, didn't I, right at the beginning I kept asking you to tell me about your youth.

HUSBAND. Why does *that* interest you?

YOUNG WIFE. Aren't you my husband? And isn't it positively unfair that I know absolutely nothing about your past?

HUSBAND. I hope you don't think I'd . . . in such bad taste . . . No, Emma! It would be profanation!

YOUNG WIFE. And yet you've . . . held any number of other young ladies in your arms, the way you're holding me now.

HUSBAND. "Young ladies!" *They* are . . .

YOUNG WIFE. There's one question you *must* answer. Or else . . . or else . . . no honeymoon.

HUSBAND. You've a way of talking . . . remember, my child, you're a mother—our little girl is sleeping in there.

YOUNG WIFE, *pressing herself to him.* But I want a boy too.

HUSBAND. Emma!

YOUNG WIFE. Oh, don't be so . . . Of course I'm your wife, but I'd like to be—your mistress, sort of.

HUSBAND. You would?

YOUNG WIFE. First, my question!

HUSBAND, *submissive*. What is it?

YOUNG WIFE. Was there a—a married woman—among them?

HUSBAND. What? How do you mean?

YOUNG WIFE. *You* know.

HUSBAND, *somewhat disturbed*. What makes you ask?

YOUNG WIFE. I'd like to know if there . . . I mean . . . there *are* women like that, I know . . . But have *you* . . .

HUSBAND, *gravely*. Do you know any such woman?

YOUNG WIFE. Well, I can't tell.

HUSBAND. Is there such a woman among your friends?

YOUNG WIFE. Well, how could I say yes—or no—and be sure?

HUSBAND. Has one of your women friends . . . People talk a lot when they . . . women among themselves . . . has one of them confessed . . . ?

YOUNG WIFE, *uncertainly*. No.

HUSBAND. Do you *suspect* that one of your friends . . .

YOUNG WIFE. Suspect . . . well . . . suspect . . .

HUSBAND. You do!

YOUNG WIFE. Definitely not, Karl. Most certainly not. Now I think it over, I wouldn't believe it of one of them.

HUSBAND. Not one?

YOUNG WIFE. Of friends—not one.

HUSBAND. Promise me something, Emma.

YOUNG WIFE. Well?

HUSBAND. Promise you'll never go around with a woman if you have the slightest suspicion that . . . her life is not beyond reproach.

YOUNG WIFE. You need a promise for that?

HUSBAND. I know, of course, that you would never *seek* contact with such women. But by *chance* you might. . . . It frequently happens that women who don't enjoy the best reputation seek the company of respectable women, partly for contrast and partly out of a certain—how shall I put it?—out of a certain nostalgia for virtue.

YOUNG WIFE. I see.

HUSBAND. Yes, I believe it's very true, what I just said. Nostalgia for virtue! For there's one thing you can be sure of: in reality all these women are very unhappy.

YOUNG WIFE. Why?

HUSBAND. How can you ask, Emma? Only imagine what sort of existence they have to lead. Full of meanness, lies, treachery—and full of danger!

YOUNG WIFE. Oh yes. I'm sure you're right.

HUSBAND. Indeed, they pay for that bit of happiness . . . that bit of . . .

YOUNG WIFE. . . . pleasure.

HUSBAND. Pleasure? What makes you call it pleasure?

YOUNG WIFE. Well, it's something, or they wouldn't do it.

HUSBAND. It's nothing. Mere intoxication.

YOUNG WIFE, *thoughtfully*. Mere intoxication.

HUSBAND. Not even intoxication. But one thing is certain—it's bought at a price!

YOUNG WIFE. Then . . . you do know what you're talking about?

HUSBAND. Yes, Emma. It's my saddest memory.

YOUNG WIFE. Who was it? Tell me. Do I know her?

HUSBAND. Emma! What are you thinking of?

YOUNG WIFE. Was it long ago? Very long? Before you married me?

HUSBAND. Don't ask. Please, don't ask.

YOUNG WIFE. But Karl!

HUSBAND. She is dead.

YOUNG WIFE. Honestly?

HUSBAND. Yes . . . It may sound ridiculous, but I have the feeling that all these women die young.

YOUNG WIFE. Did you love her very much?

HUSBAND. Can a man love a liar?

YOUNG WIFE. Then, why . . . ?

HUSBAND. Intoxication . . .

YOUNG WIFE. So it *is* . . .

HUSBAND. Please, don't talk about it. All that is long past. I've only loved one woman: you. A man can only love where he finds purity and truth.

YOUNG WIFE. Karl!

HUSBAND. Oh how safe, how good a man feels in these arms! Why didn't I know you as a child? I'm sure I'd never have looked at another woman.

YOUNG WIFE. Karl!

HUSBAND. You're beautiful . . . beautiful . . . Oh! *He puts the light out.*

*   *   *   *   *

YOUNG WIFE. You know what I can't help thinking of tonight?

HUSBAND. What, my treasure?

YOUNG WIFE. Of . . . of . . . of Venice.

HUSBAND. The first night . . .

YOUNG WIFE. Yes . . . Like that . . .

HUSBAND. What is it? Tell me.

YOUNG WIFE. Tonight . . . you love me like that.

HUSBAND. Like that.

YOUNG WIFE. Ah . . . if you could always . . .

HUSBAND, *in her arms.* Yes?

YOUNG WIFE. Oh Karl dear!

HUSBAND. What was it you wanted to say? If I could always . . . ?

YOUNG WIFE. Well, yes.

HUSBAND. Well, what would happen if I could always . . . ?

YOUNG WIFE. Then I'd always know you love me.

HUSBAND. Yes. But you know it anyhow. A man can't always be the loving husband, he must go out into a hostile world and fight the good fight! Always remember this, my child. In marriage there's a time for everything—that's the beauty of it. There aren't many who still remember their Venice after five years.

YOUNG WIFE. No.

HUSBAND. And now . . . good-night, my child.

YOUNG WIFE. Good-night!

6   THE HUSBAND AND THE LITTLE MISS

A private room in the RIEDHOF RESTAURANT; *comfortable, unobtrusive elegance; the gas stove is lit. On the table the remains of a meal: meringues with much whipped cream, fruit, cheese. White Hungarian wine in the glasses.*

The HUSBAND *smokes a Havana cigar, leans back on the corner of the sofa.*
The LITTLE MISS *sits on a chair beside him, scoops the whipped cream out of a meringue and sucks it up with satisfaction.*

HUSBAND. It's good?

LITTLE MISS, *uninterruptible.* Mm!

HUSBAND. Like another?

LITTLE MISS. No, I've eaten too much already.

HUSBAND. You've no wine left.
   He fills up her glass.

LITTLE MISS. No . . . I'll only leave it, sir.

HUSBAND. Sir? Don't be so stiff with me.

LITTLE MISS. Well, you're not so easy to get used to, sir.

HUSBAND. Sir!

LITTLE MISS. What?

HUSBAND. You said "sir" again. Come and sit by me.

LITTLE MISS. One moment—I'm not through.
   The HUSBAND *gets up, stands behind her chair and puts his arms round her, turning her head towards him.*

LITTLE MISS. What is it now?

HUSBAND. I'd like to have a kiss.

LITTLE MISS *gives him a kiss.* You're pretty fresh, you are.

HUSBAND. You only just noticed it?

LITTLE MISS. Oh, I noticed before . . . in the street. You must have quite an opinion of me.

HUSBAND. How's that?

LITTLE MISS. Going straight to a private room with you.

HUSBAND. You didn't go "straight" to the private room.

LITTLE MISS. You've a nice way of asking.

HUSBAND. You think so?

LITTLE MISS. And after all, what's wrong about it?

HUSBAND. Precisely.

LITTLE MISS. Whether you go for a walk or . . .

HUSBAND. It's much too cold for a walk, isn't it?

LITTLE MISS. It was much too cold.

HUSBAND. But in here it's nice and warm, don't you think? *He has sat down again and puts his arm round the* LITTLE MISS, *pulling her over to his side.*

LITTLE MISS, *weakly.* Hey!

HUSBAND. Now tell me . . . You'd noticed me before, hadn't you?

LITTLE MISS. Sure. In the Singer Strasse.

HUSBAND. I don't mean today. The day before yesterday and the day before that. I was following you.

LITTLE MISS. There's plenty follow me!

HUSBAND. I can imagine. But did you notice me?

LITTLE MISS. Well . . . um . . . you know what happened to me the other day? My cousin's husband followed me in the dark, and didn't recognize me.

HUSBAND. Did he speak to you?

LITTLE MISS. The idea! You think everybody's as fresh as you?

HUSBAND. It happens.

LITTLE MISS. Sure it happens.

HUSBAND. Well, what do you do?

LITTLE MISS. Me? Nothing. I just don't answer.

HUSBAND. Hm . . . you answered me.

LITTLE MISS. Well, are you mad at me?

HUSBAND *kisses her violently.* Your lips taste of whipped cream.

LITTLE MISS. Oh, they're sweet by nature.

HUSBAND. Many men have told you that, have they?

LITTLE MISS. Many men! The ideas you get!

HUSBAND. Be honest with me. How many have kissed these lips?

LITTLE MISS. Why ask? If I tell you, you won't believe me.

HUSBAND. Why not?

LITTLE MISS. Guess.

HUSBAND. Let's say—um—but you mustn't be angry!

LITTLE MISS. Why should I be?

HUSBAND. Well, at a guess . . . twenty.

LITTLE MISS *breaking away from him.* Why not a hundred while you're at it?

HUSBAND. It was only a guess.

LITTLE MISS. It was a bad guess.

HUSBAND. Let's say—ten.

LITTLE MISS, *offended*. Oh sure! A girl who lets you talk to her in the street and goes straight to a private dining room!

HUSBAND. Don't be a child. Whether people run around in the streets or sit together in a room. . . . Here we're in a restaurant, the waiter can come in any time—there's nothing to it.

LITTLE MISS. That's just what *I* thought.

HUSBAND. Have you ever been in a private dining room before?

LITTLE MISS. Well, if I must tell you the truth: yes.

HUSBAND. Well, I like that: you're honest.

LITTLE MISS. It wasn't like you think. I was with my girl friend and her fiancé, during the last Carnival.

HUSBAND. Well, it wouldn't be a tragedy if you'd been—with your boyfriend . . .

LITTLE MISS. Sure it wouldn't be a tragedy. But I haven't got a boy friend.

HUSBAND. Go on!

LITTLE MISS. Cross my heart, I haven't.

HUSBAND. You don't mean to tell me I . . .

LITTLE MISS. What? . . . There hasn't been anyone—for more than six months.

HUSBAND. I see . . . And before that? Who was it?

LITTLE MISS. What are you so inquisitive for?

HUSBAND. Because . . . I'm in love with you.

LITTLE MISS. Really?

HUSBAND. Of course. Hadn't you noticed? Come on, tell me. *He pulls her close to him.*

LITTLE MISS. Tell you what?

HUSBAND. Don't keep me begging. I'd like to know who he was.

LITTLE MISS, *laughing.* Oh, a man.

HUSBAND. Come on, come one, who was he?

LITTLE MISS. He was a little bit like you.

HUSBAND. Indeed.

LITTLE MISS. If you hadn't been so much like him . . .

HUSBAND. Well, what then?

LITTLE MISS. Now don't ask. You know what . . .

HUSBAND. So that's why you let me speak to you!

LITTLE MISS. Well, yes.

HUSBAND. Now I don't know whether to be glad or annoyed.

LITTLE MISS. If I was you, I'd be glad.

HUSBAND. Oh, surely.

LITTLE MISS. The way you talk reminds me of him too . . . and the way you look at a girl . . .

HUSBAND. What was he?

LITTLE MISS. Really, your eyes . . .

HUSBAND. What was his name?

LITTLE MISS. Don't look at me like that, no, please!
The HUSBAND *takes her in his arms. A long, hot kiss.*
The LITTLE MISS *shakes herself free and tries to get up.*

HUSBAND. What's the matter?

LITTLE MISS. Time to go home.

HUSBAND. Later.

LITTLE MISS. No, I *must* go home. Really. What do you think mother will say?

HUSBAND. You're living with your mother?

LITTLE MISS. Sure I am. What did you think?

HUSBAND. I see . . . with your mother. Just the two of you?

LITTLE MISS. Just the two . . . ?! There's five of us. Two boys and three girls.

HUSBAND. Don't sit so far away. Are you the eldest?

LITTLE MISS. No. I'm the second. First there's Kathi, she goes out to work. In a flower shop. Then there's me.

HUSBAND. What do you do?

LITTLE MISS. I'm at home.

HUSBAND. All the time?

LITTLE MISS. Well, one of us has got to be at home.

HUSBAND. Naturally. Well—and what do you tell your mother when you—come home late?

LITTLE MISS. It doesn't often happen.

HUSBAND. Tonight for example. Your mother does ask you?

LITTLE MISS. Oh, sure she does. It doesn't matter how careful I am when I get home, she wakes up every time.

HUSBAND. What will you tell her tonight?

LITTLE MISS. Oh well, I guess I'll have been to the theater.

HUSBAND. Will she believe you?

LITTLE MISS. Why shouldn't she? I often go to the theater. Only last Sunday I was at the Opera with my girl friend and her fiancé—and my older brother.

HUSBAND. Where do you get the tickets from?

LITTLE MISS. My brother's a barber.

HUSBAND. Of course, barbers . . . I suppose he's a theatrical barber?

LITTLE MISS. Why are you pumping me like this?

HUSBAND. I'm interested. And what's your other brother?

LITTLE MISS. He's still at school. He wants to be a teacher. Imagine!

HUSBAND. And you've a younger sister too?

LITTLE MISS. Yes, she's only a brat, but at that you've got to keep an eye on her. You've no idea what these girls learn at school. Do you know, the other day I caught her having a date!

HUSBAND. What?

LITTLE MISS. I did. With a boy from the school opposite. She was out walking with him in the Strozzi Gasse at half-past seven. The brat!

HUSBAND. What did you do?

LITTLE MISS. Well, she got a spanking.

HUSBAND. You are as strict as all that?

LITTLE MISS. There's no one else to do it. My older sister's in the shop, Mother does nothing but grumble—and so everything falls on me.

HUSBAND. God, you're sweet!
He kisses her and grows more tender.
And you remind me of someone, too.

LITTLE MISS. Do I? Who is she?

HUSBAND. No one in particular . . . you remind me of the time when . . . well, my youth! Come, drink up, child.

LITTLE MISS. How old are you? . . . Um . . . I don't even know your name.

HUSBAND. Karl.

LITTLE MISS. Honest? Your name's Karl?

HUSBAND. He was called Karl?

LITTLE MISS. Really, it's a miracle . . . it's too . . . No, those eyes! . . . That look!
She shakes her head.

HUSBAND. You still haven't told me who he was.

LITTLE MISS. A bad man, that's what he was, or he wouldn't have dropped me.

HUSBAND. Did you like him a lot?

LITTLE MISS. Sure I liked him a lot.

HUSBAND. I know what he was: a lieutenant.

LITTLE MISS. No, he wasn't in the Army. They wouldn't take
him. His father's got a house in the . . . but what do you
want to know for?

HUSBAND *kisses her*. Your eyes are gray really. At first I thought
they were black.

LITTLE MISS. Well, aren't they nice enough for you?
The HUSBAND *kisses her eyes*.

LITTLE MISS. Oh, no—that's something I can't stand—please,
please. . . . Oh God . . . No, let me get up . . . just for a minute, oh please!

HUSBAND, *increasingly tender*. Oh, no! No!

LITTLE MISS. But, Karl, please!

HUSBAND. How old are you? Eighteen, is it?

LITTLE MISS. Nineteen now.

HUSBAND. Nineteen . . . and I . . .

LITTLE MISS. You're thirty . . .

HUSBAND. And . . . a little more. . . . Don't let's talk of it.

LITTLE MISS. At that, he was thirty-two when I met him!

HUSBAND. How long ago?

LITTLE MISS. I can't remember. . . . You know what, there was
something in the wine!

HUSBAND. How so?

LITTLE MISS. I'm quite . . . you know . . . everything's turning
round.

HUSBAND. Hold on to me. Like this . . .
*He pulls her to him and becomes more and more tender; she
scarcely defends herself.*
I'll tell you something, treasure, now we might really go.

LITTLE MISS. Yes—home.

HUSBAND. Not home exactly.

LITTLE MISS. What do you mean? . . . Oh no, no! . . . I wouldn't
. . . What an idea!

HUSBAND. Now, listen to me, my child, next time we meet, you
know, we'll arrange it so. . . .
He has slipped to the floor, his head in her lap.
That's good; oh, that's good!

LITTLE MISS. What are you doing?
She kisses his hair.
See, there *must* have been something in the wine . . . so
sleepy . . . Hey, what happens if I can't get up? But . . . but
look, Karl! . . . If somebody comes in . . . Please . . . the
waiter!

HUSBAND. No waiter'll . . . come in here . . . not in . . . your life-
time.

⁂   ⁂   ⁂   ⁂   ⁂

The LITTLE MISS *leans back in a corner of the sofa, her eyes
shut.*
The HUSBAND *walks up and down the small room, after
lighting a cigar.*
A longish silence.

HUSBAND *looks at the girl for a long time, then says to himself.*
Who knows what sort of person she really is——God in
heaven! . . . So quickly . . . Wasn't very careful of me . . .
Hm . . .

LITTLE MISS, *without opening her eyes.* There must have been
something in that wine.

HUSBAND. How's that?

LITTLE MISS. Otherwise . . .

HUSBAND. Why blame everything on the wine?

LITTLE MISS. Where are you? Why are you so far away? Come
here to me.
The HUSBAND *goes to her, sits down.*

LITTLE MISS. Now, tell me if you really like me.

HUSBAND. But you *know*. . . .
>   *Interrupting himself quickly.*
>   Of course I do.

LITTLE MISS. You see . . . there *is* . . . Come on, tell me the truth, what was in that wine?

HUSBAND. You think I go around poisoning people?

LITTLE MISS. Look, I just don't understand. I'm not like that. . . . We've only known each other for . . . Listen, I'm not like that, cross my heart—if you believe that of me . . .

HUSBAND. There, there, don't fret so! I don't think anything bad of you. I just think you like me.

LITTLE MISS. Yes . . .

HUSBAND. After all, if two young people are alone together, and have supper, and drink wine—there doesn't have to be anything in the wine.

LITTLE MISS. Oh, I was just gabbing.

HUSBAND. But why?

LITTLE MISS, *somewhat defiantly.* Because I was ashamed! '

HUSBAND. That's ridiculous. There's no reason for it. Especially since I remind you of your first lover.

LITTLE MISS. Yes.

HUSBAND. Your first.

LITTLE MISS. Oh sure . . .

HUSBAND. Now it would interest me to know who the others were.

LITTLE MISS. There weren't any.

HUSBAND. That isn't true. It can't be true.

LITTLE MISS. Please don't nag me!

HUSBAND. A cigarette?

LITTLE MISS. No. Thank you.

HUSBAND. Do you know what time it is?

LITTLE MISS. What?

HUSBAND. Half-past eleven.

LITTLE MISS. Really.

HUSBAND. Well . . . what about your mother? Used to it, is she?

LITTLE MISS. You want to send me home already?

HUSBAND. But you wanted—yourself . . .

LITTLE MISS. Look, you're different now. What have I done to you?

HUSBAND. My dear child, what's wrong? What are you thinking of?

LITTLE MISS. It was . . . the look in your eyes, honest, cross my heart. But for that you could have gone down on your knees. . . . A lot of men have *begged* me to go to a private room with them!

HUSBAND. Well, would you like to . . . to come here again . . . soon? Or some other place . . . ?

LITTLE MISS. I don't know.

HUSBAND. Now what's *that* mean: you don't know?

LITTLE MISS. Why do you have to ask?

HUSBAND. All right—when? But first I must explain that I don't live in Vienna. I . . . just come here now and then. For a couple of days.

LITTLE MISS. Go on—you aren't Viennese?

HUSBAND. Well, yes, I'm Viennese, but I live . . . out of town.

LITTLE MISS. Where?

HUSBAND. Goodness, *that* doesn't matter, does it?

LITTLE MISS. Don't worry, I won't go there.

HUSBAND. Heavens, you can go there as much as you want. I live in Graz.

LITTLE MISS. Really?

HUSBAND. Yes. What's so astonishing about that?

LITTLE MISS. You're married, aren't you?

HUSBAND, *greatly surprised*. Whatever makes you think so?

LITTLE MISS. It looks that way to me.

HUSBAND. And if I were, it wouldn't bother you any?

LITTLE MISS. Oh, I'd like it better if you were single. But you're married. I know.

HUSBAND. Now tell me, what makes you think so?

LITTLE MISS. Oh, if a man says he doesn't live in town and hasn't always got time . . .

HUSBAND. That isn't so unlikely, is it?

LITTLE MISS. I don't believe it.

HUSBAND. And it wouldn't give you a bad conscience to seduce a married man? Make him unfaithful?

LITTLE MISS. Never mind about that—I bet your wife is no different.

HUSBAND, *very indignant*. That's enough! Such observations . . .

LITTLE MISS. I thought you didn't have a wife.

HUSBAND. Whether I have a wife or not, such observations are beyond the pale!
He has risen.

LITTLE MISS. But, Karl, what is it, Karl? Are you mad at me? Look, I didn't know you were married. I was just gabbing. Come on, let's be friends.

HUSBAND *goes to her after a couple of seconds*. You really are strange creatures.
At her side, he begins to caress her again.
Oh, the female of the species!

LITTLE MISS. No . . . don't . . . and it's so late . . .

HUSBAND. Now listen to me. We must have a serious talk. I want to see you again—many times.

LITTLE MISS. Honest?

HUSBAND. But if so, it's essential. . . . I must be able to rely on you. I can't be watching all the time.

LITTLE MISS. Oh, I can look after myself.

HUSBAND. You're . . . well, not inexperienced exactly, but you're young, and—men in general are an unscrupulous bunch.

LITTLE MISS. And how!

HUSBAND. I don't mean just in morals. . . . Well, *you* know what I mean.

LITTLE MISS. Now, really, what sort of girl do you take me for?

HUSBAND. So, if you want to love me—only me—we'll be able to fix things up somehow, even if I do live in Graz. This place isn't the right thing—someone could come in at any moment!
The LITTLE MISS *snuggles up to him.*

HUSBAND. Next time let's make it somewhere else, okay?

LITTLE MISS. Okay.

HUSBAND. Where we can't be disturbed.

LITTLE MISS. Right.

HUSBAND *embraces her with fervor.* The rest we can talk over on the way home.
He gets up, opens the door.

Waiter . . . the check!

7 THE LITTLE MISS AND THE POET

A small room, comfortably furnished, in good taste. Drapes leave it in semi-darkness. Red net curtains. A big desk littered with papers and books. Against the wall, an upright piano.

The LITTLE MISS *and the* POET *enter together. The* POET *locks the door.*

POET. Here we are, sweetheart.
He kisses her.

LITTLE MISS, *in hat and cloak.* Oh, what a nice room! Only you can't see anything!

POET. Your eyes will have to get used to semi-darkness. These sweet eyes!
He kisses her eyelids.

LITTLE MISS. These sweet eyes won't have time to get used to it.

POET. How's that?

LITTLE MISS. Because I can't stay for more than one minute.

POET. Do take your hat off.

LITTLE MISS. For one minute?

POET *pulls out her hatpin, takes the hat, puts it on one side.* And your cloak.

LITTLE MISS. What are you up to? I've got to go!

POET. First you must rest. We've been walking three hours.

LITTLE MISS. We were in the carriage.

POET. Coming home, yes. But in Weidling-am-Bach we were three solid hours on foot. Now do sit down, child . . . where-ever you like . . . at the desk. . . . No, that isn't comfortable. Sit down on the sofa. Here.
He puts her down on the sofa.
If you're very tired, you can stretch out. Like this.
He makes her lie down.
With your little head on the cushion.

LITTLE MISS, *laughing.* But I'm not a bit tired!

POET. You *think* you aren't. Right, and now if you feel sleepy, you can go to sleep. I'll keep perfectly quiet. Or I can play you a lullaby . . . one of my own.
He goes to the piano.

LITTLE MISS. Your own?

POET. Yes.

LITTLE MISS. But, Robert, I thought you were a doctor.

POET. How's that? I told you I was a writer.

LITTLE MISS. Well, writers *are* doctors, aren't they?

POET. Of philosophy? Not all writers. Not me, for instance. Why did you bring *that* up?

LITTLE MISS. Because you said the piece you were going to play was your own.

POET. Oh well . . . maybe it isn't. It doesn't matter. Does it? It never matters who's done a thing—just so long as it's beautiful—you agree?

LITTLE MISS. Oh sure . . . as long as it's beautiful!

POET. Do you know what I meant by that?

LITTLE MISS. By what?

POET. What I said just now.

LITTLE MISS, *drowsily.* Oh, sure.

POET *gets up, goes to her and strokes her hair.* You didn't understand a word.

LITTLE MISS. Now look, I'm *not* stupid.

POET. Of course you are. That's why I love you. It's a fine thing for women to be stupid. In *your* way, that is.

LITTLE MISS. Hey, don't be rude!

POET. Little angel! Isn't it nice just to lie there on a soft Persian rug?

LITTLE MISS. Oh yes. Won't you go on playing the piano?

POET. I'd rather stay with you.
  He strokes her.

LITTLE MISS. Look, can't we have the light on?

POET. Oh no . . . twilight is so comforting. Today we were bathing in sunshine all day long. Now we've come out of the bath, so to speak, and we're wrapping the twilight round us like a bathrobe.
  He laughs.
  No, it'll have to be put a little differently . . . won't it?

LITTLE MISS. Will it?

POET, *edging away from her*. It's divine, this stupidity!
   He takes out a notebook and writes a few words in it.

LITTLE MISS. What are you doing?
   Turns round to look at him.
   What are you writing down?

POET, *in an undertone*. Sun—bath—twilight—robe . . . That's it.
   He puts the notebook in his pocket, laughs.
   Nothing. And now tell me, treasure, wouldn't you like
   something to eat or drink?

LITTLE MISS. I guess I'm not thirsty. But I *am* hungry.

POET. Hm . . . now, I'd rather you were thirsty. The cognac's
   right here, but if it's food I'll have to go out and get it.

LITTLE MISS. Can't they bring it up for you?

POET. That's the difficulty. My maid isn't around any more . . .
   Never mind. I'll go. What would you like?

LITTLE MISS. It isn't worth it, I've got to go home anyway.

POET. Oho, no you don't! I'll tell you what: when we leave, we'll
   go and have supper somewhere.

LITTLE MISS. I haven't got time. And—where could we go?
   We'd be seen.

POET. You know so many people?

LITTLE MISS. It's enough if *one* of them sees us.

POET. How so?

LITTLE MISS. What do you think? If Mother heard anything . . .

POET. We could go to a place where nobody *could* see us. There
   are restaurants with private rooms after all . . .

LITTLE MISS *sings*. "Just to share a private room with you . . ."

POET. Have you ever been to a private dining room?

LITTLE MISS. As a matter of fact I have.

POET. Who was the lucky man?

LITTLE MISS. Oh, it wasn't what you think . . . I was with my girl friend and her fiancé. They took me.

POET. Really? Am I supposed to believe that?

LITTLE MISS. Suit yourself.

POET, *close to her*. Did you blush? It's dark in here. I can't make out your features.
He touches her cheek with his hand.
Even so—I recognize you.

LITTLE MISS. Well, take care you don't mix me up with another girl.

POET. Peculiar! I can't remember what you look like.

LITTLE MISS. Thank you very much.

POET, *seriously*. Do you know, it's rather spooky—I can't visualize your face—in a certain sense I've *forgotten* you. Now, if I couldn't recognize your voice either . . . what would you be? So near and yet so far—rather spooky, what?

LITTLE MISS. What are *you* talking about?

POET. Nothing, angel, nothing. Where are your lips?
He kisses her.

LITTLE MISS. Won't you put the light on?

POET. No . . .
He grows very tender.
Tell me if you love me!

LITTLE MISS. Oh, I do. I do!

POET. Have you ever loved anyone else as much?

LITTLE MISS. I told you I haven't.

POET. But . . .
He sighs.

LITTLE MISS. Well—*he* was my fiancé.

POET. I'd rather you didn't think of him.

LITTLE MISS. Oh . . . what are you doing . . . now look . . .

POET. Let's imagine we're in a castle in India.

LITTLE MISS. I'm sure people there couldn't be as naughty as
    you.

POET. How idiotic! Divine! If only you had an inkling of what
    you mean to me . . .

LITTLE MISS. Well, what?

POET. Don't push me away all the time. I'm not doing anything
    —yet.

LITTLE MISS. Listen, my corset hurts.

POET, *simply*. Take it off.

LITTLE MISS. Okay, but you mustn't be naughty.

POET. Okay.
    LITTLE MISS *rises and takes off her corset in the dark.*

POET, *sitting on the sofa in the meanwhile.* Tell me, doesn't it
    interest you at all to know my last name?

LITTLE MISS. Oh, yes—what is it?

POET. I'd better not tell you my name. I'll tell you what I call
    myself.

LITTLE MISS. What's the difference?

POET. Well, what I call myself—as a writer.

LITTLE MISS. You don't write under your real name?

POET, *close to her.*

LITTLE MISS. Ah . . . please! . . . Don't!

POET. O the sweet odor that rises from you!
    He kisses her bosom.

LITTLE MISS. You're tearing my chemise.

POET. Off with it all! Away with these . . . superfluities!

LITTLE MISS. *Robert!*

POET. Let's enter our Indian castle!

LITTLE MISS. First tell me if you really love me.

POET. I worship you!
He kisses her hotly.
My treasure, I worship you, my springtime . . . my . . .

LITTLE MISS. Robert . . . Robert . . .

   ✿   ✿   ✿   ✿

POET. That was bliss supernal . . . I call myself . . .

LITTLE MISS. Robert. *My* Robert!

POET. I call myself Biebitz.

LITTLE MISS. Why do you call yourself Biebitz?

POET. Biebitz isn't my name, it's what I call myself. You know
the name?

LITTLE MISS. No.

POET. You don't know the name Biebitz? How divine! Really?
But you're just pretending?

LITTLE MISS. Cross my heart, I've never heard it.

POET. You never go to the theatre?

LITTLE MISS. Oh, yes. Just the other day I got taken—by my girl
friend's uncle—and my girl friend—and we went to the
Opera—*Cavalleria Rusticana!*

POET. Hmm, but you don't go to the Burg Theater?

LITTLE MISS. Nobody ever gave me a ticket.

POET. I'll send you a ticket one day soon.

LITTLE MISS. Oh please! But don't forget. Make it something
funny.

POET. Yes . . . funny . . . well . . . you wouldn't like something
sad?

LITTLE MISS. Not as much.

POET. Even if it's by me?

LITTLE MISS. A play—by you? You write for the theatre?!

POET. Excuse me, I just want to light a candle. I haven't seen
you since you became mine. Angel!

He lights a candle.

LITTLE MISS. Hey, don't! I feel ashamed. Give me a blanket anyway!

POET. Later!

He walks up to her with the light and contemplates her for a long while.

LITTLE MISS *covers her face with her hands.* Robert!

POET. You're beautiful. You *are* Beauty! You are Nature herself perhaps! You are Sacred Simplicity!

LITTLE MISS. Ouch! You're dripping wax on me! Why can't you be more careful?

POET *puts the candlestick down.* You're what I've been looking for all this time. You love me—just me—you'd love me the same if I were a shop assistant. It does me good. I'll confess that up till now I couldn't get rid of a certain suspicion. Tell me, hadn't you the least idea I was Biebitz?

LITTLE MISS. Look, I don't know what you want with me. I don't know any Biebitz.

POET. Such is fame! Never mind, forget what I told you, forget even the name I told you. I'm Robert for you, and I want to remain Robert. I was joking!

Gaily.

I'm not a writer at all, I'm a shop assistant. In the evenings I play the piano for folk singers!

LITTLE MISS. Now you have me all mixed up . . . and the way you look at a girl! What's the matter, what's eating you?

POET. It's strange—it's hardly ever happened to me, my treasure —I feel like crying. You've got under my skin. Let's stay together, hm? We're going to love one another very much.

LITTLE MISS. Listen, is that true about the folk singing?

POET. Yes, but don't ask any more. If you love me, don't ask. Tell me, could you make yourself quite free for a couple of weeks?

LITTLE MISS. What do you mean, quite free?

POET. Well, away from home.

LITTLE MISS. What! How could I? What would Mother say? Anyway, everything would go wrong at home without me.

POET. I'd been thinking how lovely it would be to live with you for a few weeks quite alone, somewhere, in distant solitude, in the depths of Nature's forests. Thou Nature art my Goddess! And then, one day, farewell—to go who knows whither?

LITTLE MISS. Now you're talking of good-bye. And I thought you liked me a lot.

POET. That's just it!
He bends down and kisses her on the forehead.
Sweet creature!

LITTLE MISS. Hold me tight, I'm cold.

POET. It's time to get dressed. Wait, I'll light some more candles.

LITTLE MISS *gets up.* Don't look!

POET. No.
At the window.
Tell me, child, are you happy?

LITTLE MISS. How do you mean?

POET. In general I mean: are you happy?

LITTLE MISS. Things could be better.

POET. You don't understand me. You've told me quite enough of the state of affairs at home, I know you aren't exactly a princess. I mean, setting all that aside, do you feel you're alive? Do you feel you are really alive?

LITTLE MISS. You got a comb?

POET *goes to the dressing-table, gives her the comb, contemplates the* LITTLE MISS. God, you're enchanting to look at!

LITTLE MISS. No . . . don't!

POET. Come, stay here with me a little longer, stay and let me get something for our supper, and . . .

LITTLE MISS. But it's much too late.

POET. It's not nine yet.

LITTLE MISS. Oh well, but I've got to hurry.

POET. When shall we meet next?

LITTLE MISS. When would you like to see me?

POET. Tomorrow?

LITTLE MISS. What's tomorrow?

POET. Saturday.

LITTLE MISS. Oh, I can't make it. I've got to go see our guardian.
With my little sister.

POET. Sunday, then . . . hm . . . Sunday . . . on Sunday . . . I
must explain something to you. I'm not Biebitz, Biebitz
is a friend of mine. One day I'll introduce you to him. His
play is on next Sunday. I'll send you a ticket, and come
to the theatre to get you. You'll tell me how you like the play,
won't you?

LITTLE MISS. This Biebitz thing . . . well, I may be stupid but . . .

POET. When I know how you felt about the play, I'll really know
you.

LITTLE MISS. Okay . . . I'm ready.

POET. Let's go, then, my treasure.
They leave.

8   THE POET AND THE ACTRESS

*A room in a country inn. It is an evening in spring; meadows
and hills are lit by the moon; the windows are open. All is
still.*

The POET *and the* ACTRESS *enters; as they come in, the flame
of the candle which the* POET *is carrying goes out.*

POET. Oh!

ACTRESS. What's the matter?

POET. The candle. But we don't need it. Look, it's quite light! Marvelous!

The ACTRESS *suddenly sinks on her knees at the window, folding her hands.*

POET. What's the matter with you?

ACTRESS *remains silent.*

POET *goes to her.* What are you doing?

ACTRESS, *indignant.* Can't you see I'm praying?

POET. You believe in God?

ACTRESS. What do you think I am—an anarchist?

POET. Oh.

ACTRESS. Come here, kneel down beside me. You could use a prayer once in a while.

The POET *kneels down beside her and puts his arms round her.*

ACTRESS. You lecher!

She gets up.

And do you know to whom I was praying?

POET. To God, I presume.

ACTRESS, *with great scorn.* Oh yes? It was to you I prayed.

POET. Then why look out of the window?

ACTRESS. Tell me where you've dragged me off to, seducer.

POET. It was your own idea, my child. You wanted to go to the country. You wanted to come here.

ACTRESS. Well, wasn't I right?

POET. Yes, it's enchanting. To think it's only two hours from Vienna—and perfect solitude! What a landscape!

ACTRESS. Isn't it? You could write poetry here, if you had any talent.

POET. Have you been here before?

ACTRESS. Have I been here before? I lived here for years.

POET. With whom?

ACTRESS. Oh, with Fritz, of course.

POET. I see.

ACTRESS. I worshiped that man.

POET. You told me.

ACTRESS. Oh, I beg your pardon—I can leave if I bore you.

POET. *You* bore me? . . . You have no idea what you mean to
me. . . . You're a world in yourself. . . . You're the Divine
Spark, you're Genius . . . You are . . . The truth is, you're
Sacred Simplicity. . . . Yes, you . . . But you shouldn't talk
about Fritz—now.

ACTRESS. He was an aberration, yes . . . Oh well . . .

POET. It's good you see that.

ACTRESS. Come over and kiss me.
The POET *kisses her.*

ACTRESS. And now we're going to say good-night. Good-bye,
my treasure.

POET. What do you mean?

ACTRESS. I'm going to bed.

POET. Yes—that's all right, but this "good-night" business . . .
where am *I* going to sleep?

ACTRESS. I'm sure there are other rooms in this inn.

POET. For me the other rooms have singularly little attraction.
By the way, I'd better light up, hadn't I?

ACTRESS. Yes.

POET *lights the candle on the bedside table.* What a pretty
room . . . They're religious here, nothing but saints' pictures.
. . . Wouldn't it be interesting to spend some time among
these people—another world! How little we know of our fellow men!

ACTRESS. Stop talking bosh, and give me my pocketbook, will
you, it's on the table.

POET. Here, my own!

The ACTRESS *takes from the pocket book a small framed picture and puts it on the bedside table.*

POET. What's that?

ACTRESS. Our Lady.

POET. I beg your pardon?

ACTRESS. The Blessed Virgin.

POET. I see. You never travel without it?

ACTRESS. Never. It's my mascot. Now go, Robert.

POET. What sort of a joke is this? Don't you want me to help you?

ACTRESS. I want you to go.

POET. Will you ever take me back?

ACTRESS. Perhaps.

POET. When?

ACTRESS. Oh, in about ten minutes.

POET *kisses her.* Darling! See you in ten minutes.

ACTRESS. Where will you be?

POET. I shall walk up and down in front of the window. I love to walk at night in the open air. I get my best ideas that way. Especially when you're nearby. Wafted by your longings, as it were, floating on your art . . .

ACTRESS. You talk like an idiot.

POET, *sorrowfully.* Some women might have said—like a poet.

ACTRESS. Now go. And don't start anything with the waitress. *The* POET *departs.*

ACTRESS *undresses. She listens to the* POET *going down the wooden stairs and then to his steps beneath the open window. As soon as she is undressed, she goes to the window, looks down, sees him standing there; she calls to him in a whisper.* Come!

The POET *comes up in a hurry; rushes to her. In the meantime she has gone to bed and put out the light. He locks the door.*

ACTRESS. Well, now you may sit down by me and tell me a story.

POET *sits by her on the bed.* Shouldn't I close the window? Aren't you cold?

ACTRESS. Oh, no.

POET. What would you like me to tell you?

ACTRESS. Tell me—who are you being unfaithful to—at this moment?

POET. But I'm not being unfaithful—at this moment.

ACTRESS. Don't worry, I'm being unfaithful too.

POET. I can imagine.

ACTRESS. And who do you think it is?

POET. My dear child, I wouldn't have a notion.

ACTRESS. Guess, then.

POET. Wait a moment . . . Well, your producer.

ACTRESS. My dear, I'm not a chorus girl.

POET. Oh, it was just an idea.

ACTRESS. Guess again.

POET. Your leading man—Benno.

ACTRESS. Pooh, that man doesn't like women, didn't you know? He's having an affair with the postman.

POET. Who would have thought it?

ACTRESS. So come and kiss me.
    The POET *embraces her.*

ACTRESS. What are you doing?

POET. Don't torture me like this!

ACTRESS. Listen, Robert, I'll make a suggestion. Get in bed with me.

POET. I accept.

ACTRESS. Quickly.

POET. Well . . . if *I'd* had my way, I'd have been . . . Listen!

ACTRESS. What?

POET. The crickets are chirping outside.

ACTRESS. You must be mad, my dear, there are no crickets in these parts.

POET. But you can hear them!

ACTRESS. Oh, come on!

POET. I'm here.
He goes to her.

ACTRESS. And now lie still . . . Uh! . . . Don't move!

POET. What's the idea?

ACTRESS. I suppose you'd like to have an affair with me?

POET. I thought you might realize that sooner or later.

ACTRESS. A lot of men would like an affair with me.

POET. But at this particular moment the odds are rather strongly in my favor.

ACTRESS. Come, my cricket. From now on I'm going to call you Cricket.

POET. Fine . . .

ACTRESS. Now—who am I deceiving?

POET. Huh? Me, maybe.

ACTRESS. My child, you should have your head examined.

POET. Or maybe someone . . . you've never seen . . . someone you don't know . . . He's meant for you, but you can never find him . . .

ACTRESS. Cricket, don't talk such fantastic rot!

POET. . . . Isn't it strange . . . even you . . . and one would have thought——But no, it would just be . . . spoiling all that's best about you if one . . . Come, come, come . . .

   *   *   *   *   *

ACTRESS. That's better than acting in damn silly plays. You agree?

POET. Well, I think it's as well you have a part in a reasonable play.

ACTRESS. Meaning yours, you conceited pup.

POET. Of course.

ACTRESS, *seriously*. It really is a *wonderful* play.

POET. You see!

ACTRESS. You're a genius!

POET. By the way, why did you cancel your performance two nights ago? There was nothing wrong with you.

ACTRESS. I wanted to annoy you.

POET. Why? What had I done to you?

ACTRESS. You were conceited.

POET. In what way?

ACTRESS. Everybody in the theatre says so.

POET. Really.

ACTRESS. But I told them: that man has a *right* to be conceited.

POET. And what did they say to that?

ACTRESS. What should those people say? I never speak to them.

POET. I see.

ACTRESS. They'd like to poison me.
    Pause.
    But they won't succeed.

POET. Don't think of them. Just be happy we're here, and tell me you love me.

ACTRESS. You need further proof?

POET. Oh, that kind of thing can't be *proved*.

ACTRESS. This is just lovely! What more do you want?

POET. How many others did you try to prove it to this way? And did you love them all?

ACTRESS. Oh, no. I loved only one.

POET *embracing her*. My ...

ACTRESS. Fritz.

POET. My name is Robert. What am I to you, if it's Fritz you're thinking of?

ACTRESS. A whim.

POET. Nice to know!

ACTRESS. Tell me, aren't you proud?

POET. Why should I be proud?

ACTRESS. I think you have some reason.

POET. Oh, because of that!

ACTRESS. Yes, because of that, my pale cricket. How about the chirping? Are they still chirping?

POET. All the time. Can't you hear?

ACTRESS. I can hear. But that's frogs, my child.

POET. You're wrong: frogs croak.

ACTRESS. Certainly, they croak.

POET. But not here, my dear child. This is chirping.

ACTRESS. You're the most pigheaded creature I've ever come across. Kiss me, frog.

POET. Please don't call me that. It makes me nervous.

ACTRESS. What do you want me to call you?

POET. I've got a name: Robert.

ACTRESS. Oh, that's too dull.

POET. I must ask you to call me simply by my name.

ACTRESS. All right, Robert, kiss me ... Ah!
She kisses him.
Are you content now, frog? Ha, ha, ha!

POET. May I light myself a cigarette?

ACTRESS. Give me one.

The POET takes the cigarette case from the bedside table, takes out two, lights both and hands one to her.

ACTRESS. By the way, you never said a word about my work last night.

POET. What work?

ACTRESS. Well . . . !

POET. Oh, I see. I wasn't at the theatre.

ACTRESS. I guess you like your little joke.

POET. Not at all. When you canceled your performance the day before yesterday, I assumed that yesterday you couldn't be in full possession of our powers. So I didn't go.

ACTRESS. You missed something.

POET. Indeed?

ACTRESS. I was sensational. People turned pale.

POET. You could see them?

ACTRESS. Benno said to me "You were a goddess, darling."

POET. Hm . . . and so sick one day earlier.

ACTRESS. Yes. And do you know why? Out of longing for you.

POET. You just told me you cancelled the performance to annoy me!

ACTRESS. What do you know of my love for you? That sort of thing leaves you cold. I was in a fever for nights on end. With a temperature of 105.

POET. A high temperature just for a whim!

ACTRESS. A whim, you call it? I die for love of you, and you call it a whim?

POET. What about Fritz?

ACTRESS. What about him? What about him? I've heard too much about that . . . that cheap crook!

9 THE ACTRESS AND THE COUNT

The ACTRESS's bedroom, luxuriously furnished. It is noon; the blinds are still down; on the bedside table, a burning candle; the ACTRESS is lying in her fourposter. Numerous newspapers are strewn about on the covers.

The COUNT enters, in the uniform of a captain of Dragoons. He stops at the door.

ACTRESS. It's you, Count!

COUNT. Your good mother gave me permission, or of course I wouldn't . . .

ACTRESS. Please come right in.

COUNT. I kiss your hand. A thousand pardons—coming straight in from the street—you know, I can't see a thing. Yes . . . here we are.
Near the bed.
I kiss your hand.

ACTRESS. Sit down, my dear Count.

COUNT. Your mother said you weren't very well, Fräulein. Nothing too serious, I hope?

ACTRESS. Nothing serious? I was dying!

COUNT. Oh dear me! Not really?

ACTRESS. In any case it's very kind of you to . . . trouble to call.

COUNT. Dying! And only last night you played like a goddess!

ACTRESS. It was a great triumph, I believe.

COUNT. Colossal! People were absolutely knocked out. As for myself, well . . .

ACTRESS. Thanks for the lovely flowers.

COUNT. Not at all, Fräulein.

ACTRESS, *turning her eyes towards a large basket of flowers, which stands on a small table by the window.* There they are!

COUNT. Last night you were positively *strewn* with flowers and garlands!

ACTRESS. I left them all in my dressing room. Your basket was the only thing I brought home.

COUNT *kisses her hand.* You're very kind.
The ACTRESS *suddenly takes his hand and kisses it.*

COUNT. Fräulein!

ACTRESS. Don't be afraid, Count. It commits you to nothing!

COUNT. You're a strange creature . . . a puzzle, one might almost say.
Pause.

ACTRESS. Fräulein Birken is . . . easier to solve?

COUNT. Oh, little Birken is no puzzle. Though . . . I know her only superficially.

ACTRESS. Indeed?

COUNT. Oh, believe me. But *you* are a problem. And I've always longed for one. As a matter of fact, last night I realized what a great pleasure I'd been missing. You see, it was the first time I've seen you act.

ACTRESS. Is that true?

COUNT. Oh, yes. You see, Fräulein, it's so difficult, the theatre. By the time I get there, the best part of the play'd be over, wouldn't it?

ACTRESS. You'll have to dine earlier from now on.

COUNT. I'd thought of that. Or of not dining at all. There's not much pleasure in it, is there—dining?

ACTRESS. What do you still find pleasure in, young fogey?

COUNT. I sometimes ask myself. But I'm no fogey. There must be another reason.

ACTRESS. You think so?

COUNT. Yes. For instance, Lulu always says I'm a philosopher. What he means is: I think too much.

ACTRESS. Lulu?

COUNT. Friend of mine.

ACTRESS. He's right . . . it *is* a misfortune, all that thinking.

COUNT. I've time on my hands, that's why I think. You see, Fräulein, when they transferred me to Vienna, I thought it would be better. It'd be amusing, stimulating, the city. But it's really much the same here as up there.

ACTRESS. And where is "up there"?

COUNT. Well, down there, Fräulein, in Hungary. The small towns I used to be stationed in.

ACTRESS. What were you doing in Hungary?

COUNT. I'm telling you, dear lady—the Army.

ACTRESS. But why stay in Hungary?

COUNT. It happens, that's all.

ACTRESS. Enough to drive anyone mad, I should think!

COUNT. Oh, I don't know. In a way you have more to do there than here. You know, Fräulein, training recruits, exercising horses . . . and the surroundings aren't as bad as people say. It's really rather lovely, the big plain there. Such a sunset! It's a pity I'm not a painter. I often thought I'd paint one, if I were a painter. We had a man in our regiment, young Splany, and he could do it. Why I tell you this boring stuff I don't know, Fräulein.

ACTRESS. Please, Count! I'm highly amused.

COUNT. You know, Fräulein, it's so easy to talk to you. Lulu told me it would be. It's a thing one doesn't often meet.

ACTRESS. In Hungary!

COUNT. Or in Vienna! People are the same everywhere. Where there are more, it gets overcrowded but that's the only difference. Tell me, Fräulein, do you like people, really?

ACTRESS. Like them? I hate them! I don't want to see them. I never do see them. I'm always alone. This house is deserted!

COUNT. Just as I imagined: you're a misanthropist. It's bound to happen with artists. Moving in that more exalted sphere . . . Well, it's all right for you, at least you know why you're alive.

ACTRESS. Who told you that? I haven't the remotest idea why I'm alive!

COUNT. Not really, Fräulein . . . famous . . . celebrated . . .

ACTRESS. Is that—happiness?

COUNT. Happiness? Happiness doesn't exist. None of the things people chatter about really exist. . . . Love, for instance. It's the same with love.

ACTRESS. You may be right there.

COUNT. Enjoyment . . . intoxication . . . there's nothing wrong with them, they're real. I enjoy something, all right, and I know I enjoy it. Or I'm intoxicated, all right. That's real too. And when it's over, it's over, that's all.

ACTRESS, *grandly*. It's over!

COUNT. But as soon as you don't—I don't quite know how to say it—as soon as you stop living for the present moment, as soon as you think of later on or earlier on . . . Well, the whole thing collapses. "Later on" is sad, and "earlier on" is uncertain, in short, you just get mixed up. Don't you think so?

ACTRESS *nods, her eyes very wide open.* You pluck out the heart of the mystery, my dear Count.

COUNT. And you see, Fräulein, once you're clear about that, it doesn't matter if you live in Vienna or on the Hungarian plains or in the tiny town of Steinamanger. For example . . . where can I put my cap? . . . Oh, thanks. What were we talking about?

ACTRESS. The tiny town of Steinamanger.

COUNT. Oh, yes. Well, as I was saying, there isn't much difference. Whether I spend the evening at the Casino or the Club is all one.

ACTRESS. How does this tie in with love?

COUNT. If a man believes in it, there'll always be a girl around who loves him.

ACTRESS. Fräulein Birken, for example.

COUNT. Honestly, dear lady, I can't understand why you're always mentioning little Birken.

ACTRESS. She's your mistress after all.

COUNT. Who says that?

ACTRESS. Everyone knows.

COUNT. Except me. Remarkable.

ACTRESS. But you fought a duel on her behalf!

COUNT. Possibly I was shot dead and didn't notice.

ACTRESS. Count, you *are* a man of honor. Sit a little closer.

COUNT. If I may.

ACTRESS. Here.
She draws him closer, and runs her fingers through his hair.
I knew you would come today.

COUNT. Really? Why?

ACTRESS. I knew it last night. In the theatre.

COUNT. Oh, could you see me from the stage?

ACTRESS. My dear man, didn't you realize I was playing for you alone?

COUNT. How could that be?

ACTRESS. After I saw you in the front row, I was walking on air.

COUNT. Because of me? I'd no idea you'd noticed me.

ACTRESS. Oh, you can drive a woman to despair with that dignity of yours!

COUNT. Fräulein!

ACTRESS. "Fräulein?" At least take your saber off!

COUNT. Permit me.
He unbuckles the belt, leans the saber against the bed.

ACTRESS. And now kiss me at last.
The COUNT *kisses her. She does not let him go.*

ACTRESS. I wish I had never set eyes on you.

COUNT. No, no, it's better as it is.

ACTRESS. Count, you're a *poseur*.

COUNT. I am? Why?

ACTRESS. Many a man'd be happy to be in your shoes right now.

COUNT. *I'm* happy.

ACTRESS. Oh—I thought happiness didn't exist! Why do you
    look at me like that? I believe you're afraid of me, Count.

COUNT. I told you, Fräulein, you're a problem.

ACTRESS. Oh, don't bother me with philosophy . . . Come here.
    And ask me for something. You can have whatever you
    like. You're too handsome.

COUNT. Well, then I beg leave
    Kisses her hand.
    to return tonight.

ACTRESS. Tonight? . . . But I'm playing tonight.

COUNT. After the theatre.

ACTRESS. You ask for nothing else?

COUNT. I'll ask for everything else. After the theatre.

ACTRESS, *offended.* Then you can ask, you wretched *poseur*.

COUNT. You see, Fräulein . . . you see, my dear . . . We've been
    frank with each other till now. I'd find it all very much nicer
    in the evening, after the theatre. . . . It'll be so much more
    comfortable. . . . At present, you see, I've the feeling the
    door's going to open at any moment.

ACTRESS. This door doesn't open from the outside.

COUNT. Fräulein, wouldn't it be frivolous to spoil something
    at the start? When it might just possibly turn out to be
    beautiful?

ACTRESS. "Just possibly"!

COUNT. And to tell the truth, I find love in the morning pretty frightful.

ACTRESS. You're the craziest man I've ever come across.

COUNT. I'm not talking about ordinary females. After all, in general, it doesn't matter. But women like you, Fräulein —no, you can call me a fool as often as you like, but women like you . . . Well, one shouldn't have them before breakfast, that's all. And so . . . well . . .

ACTRESS. God, you're sweet!

COUNT. Now you see I'm right, don't you? What I have in mind . . .

ACTRESS. Tell me what you have in mind.

COUNT. What I mean is . . . I'll wait for you after the theatre, in my carriage, then we can drive off somewhere, well, and have supper and . . .

ACTRESS. I am not Fräulein Birken!

COUNT. I didn't say you were, my dear. Only, one must be in the mood! I get in the mood at supper. It's lovely to drive home after supper, and then . . .

ACTRESS. And then?

COUNT. Let events take their natural course.

ACTRESS. Come closer. Closer!

COUNT *sits down on the bed.* I must say, the perfume that comes from these pillows—mignonette, is it?

ACTRESS. It's hot in here, don't you think?
The COUNT *bends down and kisses her throat.*

ACTRESS. Oh my dear Count, this isn't on your program.

COUNT. Who says so? I have no program.
The ACTRESS *draws him to her.*

COUNT. It *is* hot.

ACTRESS. You find it so? And dark, like evening . . .
Pulling him to her.

It *is* evening, Count. It's night. . . . Shut your eyes if it's too light for you. Come! Come!
The COUNT *no longer defends himself.*

❋   ❋   ❋   ❋   ❋

ACTRESS. What's that about being in the mood, you *poseur*?

COUNT. You're a little devil.

ACTRESS. Count!

COUNT. All right, a little angel.

ACTRESS. And you should have been an actor. Really! You understand women. Do you know what I'm going to do now?

COUNT. Well?

ACTRESS. I'm going to tell you I never want to see you again.

COUNT. Why?

ACTRESS. You're too dangerous for me. You turn a woman's head. And now you stand there as if nothing has happened.

COUNT. But . . .

ACTRESS. I beg you to remember, my dear Count, that I've just been your mistress.

COUNT. Can I ever forget it?

ACTRESS. So how about tonight?

COUNT. What do you mean exactly?

ACTRESS. You intended to meet me after the theatre?

COUNT. Oh, yes, all right: let's say the day after tomorrow.

ACTRESS. The day after tomorrow? We were talking of tonight.

COUNT. There wouldn't be much sense in that.

ACTRESS. Fogey!

COUNT. You misunderstand me. I mean—how should I say—from the spiritual viewpoint.

ACTRESS. It's not your spirit that interests me.

COUNT. Believe me, it's all part of it. I don't agree that the two can be kept separate.

ACTRESS. Don't talk philosophy at me. When I want that, I read books.

COUNT. But we never learn from books.

ACTRESS. That's true. And that's why you'll be there tonight. We'll come to an agreement about the spiritual viewpoint, you . . . spiritualist!

COUNT. Then—with your permission—I'll wait with my carriage.

ACTRESS. You'll wait here. In my apartment.

COUNT. . . . After the theatre.

ACTRESS. Of course.
The COUNT *buckles on his saber.*

ACTRESS. What are you doing?

COUNT. I think it's time for me to go, Fräulein. I've been staying rather long as it is, for a formal visit.

ACTRESS. Well, it won't be a formal visit tonight!

COUNT. You think not?

ACTRESS. Just leave it to me. And now give me one more kiss, little philosopher. Here, you seducer . . . you . . . sweet thing, you spiritualist, you polecat, you . . .
After several emphatic kisses she emphatically pushes him away.
My dear Count, it was a great honor.

COUNT. I kiss your hand, Fräulein.
At the door.
Au revoir!

ACTRESS. Adieu, tiny town of Steinamanger!

10 THE COUNT AND THE WHORE

Morning, toward six o'clock. A mean little room, with one window; the dirty yellow blinds are down; frayed green curtains. A chest of drawers, with a few photographs on it and a cheap lady's hat in conspicuously bad taste. Several cheap Japanese fans behind the mirror. On the table, covered with a reddish cloth, stands a kerosene lamp, still feebly and odorously alight, with a yellow paper lampshade: next to the lamp, a jug with a little left-over beer, and a half empty glass. On the floor by the bed, untidy feminine clothing, apparently thrown off in a hurry.

The WHORE *is asleep in the bed, breathing evenly. On the sofa lies the* COUNT, *fully dressed and in a light overcoat; his hat is on the floor by the head of the sofa.*

COUNT *moves, rubs his eyes, rises with a start and, in a sitting position, looks round.* However did I get ... Oh ... So I did go home with that female. ...

He jumps up, sees her bed.

Why, here she is. To think what can happen to a man of my age! I don't remember a thing—did they carry me up? No ... I remember seeing ... When I got into the room, yes, I was still awake then, or I woke up, or ... or perhaps it's only that the room reminds me of something? ... Upon my soul, yes, I saw it last night, that's all. ...

He looks at his watch.

Last night indeed! A few hours ago. I knew something had to happen. Yesterday when I started drinking I felt that ... And what happened? Nothing ... Or did I ...? Upon my soul ... the last time I couldn't remember was ten years ago. The thing is, I was tight. If I only knew when it started ... I remember exactly going into that whores' cafe with Lulu and ... No, no ... First we left the Sacher ... and then, on the way, it started. ... Now I've got it. I was driving in my carriage with Lulu ... Silly to rack my brains. It's all one. I'll be on my way.

He rises. The lamp rocks.

Oh!

He looks at the sleeping girl.

She sleeps soundly, that one. I can't remember a thing, but I'll put the money on her bedside table—and good-bye.

He stands and looks at her a long while.

If one didn't know what she is. . . .

He again contemplates her.

I've known quite a lot of girls who didn't look so virtuous, even in their sleep. Upon my soul . . . now Lulu would say I'm philosophizing, but it's true, sleep does make us all equal, it seems to me, like his big brother—Death. . . . Hmm, I'd like to know if . . . No, I'd remember after all . . . No, no, I dropped down on the sofa right away . . . and nothing happened. . . . It's incredible how women can all look alike. . . . Let's go.

He goes to the door.

. . . Oh, there's that.

He takes out his wallet and is about to get a bill.

WHORE *wakes up.* Um . . . Who's here so early?

Recognizing him.

Hiya, son!

COUNT. Good morning. Slept well?

WHORE *stretches.* Come here. Little kiss.

COUNT *bends down, thinks better of it, pulls up short.* I was just going . . .

WHORE. Going?

COUNT. It's time really.

WHORE. You want to go like this?

COUNT, *almost embarrassed.* Well . . .

WHORE. So long, then. Come back and see us.

COUNT. Yes. Good-bye. Don't you want to shake hands?

The WHORE *pulls her hand from under the blanket and offers it.*

COUNT *takes her hand, mechanically kisses it, catches himself, and laughs.* As if she were a princess! Anyway, if one only . . .

WHORE. Why do you look at me like that?

COUNT. If one only sees the head, as now . . . when they wake up . . . they all look innocent . . . upon my soul, one really could imagine all sorts of things if the place didn't reek so of kerosene. . . .

WHORE. Yes, that lamp's a pest.

COUNT. How old are you, actually?

WHORE. Well, what do you think?

COUNT. Twenty-four.

WHORE. Oh, sure!

COUNT. Older?

WHORE. Nearly twenty.

COUNT. And how long have you been . . .

WHORE. In the business? A year.

COUNT. You did start early.

WHORE. Better too early than too late.

COUNT *sits down on her bed.* Tell me, are you happy?

WHORE. What?

COUNT. Well, I mean—how's it going? Well?

WHORE. Oh, I'm doing all right.

COUNT. I see . . . Tell me, did it ever occur to you to do something different?

WHORE. What could I do?

COUNT. Well . . . you're a pretty girl, after all, you could have a lover, for instance.

WHORE. Think I don't?

COUNT. I know—but I mean, *one,* you know: one lover—who keeps you, so you don't have to go with just any man.

WHORE. I *don't* go with just any man. I can afford to be choosy, thank goodness.
The COUNT *looks round the room.*

WHORE *notices this.* Next month we're moving into town. The Spiegel Gasse.

COUNT. We? Who?

WHORE. Oh, the madam and a couple of the other girls.

COUNT. There are others here?

WHORE. In the next room . . . can't you hear? That's Milli, she was at the café too.

COUNT. Somebody's snoring.

WHORE. That's Milli all right! She'll snore all day till ten in the evening, then she'll get up and go to the café.

COUNT. But that's an appalling sort of life!

WHORE. You said it. And the madam gets fed up with her. I'm always on the streets at twelve noon.

COUNT. What are you doing on the streets at twelve noon?

WHORE. What do you think? I'm on my beat.

COUNT. Oh, yes, I see . . . Of course . . .
He gets up, again takes out his wallet, and puts a bill on her bedside table.
Good-bye.

WHORE. Going already? . . . So long . . . Come again soon.
She turns over on her side.

COUNT *stops again.* Listen, tell me something. It doesn't mean a thing to you by now?

WHORE. What?

COUNT. I mean, you don't have fun with it any more?

WHORE *yawns.* I'm sleepy.

COUNT. It's all the same to you if a man is young or old, or if he . . .

WHORE. What are you asking all this for?

COUNT. Well . . .
Suddenly struck by a thought.

Upon my soul, now I know who you remind me of, it's . . .

WHORE. So I look like somebody, do I?

COUNT. Incredible, quite incredible—now, I beg you, please
don't say a word for at least a minute. . . .
He stares at her.
exactly the same face, exactly the same face.
He suddenly kisses her on the eyes.

WHORE. Hey!

COUNT. Upon my soul, it's a pity you aren't . . . something
else . . . you could make your fortune.

WHORE. You're like Franz.

COUNT. Who's Franz?

WHORE. Oh, the waiter at our café.

COUNT. How am I just like Franz?

WHORE. He always says I could make my fortune. And I should
marry him.

COUNT. Why don't you?

WHORE. Thank you very much . . . I don't want no marriage,
not for anything. Maybe later.

COUNT. The eyes . . . exactly the same eyes . . . Lulu'd certainly
say I'm a fool—but I'm going to kiss your eyes once more
like this. And now good-bye. God bless you. I'm going.

WHORE. So long.

COUNT, *turning at the door.* Listen . . . tell me . . . aren't you
a little bit surprised?

WHORE. Why?

COUNT. That I want nothing from you.

WHORE. There's a lot of men don't feel like it in the morning.

COUNT. Well, yes . . .
To himself.

It's too silly that I'd like her to be surprised. . . . Good-bye, then . . .

At the door.

Really, it annoys me. I know such girls are interested in nothing but the money . . . Now why do I say "such girls"? . . . At least it's nice that she doesn't pretend, it's a relief, or should be . . . Listen, I'll come again soon, you know.

WHORE, *with closed eyes.* Good.

COUNT. When are you usually in?

WHORE. I'm always in. Just ask for Leocadia.

COUNT. Leocadia . . . Right. Well, good-bye.

At the door.

I haven't got the wine out of my head yet. Isn't it the limit . . . I spend the night with one of these . . . and all I do is to kiss her eyes because she reminds me of someone. . . .

He turns to her.

Tell me, Leocadia, does it often happen that a man goes away like this?

WHORE. Like what?

COUNT. Like me.

WHORE. In the morning?

COUNT. No . . . I mean, has it occasionally happened that a man was with you—and didn't want anything?

WHORE. No. Never!

COUNT. What's the matter? Do you think I don't like you?

WHORE. Why shouldn't you like me? Last night you liked me all right.

COUNT. I like you now too.

WHORE. Last night you liked me better.

COUNT. What makes you think so?

WHORE. Don't talk silly.

COUNT. Last night . . . Tell me, didn't I drop down on the sofa right away?

WHORE. Sure you did—with me.

COUNT. With you?

WHORE. Sure—you don't remember?

COUNT. I . . . we . . . well . . .

WHORE. But you went right off to sleep after.

COUNT. I went right off . . . I see . . . So that's how it was!

WHORE. Yes, son. You must've been good and drunk if you can't remember.

COUNT. I see . . . All the same, there *is* a faint resemblance . . . Good-bye . . .
He listens.
What's the matter?

WHORE. The chambermaid's started work. Look, give her something as you go out. The front door's open, so you save on the janitor.

COUNT. Right.
In the entrance hall.
So . . . it would have been beautiful if I'd only kissed her eyes. It would almost have been an adventure. . . . Well, I suppose it wasn't to be!
The Chambermaid stands by the door and opens it for him.
Oh . . . here . . . Good-night!

CHAMBERMAID. Good morning!

COUNT. Oh, of course . . . Good morning . . . Good morning!

PURGATORY

by

W. B. YEATS

Characters

A BOY
AN OLD MAN

Scene: A ruined house and a bare tree in the background

BOY. Half-door, hall door,
    Hither and thither, day and night,
    Hill or hollow, shouldering his pack,
    Hearing you talk.

OLD MAN.   Study that house.
    I think about its jokes and stories
    I try to remember what the butler
    Said to a drunken gamekeeper
    In mid October, but I cannot.
    If I cannot, none living can.
    Where are the jokes and stories of a house,
    Its threshold gone to patch a pig-sty?

BOY. So you have come this path before?

OLD MAN. The moonlight falls upon the path,
    The shadow of a cloud upon the house,
    And that's symbolical; study that tree,
    What is it like?

BOY.   A silly old man.

OLD MAN. It's like—no matter what it's like.
    I saw it a year ago stripped bare as now,
    So I chose a better trade.
    I saw it fifty years ago
    Before the thunderbolt had riven it,
    Green leaves, ripe leaves, leaves thick as butter,
    Fat, greasy life. Stand there and look,
    Because there is somebody in that house.
    The BOY *puts down pack and stand in the doorway.*

BOY. There's nobody here.

OLD MAN.   There's somebody there.

BOY. The floor is gone, the window's gone,
    And where there should be roof there's sky,
    And here's a bit of an egg-shell thrown
    Out of a jackdaw's nest.

OLD MAN.   But there are some
  That do not care what's gone, what's left:
  The souls of Purgatory that come back
  To habitations and familiar spots.

BOY. Your wits are out again.

OLD MAN.   Re-live
  Their transgressions, and that not once
  But many times; they know at last
  The consequence of those transgressions
  Whether upon others or upon themselves;
  Upon others, others may bring help,
  For when the consequence is at an end
  The dream must end; if upon themselves,
  There is no help but in themselves
  And in the mercy of God.

BOY.   I have had enough!
  Talk to the jackdaws, if talk you must.

OLD MAN. Stop! Sit there upon that stone.
  That is the house where I was born.

BOY. The big old house that was burnt down?

OLD MAN. My mother that was your grand-dam owned it,
  This scenery and this countryside,
  Kennel and stable, horse and hound—
  She had a horse at the Curragh, and there met
  My father, a groom in the training stable,
  Looked at him and married him.
  Her mother never spoke to her again,
  And she did right.

BOY.   What's right and wrong?
  My granddad got the girl and the money.

OLD MAN. Looked at him and married him,
  And he squandered everything she had.
  She never knew the worst, because
  She died in giving birth to me,
  But now she knows it all, being dead.
  Great people lived and died in this house;
  Magistrates, colonels, members of Parliament,
  Captains and Governors, and long ago

Men that had fought at Aughrim and the Boyne.
Some that had gone on government work
To London or to India came home to die,
Or came from London every spring
To look at the may-blossom in the park.
They had loved the trees that he cut down
To pay what he had lost at cards
Or spent on horses, drink, and women;
Had loved the house, had loved all
The intricate passages of the house,
But he killed the house; to kill a house
Where great men grew up, married, died,
I here declare a capital offence.

BOY. My God, but you had luck! Grand clothes,
   Any maybe a grand horse to ride.

OLD MAN. That he might keep me upon his level
He never sent me to school, but some
Half-loved me for my half of her:
A gamekeeper's wife taught me to read,
A Catholic curate taught me Latin.
There were old books and books made fine
By eighteenth-century French binding, books
Modern and ancient, books by the ton.

BOY. What education have you given me?

OLD MAN. I gave the education that befits
A bastard that a pedlar got
Upon a tinker's daughter in a ditch.
When I had come to sixteen years old
My father burned down the house when drunk.

BOY. But what is my age, sixteen yeears old,
   At the Puck Fair.

OLD MAN.   And everything was burnt;
   Books, library, all were burnt.

BOY. Is what I have heard upon the road the truth,
   That you killed him in the burning house?

OLD MAN. There's nobody here but our two selves?

BOY. Nobody, Father.

OLD MAN.   I stuck him with a knife,
    That knife that cuts my dinner now,
    And after that I left him in the fire.
    They dragged him out, somebody saw
    The knife wound but could not be certain
    Because the body was all black and charred.
    Then some that were his drunken friends
    Swore they would put me upon trial,
    Spoke of quarrels, a threat I had made.
    The gamekeeper gave me some old clothes,
    I ran away, worked here and there
    Till I became a pedlar on the roads,
    No good trade, but good enough
    Because I am my father's son,
    Because of what I did or may do.
    Listen to the hoofbeats! Listen, listen!

BOY. I cannot hear a sound.

OLD MAN.   Beat! Beat!
    This night is the anniversary
    Of my mother's wedding night,
    Or of the night wherein I was begotten.
    My father is riding from the public-house,
    A whiskey-bottle under his arm.
    A window is lit showing a young girl.
    Look at the window; she stands there
    Listening, the servants are all in bed,
    She is alone, he has stayed late
    Bragging and drinking in the public-house.

BOY. There's nothing but an empty gap in the wall.
    You have made it up. No, you are mad!
    You are getting madder every day.

OLD MAN. Its louder now because he rides
    Upon a gravelled avenue
    All grass today. The hoof-beat stops,
    He has gone to the other side of the house,
    Gone to the stable, put the horse up.
    She has gone down to open the door.
    This night she is no better than her man
    And does not mind that he is half drunk,

She is mad about him. They mount the stairs,
She brings him into her own chamber.
And that is the marriage-chamber now.
The window is dimly lit again.

Do not let him touch you! It is not true
That drunken men cannot beget,
And if he touch he must beget
And you must bear his murderer.
Deaf! Both deaf! It I should throw
A stick or a stone they would not hear;
And that's a proof my wits are out.
But there's a problem: she must live
Through everything in exact detail,
Driven to it by remorse, and yet
Can she renew the sexual act
And find no pleasure in it, and if not,
If pleasure and remorse must both be there,
Which is the greater?
                I lack schooling.
Go fetch Tertullian; he and I
Will ravel all that problem out
Whilst those two lie upon the mattress
Begetting me.
                Come back! Come back!
And so you thought to slip away,
My bag of money between your fingers,
And that I could not talk and see!
You have been rummaging in the pack.
The light in the window has faded out.

BOY. You never gave me my right share.

OLD MAN. And had I given it, young as you are,
You would have spent it upon drink.

BOY. What if I did? I had a right
To get it and spend it as I chose.

OLD MAN. Give me that bag and no more words.

BOY. I will not.

OLD MAN.   I will break your fingers.
They struggle for the bag. In the struggle it drops, scattering

the money. The OLD MAN *staggers but does not fall. They
stand looking at each other. The window is lit up. A man
is seen pouring whiskey into a glass.*

BOY. What if I killed you? You killed my granddad,
Because you were young and he was old.
Now I am young and you are old.

OLD MAN, *staring at window.* Better-looking, those sixteen
years——

BOY. What are you muttering?

OLD MAN.   Younger—and yet
She should have known he was not her kind.

BOY. What are you saying? Out with it!
    OLD MAN *points to window.*
My God! The window is lit up
And somebody stands there, although
The floorboards are all burnt away.

OLD MAN. The window is lit up because my father
Has come to find a glass for his whiskey.
He leans there like some tired beast.

BOY. A dead, living, murdered man!

OLD MAN. "Then the bride-sleep fell upon Adam":
Where did I read those words?
                              And yet
There's nothing leaning in the window
But the impression upon my mother's mind;
Being dead she is alone in her remorse.

BOY. A body that was a bundle of old bones
Before I was born, Horrible! Horrible!
    He covers his eyes.

OLD MAN. That beast there would know nothing, being nothing,
If I should kill a man under the window
He would not even turn his head.
    He stabs the BOY.
My father and my son on the same jackknife!
That finishes—there—there—there—
    He stabs again and again. The window grows dark.

"Hush-a-bye baby, thy father's knight,
Thy mother a lady, lovely and bright."
No, that is something that I read in a book,
And if I sing it must be to my mother,
And I lack rhyme.
The stage has grown dark except where the tree stands in
white light.

Study that tree.
It stands there like a purified soul,
All cold, sweet, glistening light.
Dear mother, the window is dark again,
But you are in the light because
I finished all that consequence.
I killed that lad because had he grown up
He would have struck a woman's fancy,
Begot, and passed pollution on.

I am a wretched foul old man
And therefore harmless. When I have stuck
This old jack-knife into a sod
And pulled it out all bright again,
And picked up all the money that he dropped,
I'll to a distant place, and there
Tell my old jokes among new men.
He cleans the knife and begins to pick up money.

Hoof-beats! Dear God,
How quickly it returns—beat—beat—!

Her mind cannot hold up that dream.
Twice a murderer and all for nothing,
And she must animate that dead night
Not once but many times!

O God,
Release my mother's soul from its dream!
Mankind can do no more. Appease
The misery of the living and the remorse of the dead.

MOTHER COURAGE

A Chronicle
of the Thirty Years' War
by

BERTOLT BRECHT

English Version by
Eric Bentley

Characters (*in order of appearance*)

There are 32 roles plus four "voices off" and three supers. But much doubling is possible; in fact, of all the actors, only the seven principals cannot double; these seven are Mother Guts, her three children, Cook, Chaplain, Yvette—even one of the children, Swiss Cheese, *could* double if absolutely necessary.

Prologue

MOTHER GUTS   SWISS CHEESE
EILIF   CATHERINE

Scene One

RECRUITING OFFICER   SERGEANT

Scene Two

COOK   COMMANDER   CHAPLAIN

Scene Three

ORDNANCE OFFICER   SERGEANT
YVETTE POTTIER   ONE EYE
SOLDIER   COLONEL
(TWO SUPERS)

Scene Four

CLERK   OLDER SOLDIER   YOUNGER SOLDIER

Scene Five

FIRST SOLDIER   PEASANT
SECOND SOLDIER   PEASANT WOMAN

Scene Six

SOLDIER (*singing*)

Scene Seven: no new characters

Scene Eight

OLD WOMAN   VOICES (*two*)
YOUNG MAN   SOLDIER
(ONE SUPER)

Scene Nine

VOICE

Scene Ten

VOICE (*girl singing*)

Scene Eleven

LIEUTENANT   OLD PEASANT
FIRST SOLDIER   PEASANT WOMAN
SECOND SOLDIER   YOUNG PEASANT

Scene Twelve: no new characters

THE TIME: 1624–1636; THE PLACE: *Sweden, Poland, Germany*

PROLOGUE

MOTHER COURAGE *sits on her wagon singing. Her dumb daughter* CATHERINE *sits beside her playing the mouth organ. The wagon is drawn by her two sons,* EILIF *and* SWISS CHEESE, *who join in the refrains.**

Captains and Colonels, cease your drumming!
Let all your infantry be still!
For Courage in her wagon's coming
And she has got good boots to sell
These fellows never will adore you
(Guns on their backs, lice in their hair)
But since they'll soon be dying for you
Right now they need good boots to wear

> *The spring is here, get out of bed*
> *The snow melts fast, green buds arrive*
> *You'll sleep forever when you're dead*
> *But if you're not, then look alive!*

To die for you your men are willing
But cannot fight unless they feed
And Courage no man's blood is spilling
Just wine for soul's and body's need
Cannon is rough on empty bellies
First you should have them taste my fare
Then let them go and find where hell is
And take my blessing with them there

> *The spring is here, get out of bed*
> *The snow melts fast, green buds arrive*
> *You'll sleep forever when you're dead*
> *But if you're not, then look alive!*

* Where there is a revolving stage, the wagon is placed on it. If the wagon moves one way and the turntable the other way, the wagon can, for a while, be stationary in relation to the audience.

1

SPRING, 1624. IN DALARNA, SWEDEN, KING
GUSTAVUS ADOLPHUS IS RECRUITING FOR
THE CAMPAIGN IN POLAND. THE PROVI-
SIONER ANNA FIERLING, KNOWN AS CAN-
TEEN ANNA OR MOTHER COURAGE, LOSES
A SON.*

*A highway in the neighborhood of a town. A top Sergeant
and a Recruiting Officer stand shivering.*

OFFICER. How the hell can you line up a squadron in *this* place?
You know what I keep thinking about, Sergeant? Suicide.
I'm supposed to slap four platoons together by the twelfth—
four platoons the Chief's asking for! And they're so friendly
around here I'm scared to sleep nights. Suppose I do get my
hands on some character and squint at him so I don't notice
he's chicken breasted and has varicose veins. I get him drunk
and relaxed, he signs on the dotted line. I pay for the drinks,
he steps outside for a minute. I get a hunch I should follow
him to the door, and am I right! Off he's shot like a louse
from a scratch. You can't take a man's word any more, Sergeant. There's no loyalty left in the world, no trust, no faith,
no sense of honor. I'm losing my confidence in mankind, Sergeant.

SERGEANT. What they could use round here is a good war. What
else can you expect with peace running wild all over the
place? You know what the trouble with peace is? No organization. When do you get organization? In a war. Peace is
one big waste of equipment. Anything goes, no one gives a
god damn. See the way they eat? Cheese on rye, bacon on
the cheese? Disgusting! How many horses they got in this
town? How many young men? Nobody knows! They haven't
bothered to count 'em!! That's peace for you!!! I been

*The scene headings in block capitals are projected on a
front curtain. In the scene itself the location is indicated by
large black letters hanging from the flies (e.g. SWEDEN in
this first scene).

in places where they haven't had a war in seventy years and you know what? The people can't remember their own names! They don't know who they are! It takes a war to fix all that. In a war everyone registers, everybody's name's on a list, their shoes are stacked, their corn's in the bag, you count it all up—cattle, men, et cetera—and take it away! Yeah, that's the story—no organization, no war!

OFFICER. It's the God's truth.

SERGEANT. Course, a war's like every real good deal, hard to get going. But when it's on the road, it's a pisser—everybody's scared off peace—like a crapshooter that keeps fading to cover his loss. Course, *until* it gets going, they're just as scared off war—afraid to try anything new.

OFFICER. Look, a wagon! Two women and a couple of young punks. Stop the old lady, Sergeant. And if there's nothing doing this time, you won't catch *me* freezing my ass in the April wind!

MOTHER COURAGE *entering with her three children as in the prologue.* Good day to you, Sergeant!

SERGEANT *barring the way.* Good day! Who do you think *you* are?

MOTHER COURAGE. Tradespeople!
    She prepares to go.

SERGEANT. Halt! Where are you riffraff from?

EILIF. The Second Protestant Regiment.

SERGEANT. Where are your papers?

MOTHER COURAGE. Papers?

SWISS CHEESE. But this is Mother Courage!

SERGEANT. Never heard of her. Where'd she get a name like that?

MOTHER COURAGE. They call me Mother Courage because I was afraid I'd be ruined, so I drove through the bombardment of Riga like a madwoman, with fifty loaves of bread in my cart. They were getting moldy, I couldn't please myself.

SERGEANT. No funny business! Where are your papers?

MOTHER COURAGE, *rummaging among a mass of papers in a tin box, and clambering down from her cart*. Here, Sergeant! Here's a whole Bible I got in Altötting to wrap cucumbers in, and a map of Moravia, God knows if I'll ever get there, it's good enough for the cat if I don't. And here's a document to say my horse hasn't got hoof and mouth disease; too bad he died on us, he cost fifteen gilders, thank God I didn't pay it. Is that enough paper?

SERGEANT. Are you making a pass at me? Well, you got another guess coming. You got to have a license and you know it.

MOTHER COURAGE. Show a little respect for a lady and don't go telling these grown children of mine I'm making a pass at you, it's not proper, what would I want with *you*? My license in the Second Protestant Regiment is an honest face, even if *you* wouldn't know how to read it. I'll have no rubber stamp on it neither.

OFFICER. There's insubordination for you, my dear Sergeant!
To MOTHER COURAGE.
Do you know what we need in the army?
MOTHER COURAGE *starts to reply but he doesn't let her*.
Discipline!

MOTHER COURAGE. I'd have said frankfurters.

SERGEANT. Name?

MOTHER COURAGE. Anna Fierling.

SERGEANT. So you're all Fierlings?

MOTHER COURAGE. What do you mean? I was talking about me.

SERGEANT. And I was talking about your children!

MOTHER COURAGE. Must they all have the same name?
Indicating the elder son.
This boy, for instance, his name is Eilif Noyocki—for the good reason that his father always said his name was Koyocki or Moyocki. The boy remembers him to this day, only it's another one he remembers to this day, a Frenchman with a pointed beard. Anyhow he certainly has his father's brains—that man would have the pants off a farmer's behind before he knew what had happened. So we all have our own names.

SERGEANT. You're all called something different?

MOTHER COURAGE. Are you pretending you don't get it?

SERGEANT, *indicating Swiss Cheese*. He's Chinese, I suppose?

MOTHER COURAGE. Wrong again. A Swiss.

SERGEANT. After the Frenchman?

MOTHER COURAGE. Frenchman? I don't know any Frenchman.
Don't confuse the issue or we'll be here all day. He's a Swiss
but he happens to be called Feyos, a name that has nothing
to do with his father, who was called something else; he was
a military engineer, if you please, and a drunkard.
    SWISS CHEESE *nods, beaming, and even* CATHERINE *is
    amused.*

SERGEANT. Then how come his name's Feyos?

MOTHER COURAGE. No harm meant, Sergeant, but you have no
imagination. Of course he's called Feyos—when he came I
was with a Hungarian, he didn't mind a bit, he had a floating kidney, though he never touched a drop, he was a very
honest man. The boy takes after him.

SERGEANT. But he wasn't his father!

MOTHER COURAGE. I said he took after him. I call him Swiss
Cheese.
    Indicating her daughter.
She's called Catherine Haupt. Half German.

SERGEANT. A nice family I must say.

MOTHER COURAGE. We've seen the whole world together, my
wagon and me.

SERGEANT, *writing*. We'll need all that in writing.

OFFICER, *to* EILIF. And you two oxen pull the cart. Jacob Ox and
Esau Ox! Do you ever get out of harness?

EILIF. Can I smack him in the puss, mother? I'd like to.

MOTHER COURAGE. No, you can't, you stay where you are. And
now, gentlemen, what about a fine pair of pistols? Or a belt—
yours is practically worn through, sergeant.

SERGEANT. I'm after something else. I see these boys are straight as birch trees, broad in the chest, strong of limb—what are specimens like that doing out of the army I'd like to know?

MOTHER COURAGE, *rapidly*. It's no use, sergeant: the soldier's life is not for sons of mine!

OFFICER. Why not? It means money. It means fame. Peddling boots is woman's work.

To EILIF.

Just step up here and let me see if that's muscle or chicken fat.

MOTHER COURAGE. Chicken fat. Give him a good hard look and he'll fall over.

OFFICER. And kill a calf while he's falling if there's one in the way.

He tries to hustle EILIF *off.*

MOTHER COURAGE. Will you let him alone? He's not for you!

OFFICER. He called my face a puss, that's an insult. The two of us will now go out in the field and settle this affair like men of honor.

EILIF. Don't worry, I can handle him, Mother.

MOTHER COURAGE. Stay here, you trouble maker! Never happy unless you're in a fight.

To the OFFICER.

He has a knife in his boot and he knows how to use it.

OFFICER. I'll draw it out of him like a milk tooth. Come on, young fellow!

MOTHER COURAGE. Officer, I'll report you to the Colonel, he'll throw you in jail. The lieutenant is courting my daughter!

SERGEANT. Take it easy, brother.

To MOTHER COURAGE.

What have you got against the service? Wasn't his father a soldier? Didn't he die a soldier's death? You said so yourself.

MOTHER COURAGE. Yes, he' dead, but this one's just a baby, and you'll lead him to the slaughter for me, I know you. You'll get five gilders for him.

OFFICER. First thing you know, you'll have a new cap and knee boots, how about it?

EILIF. Not from you, thanks.

MOTHER COURAGE. "Come on, let's go fishing," said the angler to the worm.

To SWISS CHEESE.

Run and tell everybody they're trying to steal your brother!

She draws a knife.

Now try and steal him! And I'll let you have it, I'll cut you down like dogs! Using *him* in your war! We sell linen, we sell ham, we're peaceful people!

SERGEANT. You're peaceful all right, your knife proves it. Why, you should be ashamed of yourself. Give me that knife, you hag! You admit you live off the war, what else *would* you live off? Tell me: how can we have a war without soldiers?

MOTHER COURAGE. Do they have to be mine?

SERGEANT. So that's it. The war should swallow the pits and spit out the peach, huh? Your brood should get fat off the war, and the poor war shouldn't ask a think in return; it can look after itself, huh? Call yourself Mother Courage and then get scared of the war—your breadwinner? Your sons aren't scared, I know that much.

EILIF. No war can scare me.

SERGEANT. Why should it? Look at me: the soldier's life hasn't done me any harm, has it? I enlisted at seventeen.

MOTHER COURAGE. You haven't reached seventy.

SERGEANT. I will, though.

MOTHER COURAGE. Above ground?

SERGEANT. Are you trying to rile me, telling me I'll die?

MOTHER COURAGE. Suppose it's the truth? Suppose I can see it's your fate? Suppose I know you're just a corpse on furlough?

SWISS CHEESE. She has second sight. Everyone says so. She can look into the future.

OFFICER. Then go look into the sergeant's future, it might amuse him.

SERGEANT. I don't believe in that stuff.

MOTHER COURAGE. Your helmet!
He gives her his helmet.

SERGEANT. It means about as much as a crap in the grass. But anything for a laugh.

MOTHER COURAGE *takes a sheet of parchment and tears it in two pieces.* Eilif, Swiss Cheese, and Catherine, so should we all be torn asunder if we let ourselves be drawn too deep into the war!
To the SERGEANT.
For you, I'll make an exception, and do it free. Death is black. I draw a black cross on this piece of paper.

SWISS CHEESE. And the other she leaves blank, see?

MOTHER COURAGE. Then I fold them, put them in the helmet, and shuffle them up—mixed up like we all are from our mother's womb on. And now you draw and find out the answer.
The SERGEANT *hesitates.*

OFFICER, *to* EILIF. I don't take just anybody, I'm particular, they all say so. And you're full of punch, I like that.

SERGEANT, *fishing into the helmet.* It's a lot of bunk. Hogwash!

SWISS CHEESE. He's drawn the black cross. His number's up!

OFFICER. Don't let them frighten you, there aren't enough bullets to go round.

SERGEANT, *hoarsely.* You swindled me.

MOTHER COURAGE. You swindled yourself, the day you enlisted. And now we must drive on, there isn't a war every day in the week, we got to get to work.

SERGEANT. Hell and damnation, you're not getting away with this. We're taking that bastard of yours with us, we'll make a soldier of him.

EILIF. I'd like that, mother.

MOTHER COURAGE. Shut up, you Finnish devil!

EILIF. And Swiss Cheese would like to be a soldier too.

MOTHER COURAGE. That's news to me. I see I'll have to draw lots for all three of you.

She goes to the back to draw crosses on the slips.

OFFICER, *to Eilif.* People 've been saying the Swedish soldier is religious. That's malicious gossip, I can't tell you how much damage it's done us. We only sing on Sunday. One verse of a hymn. And then only if you have a voice.

MOTHER COURAGE *returns with the slips and throws them into the* SERGEANT's *helmet.* Run away from their mother would they, the devils, and off to war like a cat to cream? Just let me consult these slips and they'll see the world's no promised land with its "Join up, son, you're officer material!"

She thrusts the helmet at EILIF.

There, take yours, Eilif.

He does so. As he unfolds the paper she snatches it from him.

There you are, a cross! If he's a soldier, his number's up, that's for sure.

OFFICER, *still talking to Eilif.* If you're wetting your pants, I'll try your brother.

MOTHER COURAGE. Now take yours, Swiss Cheese. You're a safer bet because you're my *good* boy.

He draws his lot.

Why do you look so strangely at it? It *must* be blank.

She takes it from him.

A cross? Oh, Swiss Cheese, there's no saving you either—unless you're a good boy through and through every minute of every day! Just look, sergeant, a black cross, isn't it?

SERGEANT. Another cross. But I don't see why *I* got one, I always stay well in the rear.

To the OFFICER.

It can't be a trick, it gets her own children.

MOTHER COURAGE, *to* CATHERINE. And now all I have left is you, you're a cross in yourself, but you have a kind heart.

She holds the helmet up but takes the paper herself.

Oh! I could give up in despair! I can't be right, I must have made a mistake. Don't be *too* kind, Catherine, don't be too kind, there's a cross in your path!

Breaking the mood.

So now you all know: always be very careful! And now we'll
get in and drive on.
She climbs on to the wagon.

OFFICER, *to* SERGEANT. Do something.

SERGEANT. I don't feel so well.

OFFICER. Try doing business with her.
Aloud.
That belt, sergeant, you could at least take a look at it, after
all they live by trade, don't they, these good people? Hey,
you! The sergeant will buy the belt!

MOTHER COURAGE. Half a gilder. Worth four times the price.

SERGEANT. It's not even a new one. But there's too much wind
here, I'll go look at it behind your wagon.

MOTHER COURAGE. It doesn't seem windy to me.

SERGEANT. Hey, maybe it is worth half a gilder at that, there's
silver on it.

MOTHER COURAGE *following him* evenly *back of the wagon.* A solid six
ounces worth.

OFFICER, *to* EILIF. I can let you have some cash in advance,
come on!
EILIF is undecided.

MOTHER COURAGE, *behind the wagon with the* SERGEANT. Half
a gilder then, quick.

SERGEANT. I still don't see why I had to draw a cross. I told you
I always stay in the rear, it's the only place that's safe. You
send the others on ahead to win the laurels of victory or the
glory of heroic defeat as the case may be. You've ruined my
afternoon.

MOTHER COURAGE. You mustn't take on so. Here, have a shot of
brandy.
She gives him some.
And go right on staying in the rear. Half a gilder.

OFFICER. *Has taken* EILIF *by the arm and is drawing him up-*
stage. Ten gilders in advance and you're a soldier of the king,
my lad, a stout fellow! The women'll be mad about you.

And you can smack me in the puss because I insulted you.
Both leave.
CATHERINE *makes harsh noises.*

MOTHER COURAGE. Coming, Catherine, coming! The sergeant's
just paying his bill.
She bites the half gilder.
To me, Sergeant, all money is suspect, but your half gilder's
okay. Now we'll be off. Where's Eilif?

SWISS CHEESE. Gone with the recruiting officer.

MOTHER COURAGE *stops in her tracks, a pause, then.* Oh, you
simpleton!
To CATHERINE.
And you could do nothing about it, you're dumb.

SERGEANT. Take a shot yourself, mother. That's how it goes.
Your son's a soldier, he might do worse.

MOTHER COURAGE *motions* CATHERINE *down from the wagon.*
You must help your brother now, Catherine.
*Brother and sister get into harness together and pull the
wagon,* MOTHER COURAGE *beside them.*

SERGEANT, *looking after them.*
If from the war you'd like to borrow
Remember: the debt must be paid tomorrow!

2

IN THE YEARS 1625 AND 1626 MOTHER
COURAGE JOURNEYS THROUGH POLAND IN
THE BAGGAGE TRAIN OF THE SWEDISH
ARMY. SHE MEETS HER SON AGAIN BEFORE
WALLHOF CASTLE. OF THE SUCCESSFUL
SALE OF A CAPON AND GREAT DAYS FOR THE
BRAVE SON.

*Tent of the Swedish Commander. Kitchen next to it. Sound
of cannon. The* COOK *is quarrelling with* MOTHER COURAGE
who is trying to sell him a capon.

COOK, *who has a Dutch accent.* Sixty hellers for that paltry poultry?

MOTHER COURAGE. Paltry poultry? Why, he's the fattest fowl you ever saw! I see no reason why I shouldn't get sixty hellers for him—this Commander can eat till the cows come home.

COOK. They're ten hellers a dozen on every street corner.

MOTHER COURAGE. A capon like this on every street corner! With a siege going on and people all skin and bones? Maybe you can get a field rat! I said maybe. Because we're all out of *them* too. Didn't you see the soldiers running five deep after one hungry little field rat? All right then, in a siege, my price for a giant capon is fifty hellers.

COOK. But we're not "in a siege," we're doing the besieging, it's the other side that's "in a siege" . . .

MOTHER COURAGE. A fat lot of difference that makes, *we* don't have a thing to eat either. They took everything in the town with them before all this started, and now they've nothing to do but eat and drink. It's us I'm worried about. Look at the farmers round here, they haven't a thing.

COOK. Sure they have. They hide it.

MOTHER COURAGE. They have not! They're ruined. They're so hungry I've seen 'em digging up roots to eat. I could boil your leather belt and make their mouths water with it. That's how things are round here. And I'm supposed to let a capon go for forty hellers!

COOK. Thirty. Not forty, I said thirty hellers.

MOTHER COURAGE. I know *your* problem: if you don't find something to eat and quick, the Chief will—cut—your—fat—head —off!

COOK. All right, just watch.
He takes a piece of beef and lays his knife on it.
Here's a piece of beef, I'm going to roast it. I give you one more chance.

MOTHER COURAGE. Roast it, go ahead, it's only one year old.

COOK. One *day* old! Yesterday it was a cow. I saw it running around.

MOTHER COURAGE. In that case it must have started stinking before it died.

COOK. I don't care if I have to cook it five hours.
He cuts into it.

MOTHER COURAGE. Put plenty of pepper in.

The SWEDISH COMMANDER, *a Chaplain and* EILIF *enter the tent.*

COMMANDER, *clapping* EILIF *on the shoulder.* In the Commander's tent with you, Eilif my son! Sit at my right hand, you happy warrior! You've played a hero's part, you've served the Lord in his own Holy War, *that's* the thing! And you'll get a gold bracelet out of it when we take the town if *I* have any say in the matter! We come to save their souls and what do they do, the filthy, irreligious sons of bitches? Drive their cattle away from *us*, while they stuff their priests with beef at both ends! But you showed 'em. So here's a can of red wine for you, we'll drink together!
They do so.
The chaplain gets the dregs, he's religious. Now what would you like for dinner, my hearty?

EILIF. How about a slice of meat?

COOK. Nothing to eat, so he brings company to eat it!
MOTHER COURAGE *makes him stop talking, she wants to listen.*

COMMANDER. Cook, meat!

EILIF. Tires you out, skinning peasants. Gives you an appetite.

MOTHER COURAGE. Dear God, it's my Eilif!

COOK. Who?

MOTHER COURAGE. My eldest. It's two years since I saw him, he was stolen from me right off the street. He must be in high favor if the Commander's invited him to dinner. And what do you have to eat? Nothing. You hear what the Commander's guest wants? Meat! Better take my advice, buy the capon. The price is one gilder.

COMMANDER *who has sat down with* EILIF *and the* CHAPLAIN, *roaring.* Cook! Dinner, you pig, or I'll have your head!

COOK. This is blackmail. Give me the damn thing!

MOTHER COURGE. Paltry poultry like this?

COOK. You were right. Give it here. It's highway robbery, fifty
hellers.

MOTHER COURAGE. I said one gilder. Nothing's too high for my
eldest, the Commander's guest of honor.

COOK. Well, you might at least pluck the damn thing till I have
a fire going.

MOTHER COURAGE, *sitting down to pluck the capon.* I can't wait
to see his face when he sees me.

COMMANDER. Have another glass, my son, it's my favorite
Falernian. There's only one cask left—two at the most—but
it's worth it to meet a soldier that still believes in God! Our
chaplain here just looks on, he only preaches, he hasn't a clue
how anything gets done. So now, Eilif my son, give us the
details: tell us how you fixed the peasants and grabbed the
twenty bullocks.

EILIF. Well, it was like this. I found out that the peasants had
hidden their oxen and—on the sly and chiefly at night—had
driven them into a certain wood. The people from the town
were to pick them up there. I let them get their oxen in
peace—they ought to know better than me where they are, I
said to myself. Meanwhile I made my men crazy for meat.
Their rations were short and I made sure they got shorter.
Their mouths'd water at the sound of any word beginning
with M, like mother.

COMMANDER. Smart kid.

EILIF. Not bad. The rest was a snap. Only the peasants had
clubs and outnumbered us three to one and made a murder-
ous attack on us. Four of them drove me into a clump of
trees, knocked my good sword from my hand, and yelled,
"Surrender!" What now, I said to myself, they'll make mincemeat of me.

COMMANDER. What did you do?

EILIF. I laughed.

COMMANDER. You what?

EILIF. I laughed. And so we got to talking. I came right down to business and said: "Twenty gilders an ox is too much, I bid fifteen." Like I wanted to buy. That foxed 'em. So while they were scratching their heads, I reached for my good sword and cut 'em to pieces. Necessity knows no law, huh?

COMMANDER. What do *you* say, keeper of souls?

CHAPLAIN. Strictly speaking, that saying is not in the Bible. Our Lord made five hundred loaves out of five so that no such necessity would arise. When he told men to love their neighbors, their bellies were full. Nowadays things are different.

COMMANDER, *laughing*. Quite different. A swallow of wine for those wise words, you pharisee!

To EILIF.

You cut 'em to pieces in a good cause, our fellows were hungry and you gave 'em to eat. Doesn't it say in the Bible "Whatsoever thou doest to the least of these my children, thou doest unto me?" And what *did* you do to 'em? You got 'em the best steak dinner they ever tasted.

EILIF. I reached for my good sword and cut 'em to pieces.

COMMANDER. You have the makings of a Julius Caesar, why, you should be presented to the King!

EILIF. I've seen him—from a distance of course. He seemed to shed a light all around. I must try to be like him!

COMMANDER. I think you're succeeding, my boy! Oh, Eilif, you don't know how I value a brave soldier like you!
He takes him to the map.
Take a look at our position, Eilif, it isn't all it might be, is it?

MOTHER COURAGE, *who has been listening and is now plucking angrily at her capon.* He must be a very bad commander.

COOK. Just a greedy one. Why bad?

MOTHER COURAGE. Because he needs *brave* soldiers, that's why. If his plan of campaign was any good, why would he need *brave* soldiers, wouldn't plain, ordinary soldiers do? Whenever there are great virtues, it's a sure sign something's wrong.

COOK. You mean, it's a sure sign something's right.

MOTHER COURAGE. I mean what I say. Listen. When a king is a stupid king and leads his soldiers into a trap, they need this virtue of courage. When he's tight fisted and hasn't enough soldiers, the few he does have need the heroism of Hercules —another virtue. And if he's a sloven and doesn't give a damn about anything, they have to fend for themselves and be wise as serpents or they're through. Loyalty's another virtue and you need plenty of it if the king's always asking too much of you. But in a good country the virtues wouldn't be necessary. Everybody could be quite ordinary, middling, and, for all of me, cowards.

COMMANDER. I bet our father was a soldier.

EILIF. I've heard he was a great soldier. My mother warned me. I know a song about that.

COMMANDER. Sing it to us.
Roaring.
Bring that meat!

EILIF. It's called THE SONG OF THE SOLDIER BOY.
He sings and at the same time does a war dance with his sabre.

"A chopper will chop and a cleaver will cleave
"If you fall into ice it will freeze you
"What can we do with ice? Keep off, son, be wise!"
Said the old woman to the soldier boy
But the brave lad, he was after some fun
And he heard the drum roll and he picked up his gun
"We know our parade ground will please you
"Then it's up to the northward and it's down to the south
"With a knife at your side and a smile on your mouth"
Whispered the sergeant to the soldier boy

"Woe to him who defies the advice of the wise!
"Just listen to me I implore you!
"O beware, my young friend, unhappy's the end!"
Said the old woman to the soldier boy
But the brave lad with his knife at his side
Laughed aloud in her face and stepped into the tide

"O life of great deeds, we adore you!
"When white shines the moon over yonder church tower
"We are all coming back, you can pray for that hour!"
Whispered the sergeant to the old woman

MOTHER COURAGE, *taking up the song and beating time with her wooden spoon.*
"You are gone like the wind! But the cold stays behind!
"And all your great deeds will now warm us
"How fast the wind flies! God preserve him alive!"
Prayed the good woman for the soldier boy
And so the brave lad with his knife at his side
And his gun in his hand was swept out by the tide
And was lost in the waters enormous
Over the church tower, see the moon shining white
But the brave lad floats along with the ice
And is lost in the waters enormous

"You are gone like the wind! But the cold stays behind!
"And all your great deeds will not warm us!
"Woe to him who defies the advice of the wise!"
Said the old woman to the soldier boy

COMMANDER. What a kitchen I've got! There's no end to the liberties they take!

EILIF *has entered the kitchen and embraced his mother.* To see you again! Where are the others?

MOTHER COURAGE, *in his arms.* Happy as ducks in a pond. Swiss Cheese is paymaster with the Second Protestant Regiment, so at least he isn't in the fighting, I couldn't keep him out altogether.

EILIF. Are your feet holding up?

MOTHER COURAGE. I've a bit of trouble getting my shoes on in the morning.

COMMANDER, *who has come over.* So, you're his mother! I hope you have more sons for me like this fellow.

EILIF. If I'm not the lucky one: you sit there in the kitchen and hear your son being feasted!

MOTHER COURAGE. Yes. I heard all right.
Gives him a box on the ear.

EILIF. Because I took the oxen?

MOTHER COURAGE. No. Because you didn't surrender when the four peasants let fly at you and tried to make mincemeat of you! Didn't I teach you to take care of yourself? Finnish devil!

The COMMANDER *and the* CHAPLAIN *stand laughing in the doorway.*

3

THREE YEARS PASS AND MOTHER COURAGE, WITH PARTS OF A FINNISH REGIMENT, IS TAKEN PRISONER. HER DAUGHTER IS SAVED, HER WAGON LIKEWISE, BUT HER HONEST SON DIES.

A camp. The regimental flag is flying from a pole. After-noon. All sorts of wares hanging on the wagon. MOTHER COURAGE's *clothes line is tied to the wagon at one end, to a cannon at the other. She and* CATHERINE *are folding the wash on the cannon. At the same time she is bargaining with an* ORDNANCE OFFICER *over a bag of bullets.* SWISS CHEESE, *paymaster's uniform now, looks on.* YVETTE POTTIER, *a very good-looking young person, is sewing at a colored hat, a glass of brandy before her. She is in stocking feet. Her red boots are near by.*

OFFICER. I'm letting you have the bullets for two gilders. Dirt cheap. 'Cause I need the money. The Colonel's been drinking with the officers for three days and we're out of liquor.

MOTHER COURAGE. They're army property. If they find 'em on me, I'll be courtmartialled. You sell your bullets, you bastards, and send your men out to fight with nothing to shoot with.

OFFICER. Aw, come on, one good turn deserves another.

MOTHER COURAGE. I won't take army stuff. Not at *that* price.

OFFICER. You can resell 'em for five gilders, maybe eight, to the Ordnance Officer of the Fourth Regiment. All you have to do is give him a receipt for twelve. He hasn't a bullet left.

MOTHER COURAGE. Why don't you do it yourself?

OFFICER. I don't trust him. We're friends.

MOTHER COURAGE *takes the bag.* Give it here.
> *To* CATHERINE.
Take it round the back and pay him a gilder and a half.
> *As the* OFFICER *protests.*
I said a gilder and a half!
> CATHERINE *drags the bag away. The* OFFICER *follows.*
> MOTHER COURAGE *speaks to* SWISS CHEESE.
Here's your underwear back, take care of it; it's October
now, autumn may come at any time; I purposely don't say
it must come, I've learnt from experience there's nothing
that must come, not even the seasons. But your books *must*
balance now you're the regimental paymaster. *Do* they
balance?

SWISS CHEESE. Yes, Mother.

MOTHER COURAGE. Don't forget they made you paymaster because you're honest and so simple you'd never think of
running off with the cash. Don't lose that underwear.

SWISS CHEESE. No, Mother. I'll put it under the mattress.
> *He starts to go.*

OFFICER. I'll go with you, paymaster.

MOTHER COURAGE. Don't teach him how to finagle!
> *Without a good-bye the* OFFICER *leaves with* SWISS CHEESE.

YVETTE, *waving to him.* You might at least say good-by!

MOTHER COURAGE, *to* YVETTE. I don't like that. *He's* no sort of
company for my Swiss Cheese. But the war's not making a
bad start. Before all the different countries get into it, four
or five years'll have gone by like nothing. If I look ahead and
make no mistakes, business will be good. Don't you know
you shouldn't drink in the morning with your illness?

YVETTE. Who says I'm ill? That's libel!

MOTHER COURAGE. They all say so.

YVETTE. They're all liars. I'm desperate, Mother Courage. They all avoid me like a stinking fish. Because of those lies. So what am I fixing my hat for?

She throws it down.

That's why I drink in the morning; I never used to, it gives you crow's feet, but now it's all one, every man in the regiment knows me. I should have stayed home when my first was unfaithful. But pride isn't for the likes of us, you eat dirt or down you go.

MOTHER COURAGE. Now don't you start in again with your friend Peter and how it all happened—in front of my innocent daughter.

YVETTE. She's the one that should hear it. So she'll get hardened against love.

MOTHER COURAGE. That's something no one ever gets hardened against.

YVETTE. He was an army cook, blonde, a Dutchman, but thin. Catherine, beware of thin men! I wasn't. I didn't even know he'd had another girl before me and she called him Peter Piper because he never took his pipe out of his mouth the whole time, it meant so little to him.

She sings THE SONG OF FRATERNIZATION.

When I was hardly seventeen
The foe came to our land
And laying aside his sabre
He gave me gently his right hand
> *First came the May Day rite*
> *Then came the May Day night*
> *The regiment well organized*
> *Presented arms, then stood at ease*
> *Then took us off behind the trees*
> *And there we fraternized*

Our foes they came in plenty
A cook was my own foe
I hated him by daylight
At night I loved my soldier so
> *First came the May Day rite*
> *Then came the May Day night*
> *The regiment well organized*
> *Presented arms, then stood at ease*
> *Then took us off behind the trees*
> *And there we fraternized*

The feeling in my bosom
Was like a heavenly dove
Though the folk all around were saying
That I despised my own true love
> *First came the May Day rite*
> *Then came the May Day night*
> *The regiment well organized*
> *Presented arms, then stood at ease*
> *Then took us off behind the trees*
> *And there we fraternized*

I made the mistake of running after him, I never found him.
It's ten years ago now.
With swaying gait she goes behind the wagon.

MOTHER COURAGE. You're leaving your hat.

YVETTE. For the birds.

MOTHER COURAGE. Let this be a lesson to you, Catherine, never
start anything with a soldier. Love *is* like a heavenly dove,
so watch out! He tells you he'd like to kiss the ground under
your feet—did you wash 'em yesterday, while we're on the
subject? And then if you don't look out, your number's up,
you're his slave for life. Here comes the Commander's Cook,
what's biting *him?*
Enter the COOK *and the* CHAPLAIN.

CHAPLAIN. I bring a message from your son Eilif. The Cook
came with me. You've made, ahem, an impression on him.

COOK. I thought I'd get a little whiff of the balmy breeze.

MOTHER COURAGE. Get it then, and welcome. But what does
Eilif want? I've no money to spare.

CHAPLAIN. Actually, I have something to tell his brother, the
paymaster.

MOTHER COURAGE. He isn't here. And he isn't anywhere else
either. He's not his brother's paymaster, and he's not going
to lead him into temptation.
She takes money from the purse at her belt.
Give him this. It's a sin. He's speculating in mother love,
he ought to be ashamed of himself.

COOK. Not for long. He has to go with his regiment now—to his
death maybe. Send some more money, or you'll be sorry.

You women are hard—and sorry afterwards. A glass of brandy wouldn't cost very much, but you don't give it, and six feet under goes your man and you can't dig him up again.

CHAPLAIN. All very touching, my dear Cook, but to fall in this war is not a misfortune, it's a blessing. This is a holy war. Not just any old war but a religious one, and therefore pleasing unto God.

COOK. Sure. In one sense it's a war because there's fleecing, bribing, plundering, not to mention a little raping, but it's different from all other wars because it's a holy war. That's clear. All the same, it makes you thirsty.

CHAPLAIN, *to* MOTHER COURAGE, *pointing at the Cook*. I tried to hold him off but he said you'd bewitched him. He dreams about you.

COOK, *lighting a clay pipe*. Brandy from the fair hand of a lady, that's for me. And don't embarrass me any more: the stories the chaplain was telling on the way over still have me blushing.

MOTHER COURAGE. A man of his cloth! I must get you both something to drink or you'll be making improper advances out of sheer boredom.

CHAPLAIN. That is indeed a temptation, said the Court Chaplain, and gave way to it.
Turning toward CATHERINE *as he strolls around.*
And who is this captivating young person?

MOTHER COURAGE. She's not a captivating young person, she's a respectable young person.
The CHAPLAIN *and the* COOK *go with* MOTHER COURAGE *behind the cart.*

MOTHER COURAGE. The trouble here in Poland is that the Poles *would* keep meddling. It's true our Swedish King moved in on them with man, beast, and wagon, but instead of maintaining the peace the Poles were always meddling in their own affairs. They attacked the Swedish King when he was in the act of peacefully withdrawing. So they were guilty of a breach of the peace and their blood is on their own heads.

:HAPLAIN. Anyway, our Gustavus Adolphus was thinking of nothing but their freedom. The German Kaiser enslaved them all, Poles and Germans alike, so our King *had* to liberate them.

:OOK. Just what *I* think. Your health! Your brandy is first rate, I'm never mistaken in a face.

CATHERINE *looks after them, leaves the washing, and goes to the hat, picks it up, sits down, and takes up the red boots.*

And the war is a holy war.

Singing while CATHERINE *puts the boots on.*

"A mighty fortress is our God . . ." *He sings a verse or so of Luther's hymn.* And talking of King Gustavus, this freedom he tried to bring to Germany cost him a pretty penny. Back in Sweden he had to levy a salt tax, the poorer folks didn't like it a bit. Then, too, he had to lock up the Germans and even cut their heads off, they clung so to slavery and their Kaiser. Of course, if no one had *wanted* to be free, the King wouldn't have had any fun. First it was just Poland he tried to protect from bad men, specially the Kaiser, then his appetite grew with eating, and he ended protecting Germany too.

:HAPLAIN. He had one thing in his favor anyway: the Word of God. Or they could have said he did it all for himself and for profits. He has a clear conscience, that man.

:OOK, *with heavy irony.* Yes. He always put conscience first.

:HAPLAIN. It's plain you're no Swede, or you'd speak differently of the Hero King!

.MOTHER COURAGE. What's more, you eat his bread.

:OOK. I don't eat his bread. I bake his bread.

.MOTHER COURAGE. He can never be conquered, and I'll tell you why: his men believe in him.

Earnestly.

To hear the big fellows talk, they wage the war from fear of God and for all things bright and beautiful, but just look into it, and you'll see they're not so silly: they want a good profit out of it, or else the little fellows like you and me wouldn't back'em up.

:OOK. Surely.

CHAPLAIN, *indicating the Protestant flag*. And as a Dutchman
you'd do well to see which flag's flying here before you express an opinion!

MOTHER COURAGE. All good Protestants for ever!

COOK. A health!

> CATHERINE *has begun to strut around with* YVETTE's *hat on,
> copying* YVETTE's *sexy walk.*
> *Suddenly cannon and shots. Drums.* MOTHER COURAGE, *the*
> COOK, *and the* CHAPLAIN *rush round to the front of the cart,
> the two last with glasses in their hands. The Ordnance*
> OFFICER *and a* SOLDIER *come running to the cannon and
> try to push it along.*

MOTHER COURAGE. What's the matter? Let me get my wash off
that gun, you slobs!

> *She tries to do so.*

OFFICER. The Catholics! Surprise attack! We don't know if we
can get away!

> *To the* SOLDIER.

Get that gun!

> *Runs off.*

COOK. For heaven's sake! I must go to the Commander. Mother
Courage, I'll be back in a day or two—for a short conversation.

> *Rushes off.*

MOTHER COURAGE. Hey, you're leaving your pipe!

COOK, *off*. Keep it for me, I'll need it!

MOTHER COURAGE. This *would* happen when we were just
making money.

CHAPLAIN. Well, I must be going too. Yes, if the enemy's so
close, it can be dangerous. "Blessed are the peacemakers,"
a good slogan in wartime! If only I had a cloak.

MOTHER COURAGE. I'm lending no cloaks. Not even to save a
life I'm not. I've had experience in that line.

CHAPLAIN. But I'm in special danger. Because of my religion!

MOTHER COURAGE *brings him a cloak*. It's against my better
judgment. Now run!

CHAPLAIN. I thank you, you're very generous, but maybe I'd better stay and sit here. If I run, I might attract the enemy's attention. I might arouse suspicion.

MOTHER COURAGE *to the* SOLDIER. Let it alone, you dope, who's going to pay you for this? It'll cost *you* your life, let me hold it for you.

SOLDIER, *running away.* You're my witness: I tried!

MOTHER COURAGE. I'll swear to it!

Seeing CATHERINE *with the hat.*

What on earth are you up to—with a whore's hat! Take it off this minute! Are you crazy? With the enemy coming?

She tears the hat off her head.

Do you want them to find you and make a whore of you? And she has the boots on too, straight from Babylon, I'll soon fix that.

She tries to get them off.

Oh God, Chaplain, help me with these boots, I'll be right back!

She runs to the wagon.

YVETTE, *entering and powdering her face.* What's that you say; the Catholics are coming? Where's my hat? Who's been trampling on it!? I can't run around in that, what will they think of me? And I've no mirror either.

To the CHAPLAIN, *coming very close.*

How do I look—too much powder?

CHAPLAIN. Just, er, right.

YVETTE. And where are my red boots?

She can't find them because CATHERINE *is hiding her feet under her skirt.*

I left them here! Now I've got to go barefoot to my tent, it's a scandal!

Exit.

SWISS CHEESE *comes running in carrying a cash box.*

MOTHER COURAGE *enters with her hands covered with ashes.*

To CATHERINE. Ashes!

To SWISS CHEESE.

What you got there?

SWISS CHEESE. The regimental cash box.

MOTHER COURAGE. Throw it away! Your paymastering days are over!

SWISS CHEESE. It's a trust!
He goes to the back.

MOTHER COURAGE, *to the* CHAPLAIN. Off with your pastor's coat, Chaplain, or they'll recognize you, cloak or no cloak.
She is rubbing ashes into CATHERINE's *face.*
Keep still. A little dirt, and you're safe. When a soldier sees a clean face, there's one more whore in the world. Specially a Catholic soldier. That should do, it looks like you've been rolling in muck. Don't tremble. Nothing can happen to you now.
To SWISS CHEESE.
Where have you left that cash?

SWISS CHEESE. I thought I'd just put it in the wagon.

MOTHER COURAGE, *horrified.* What!? In my wagon? God punish you for a prize idiot! If I just look away for a moment! They'll hang all three of us!

SWISS CHEESE. Then I'll put it somewhere else. Or escape with it.

MOTHER COURAGE. You'll stay right here. It's too late.

CHAPLAIN, *still changing his clothes.* For Heaven's sake: the Protestant flag!

MOTHER COURAGE, *taking down the flag.* I don't notice it any more, I've had it twenty-five years.
The sound of cannon grows.
Here the curtain is lowered.
Three days later. Morning. The cannon is gone. MOTHER COURAGE, CATHERINE, *the* CHAPLAIN *and* SWISS CHEESE *sit anxiously eating.*

SWISS CHEESE. This is the third day I've been sitting here doing nothing, and the Sergeant, who's always been patient with me, may be slowly beginning to ask, "Where on earth is Swiss Cheese with that cash box?"

MOTHER COURAGE. Be glad they're not on the scent.

CHAPLAIN. What about me? I can't hold service here or I'll
be in hot water. It is written, "Out of the abundance of the
heart, the tongue speaketh." But woe is me if *my* tongue
speaketh!

MOTHER COURAGE. That's how it is. Here you sit—one with his
religion, the other with his cash box, I don't know which is
more dangerous.

CHAPLAIN. We're in God's hands now!

MOTHER COURAGE. I hope we're not as desperate as *that*, but it
is hard to sleep at night. 'Course it'd be easier if *you* weren't
here, Swiss Cheese, all the same I've not done badly. When
they questioned me, I always asked where I could buy holy
candles a bit cheaper. I know these things because Swiss
Cheese's father was a Catholic and made jokes about it.
They didn't quite believe me but they needed a canteen,
so they winked an eye. Maybe it's all for the best. We're pris-
oners. But so are lice in fur.

CHAPLAIN. The milk is good. As far as quantity goes, we may
have to reduce our Swedish appetites somewhat. We are
defeated.

MOTHER COURAGE. Who's defeated? The defeats and victories
of the fellows at the top aren't always defeats and victories
for the fellows at the bottom. Not at all. There've been cases
where a defeat is a victory for the fellows at the bottom, it's
only their honor that's lost, nothing serious. In Livonia once,
our Chief took such a knock from the enemy, in the con-
fusion I got a fine gray mare out of the baggage train, it
pulled my wagon seven months—till we won and there was
inventory. But in general both defeat and victory are a
costly business for us that haven't got much. The best thing
is for politics to kind of get stuck in the mud.
To SWISS CHEESE.
Eat!

SWISS CHEESE. I don't like it. How will the Sergeant pay his
men?

MOTHER COURAGE. Soldiers in flight don't get paid.

SWISS CHEESE. Well, they could claim to be. No pay, no flight. They can refuse to budge.

MOTHER COURAGE. Swiss Cheese, your sense of duty worries me. I've brought you up to be honest because you're not very bright. But don't go too far! And now I'm going with the Chaplain to buy a Catholic flag and some meat. A good thing they let me continue in business. In business you ask what price, not what religion. Protestant pants keep you just as warm.

She disappears into the wagon.

CHAPLAIN. She's worried about the cash box. Up to now they've ignored us—as if we were part of the wagon—but can it last?

SWISS CHEESE I can get rid of it.

CHAPLAIN. That's almost *more* dangerous. Suppose you're seen. They have spies. Yesterday morning one jumped out of the very hole I was relieving myself in. I was so off guard I almost broke out in prayer—*that* would have given me away all right! I believe their favorite way of finding a Protestant is smelling his, um, excrement. The spy was a little brute with a bandage over one eye.

MOTHER COURAGE, *clambering out of the wagon with a basket.* I've found you out, you shameless hussy!

She holds up YVETTE's *red boots in triumph.*

Yvette's red boots! She just snitched them—because you went and told her she was a captivating person.

She lays them in the basket.

Stealing Yvette's boots! But *she* disgraces herself for money, *you* do it for nothing—for pleasure! Save your proud peacock ways for peacetime!

CHAPLAIN. I don't find her proud.

MOTHER COURAGE. I like her when people say "I never noticed the poor thing." I like her when she's a stone in Dalarna where there's nothing but stones.

To SWISS CHEESE.

Leave the cash box where it is, do you hear? And pay attention to your sister, she needs it. Between the two of you, you'll be the death of me yet; I'd rather take care of a bag of fleas.

She leaves with the CHAPLAIN.

CATHERINE *clears the dishes away.*

SWISS CHEESE. Not many days more when you can sit in the sun in your shirtsleeves.

CATHERINE *points to a tree.*

Yes, the leaves are yellow already.

With gestures, CATHERINE *asks if he wants a drink.*

I'm not drinking, I'm thinking.

Pause.

She says she can't sleep. So I *should* take the cash box away. I've found a place for it. I'll keep it in the mole hole by the river till the time comes. I might get it tonight before sunrise and take it to the regiment. How far can they have fled in three days? The Sergeant's eyes'll pop out of his head. "You've disappointed me most pleasantly, Swiss Cheese," he'll say, "*I* trust you with the cash box and *you* bring it back!" Yes, Catherine, I *will* have a glass now!

When CATHERINE *reappears behind the wagon two men confront her. One of them is a sergeant. The other doffs his hat and flourishes it in a showy greeting. He has a bandage over one eye.*

THE MAN WITH THE BANDAGE. Good morning, young lady. Have you seen a staff officer from the Second Protestant Regiment?

Terrified, CATHERINE *runs away, spilling her brandy. The two men look at each other and then withdraw after seeing* SWISS CHEESE.

SWISS CHEESE, *starting up from his reflections.* You're spilling it! What's the matter with you, can't you see where you're going? I don't understand you. Anyway, I must be off, I've decided it's the thing to do.

He stands up. She does all she can to make him aware of the danger he is in. He only pushes her away.

I'd like to know what you mean. I know you mean well, poor thing, you just can't get it out. And don't trouble yourself about the brandy; I'll live to drink so much of it, what's one glass?

He takes the cash box out of the wagon and puts it under his coat.

I'll be right back. But don't hold me up or I'll have to scold you. Yes, I know you mean well. If you only could speak! *When she tries to hold him back he kisses her and pulls himself free. Exit. She is desperate and runs up and down, emitting little sounds.* MOTHER COURAGE *and the* CHAPLAIN *return.* CATHERINE *rushes at her mother.*

MOTHER COURAGE. What *is* it, what *is* it, Catherine? Control yourself! Has someone done something to you? Where is Swiss Cheese?

To the CHAPLAIN.

Don't stand around, get that Catholic flag up!

She takes a Catholic flag out of her basket and the CHAPLAIN *runs it up the pole.*

CHAPLAIN, *bitterly.* All good Catholics forever!

MOTHER COURAGE. Now, Catherine, calm down and tell all about it, your mother understands. What, that little bastard of mine's taken the cash box away? I'll box his ears for him, the rascal! Now take your time and don't try to talk, use your hands. I don't like it when you howl like a dog, what'll the Chaplain think of you? See how shocked he looks. A man with one eye was here?

CHAPLAIN. That fellow with one eye is an informer! Have they caught Swiss Cheese?

CATHERINE *shakes her head, shrugs her shoulders.*

This is the end.

Voices off. The two men bring in SWISS CHEESE.

SWISS CHEESE. Let me go. I've nothing on me. You're breaking my shoulder! I am innocent.

SERGEANT. This is where he comes from. These are his friends.

MOTHER COURAGE. Us? Since when?

Putting things in her basket.

SWISS CHEESE. I don't even know 'em. I was just getting my lunch here. Ten hellers it cost me. Maybe you saw me sitting on that bench. It was too salty.

SERGEANT. Who *are* you people, anyway?

MOTHER COURAGE. Law abiding citizens! It's true what he says. He bought his lunch here. And it was too salty.

SERGEANT. Are you pretending you don't know him?

MOTHER COURAGE. I can't know all of them, can I? *I* don't ask, "What's your name and are you a heathen?" If they pay up, they're not heathens to me. Are you a heathen?

SWISS CHEESE. Oh, no!

CHAPLAIN. He sat there like a law-abiding chap and never once opened his mouth. Except to eat. Which is necessary.

SERGEANT. Who do you think *you* are?

MOTHER COURAGE. Oh, he's my barman. And you're thirsty, I'll bring you a glass of brandy; you must be footsore and weary!

SERGEANT. No brandy on duty.

To SWISS CHEESE.

You were carrying something. You must have hidden it by the river. We saw the bulge in your shirt.

MOTHER COURAGE. Sure it was him?

SWISS CHEESE. I think you mean another fellow. There *was* a fellow with something under his shirt, I saw him. I'm the wrong man.

MOTHER COURAGE. I think so too. It's a misunderstanding. Could happen to anyone. Oh, I know what people are like, I'm Mother Courage, you've heard of me, everyone knows about me, and I can tell you this: he looks honest.

SERGEANT. We're after the regimental cash box. And we know what the man looks like who's been keeping it. We've been looking for him two days. It's you.

SWISS CHEESE. No, it's not!

SERGEANT. And if you don't shell out, you're dead, see? Where is it?

MOTHER COURAGE, *urgently*. 'Course he'd give it to you to save his life. He'd up and say, I do have it, here it is, you're stronger than me. He's not *that* stupid. Speak, little stupid, the Sergeant's giving you a chance!

SWISS CHEESE. What if I don't have it?

SERGEANT. Come with us. We'll get it out of you.
They take him off.

MOTHER COURAGE, *shouting after them*. He'd tell you! He's not *that* stupid! And leave his shoulder alone!!
She runs after them.
The curtain falls again.
The same evening. The CHAPLAIN *and* CATHERINE *are waiting.*

MOTHER COURAGE *entering, excited*. It's life and death. But the Sergeant will still listen to us. The only thing is, he mustn't know it's our Swiss Cheese, or they'll say we helped him. It's only a matter of money, but where can *we* get money? Wasn't Yvette here? I met her on the way over. She's picked up a Colonel! Maybe he'll buy her a canteen business!

CHAPLAIN. You'd sell the wagon, everything?

MOTHER COURAGE. Where else would I get the money for the Sergeant?

CHAPLAIN. What are you to live off?

MOTHER COURAGE. That's just it.
Enter YVETTE POTTIER *with a hoary old* COLONEL.

YVETTE, *embracing* MOTHER COURAGE. *Dear* Mistress Courage, we meet again!
Whispering.
He didn't say no.
Aloud.
This is my friend, my, um, business adviser. I happened to hear you might like to sell your wagon. Due to special circumstances. I'd like to think about it.

MOTHER COURAGE. I want to pawn it, not sell it. And nothing hasty. In war time you don't find another wagon like that so easy.

YVETTE, *disappointed*. Only pawn it? I thought you wanted to sell, I don't know if I'm interested.
To the COLONEL.
What do *you* think, my dear?

COLONEL. I quite agree with you, honey bun.

1OTHER COURAGE. It's only for pawn.

VETTE. I thought you *had* to have the money.

1OTHER COURAGE, *firmly*. I do have to have it. But I'd rather wear my feet off looking for an offer than just sell. We live off the wagon.

OLONEL. Take it, take it!

VETTE. My friend thinks I should go ahead, but I'm not sure— if it's only for pawn. You think we should buy it outright, don't you?

OLONEL. I do, bunny, I do!

1OTHER COURAGE. Then you must find something that's for sale.

VETTE. Yes, we can go around looking for something, I *love* going around looking, I *love* going around with you, Poldy . . .

OLONEL. Really? You do?

VETTE. Oh, it's *lovely!* I could take *weeks* of it!

OLONEL. Really? You could?

VETTE. If you get the money, when are you thinking of paying it back?

1OTHER COURAGE. In two weeks. Maybe in one.

VETTE. I can't make up my mind. Poldy, advise me, *chéri!*
She takes the COLONEL *to one side.*
She'll *have* to sell, don't worry. That lieutenant—the blond one—you know the one I mean—he'll lend me the money. He's *mad* about me, he says I remind him of someone. What do you advise?

OLONEL. Oh, I have to warn you against *him*. He's no good. He'll exploit the situation. I told you, bunny, I told you *I'd* buy you something, didn't I tell you that?

VETTE. I simply can't let you!

OLONEL. Oh, please, please!

VETTE. Well, if you think the lieutenant might exploit the situation I *will* let you!

COLONEL. I do think so.

YVETTE. So you advise me to?

COLONEL. I do, bunny, I do!

YVETTE, *returning to* MOTHER COURAGE. My friend says a
right. Write me out a receipt saying the wagon's mine whe
the two weeks are up—with everything in it. I'll just ru
through it all now, the two hundred gilders can wait.
To the COLONEL.
You go on ahead to the camp, I'll follow, I must go over a
this so nothing'll be missing later from *my* wagon!

COLONEL. Wait, I'll help you up!
He does so.
Come soon, honey-bunny!
Exit

MOTHER COURAGE. Yvette, Yvette!

YVETTE. There aren't many boots left!

MOTHER COURAGE. Yvette, this is no time to go through th
wagon, yours or not yours. You promised you'd talk to th
Sergeant about Swiss Cheese. There isn't a minute to los
He's up before the court martial one hour from now.

YVETTE. I just want to check through these shirts.

MOTHER COURAGE *dragging her down the steps by the skirt.* Yo
hyena, Swiss Cheese's life's at stake! And don't say who th
money comes from. Pretend he's your sweetheart, fo
heaven's sake, or we'll all get it for helping him.

YVETTE. I've arranged to meet One Eye in the bushes. He mus
be there by now.

CHAPLAIN. And don't hand over all two hundred, a hundre
and fifty's sure to be enough.

MOTHER COURAGE. I'll thank you to keep your nose out of this
I'm not doing *you* out of your porridge. Now run, and n
haggling, remember his life's at stake.
She pushes YVETTE *off.*

CHAPLAIN. I didn't want to talk you into anything, but what ar we going to live on? You have an unmarriageable daughter round your neck.

MOTHER COURAGE. I'm counting on that cash box, smart alec. They'll pay his expenses out of it.

CHAPLAIN. You think she can work it?

MOTHER COURAGE. It's to her interest: I pay out the two hundred and she gets the wagon. She knows what she's doing, she won't have her colonel on the string forever. Catherine, go and clean the knives, use pumice stone.

To the CHAPLAIN.

And don't *you* stand around like Jesus in Gethsemane. Get a move on, wash those glasses. There'll be over fifty cavalrymen here tonight, can't you just hear them grumbling, "Isn't walking terrible, oh my poor feet!" I think they'll let us have him. Thanks be to God they're corruptible. They're not wolves, they're human and after money. God is merciful, and men are bribable, that's how His will is done on earth as it is in Heaven. Corruption is our only hope. As long as there's corruption, there'll be merciful judges and even the innocent may get off!

YVETTE *comes panting in.* They'll do it for two hundred if you make it snappy, these things change from one minute to the next. I'd better take One Eye to my colonel right now. He confessed he had the cash box, they put the thumb screws on him. But he threw it in the river when he noticed them coming up behind him. So it's gone. Shall I run and get the money from my colonel?

MOTHER COURAGE. The cash box gone? How'll I ever get my two hundred back?

YVETTE. So you thought you could get it from the cash box? I *would* have been sunk. Not a hope, Mother Courage. If you want your Swiss Cheese, you'll have to pay. Or should I let the whole thing drop, so you can keep your wagon?

MOTHER COURAGE. What can I do? I *can't* pay two hundred. You *should* have haggled with them. I must hold on to something, or any passer-by can kick me in the ditch. Go and say I'll pay a hundred and twenty or the deal's off. Even at that I lose the wagon.

YVETTE. They won't do it. And anyway, One Eye's in a hurry. He looks over his shoulder the whole time, he's so worked up. Hadn't I better give them the whole two hundred?

MOTHER COURAGE, *desperate*. I can't pay it! I've been working thirty years. She's twenty-five and still no husband, I have her to think of. So leave me alone, I know what I'm doing. A hundred and twenty or no deal.

YVETTE. You know best.

Runs off.

MOTHER COURAGE *turns away and slowly walks a few paces to the rear. Then she turns round, looks neither at the* CHAPLAIN *nor her daughter, and sits down to help* CATHERINE *polish the knives.*

MOTHER COURAGE. You'll have your brother back. I *will* pay two hundred—if I have to. With eighty gilders we could pack a hamper with goods and begin over. It wouldn't be the end of the world.

CHAPLAIN. The Bible says, the Lord will provide.

MOTHER COURAGE, *to* CATHERINE. You must rub them dry.

YVETTE *comes running on.* They won't do it. I warned you. He said the drums would roll any second now and that's the sign a verdict has been pronounced. I offered a hundred and fifty, he didn't even shrug his shoulders. I could hardly get him to stay there while I came to you.

MOTHER COURAGE. Tell him, I'll pay two hundred. Run!

YVETTE *runs.* MOTHER COURAGE *sits, silent. The* CHAPLAIN *has stopped doing the glasses.*

I believe—I haggled too long.

In the distance, a roll of drums. The CHAPLAIN *stands up and walks toward the rear.* MOTHER COURAGE *remains seated. It grows dark. It gets light again.* MOTHER COURAGE *has not moved.*

YVETTE, *appears, pale.* Now you've done it—with your haggling. You can keep the wagon now. He got eleven bullets, that's all. I don't know why I still bother about you, you don't deserve it, but I just happened to learn they don't think the cash box is really in the river. They suspect it's here, they think you're connected with him. I think they mean to bring him here to see if you give yourself away when you see him. I warn you not to know him or we're in for it. And I better tell you straight, they're right behind me. Shall I keep Catherine away?

MOTHER COURAGE *shakes her head.*

Does she know? Maybe she never heard the drums or didn't understand.

MOTHER COURAGE. She knows. Bring her.

YVETTE *brings* CATHERINE, *who walks over to her mother and stands by her.* MOTHER COURAGE *takes her hand. Two men come on with a stretcher; there is a sheet on it and something underneath. Beside them, the* SERGEANT. *They put the stretcher down.*

SERGEANT. Here's a man we don't know the name of. But he has to be registered to keep the records straight. He bought a meal from you. Look at him, see if you know him.

He pulls back the sheet.

Do you know him?

MOTHER COURAGE *shakes her head.*

What? You never saw him before he took that meal?

MOTHER COURAGE *shakes her head.*

Lift him up. Throw him on the junk heap. He has no one that knows him.

They carry him off.

4

MOTHER COURAGE *sings the song of the Great Capitulation.*

Outside an officer's tent. MOTHER COURAGE *waits. A* CLERK *looks out of the tent.*

CLERK. You want to speak to the captain? I know you. You had a Protestant paymaster with you, he was hiding out. Better make no complaint here.

MOTHER COURAGE. I will too! I'm innocent and if I give up it'll look like I have a bad conscience. They cut everything in my wagon to ribbons with their sabres and then claimed a fine of five thalers for nothing and less than nothing.

CLERK. For your own good, keep your trap shut. We haven't many canteens, so we let you stay in business, especially if you've a bad conscience and have to pay a fine now and then.

MOTHER COURAGE. I'm going to lodge a complaint.

CLERK. As you wish. Wait here till the captain has time. *Withdraws into the tent.*

YOUNG SOLDIER *comes storming in.* Screw the captain! Where *is* the son-of-a-bitch? Snitching my reward, spending it on brandy for his whores, I'll rip his belly open!

OLDER SOLDIER, *coming after him.* Shut your hole, you'll wind up in the stocks.

YOUNG SOLDIER. Come out, you thief, I'll make lamb chops out of you! I was the only one in the squad who swam the river and *he* grabs my money, I can't even buy a beer. Come on out! And let me slice you up!

OLD SOLDIER. Holy Christ, he'll destroy himself!

YOUNG SOLDIER. Let me go or I'll run *you* down too. This thing has got to be settled!

OLDER SOLDIER. Saved the colonel's horse and didn't get the reward. He's young, he hasn't been at it long.

MOTHER COURAGE. Let him go. He doesn't have to be chained, he's not a dog. Very reasonable to want a reward. Why else should he want to shine?

YOUNG SOLDIER. He's in there pouring it down! You're all chickens. I done something special, I want the reward!

MOTHER COURAGE. Young man, don't scream at *me*, I have my own troubles.

YOUNG SOLDIER. He's whoring on my money and I'm hungry! I'll murder him!

MOTHER COURAGE. I understand: you're hungry. You're angry; I understand that too.

YOUNG SOLDIER. It's no use you talking, I won't stand for injustice!

MOTHER COURAGE. You're quite right. But how long for? How long won't you stand injustice for? One hour? Or two? You haven't asked yourself that, have you? And yet it's the main thing. It's a misery to sit in the stocks. Especially if you leave it till then to decide you do stand for injustice.

YOUNG SOLDIER. I don't know why I listen to you. Screw that captain! Where is he?

MOTHER COURAGE. You listen because you know I'm right. Your rage has calmed down already. It was a short one and you'd need a long one. But where would you find it?

YOUNG SOLDIER. Are you trying to say it's not right to ask for the money?

MOTHER COURAGE. Just the opposite. I only say, your rage won't last. You'll get nowhere with it, it's a pity. If your rage was a long one, I'd urge you on. Slice him up, I'd advice you. But what's the use if you *don't* slice him up because you feel your tail between your legs? You stand there and the captain lets you have it.

OLDER SOLDIER. You're quite right, he's nuts.

YOUNG SOLDIER. All right, we'll see whether I slice him up or not. *Draws his sword.*
When he comes out, I slice him up!

CLERK, *looking out.* The captain will be right out.
In the tone of military command:
Be seated!
The YOUNG SOLDIER *sits.*

MOTHER COURAGE. What did I tell you? They know us inside out, they know their business. Be seated! And we sit. Oh, you needn't be embarrassed in front of me, I'm no better. We don't stick our necks out, do we? We're too well paid to keep 'em in. Let me tell you about the Great Capitulation.

She sings THE SONG OF THE GREAT CAPITULATION.

I believed once I was something special   to individual
In the spring of life when I was young and free

(Not like your ordinary, run-of-the-mill girl with my looks
and my talent and my love of higher things!)*
And I bade them take the cook's hair out of my porridge:
None was more particular than me
(All or nothing, or anyway not the second best, I am the
master of my fate, I'll take no orders from no one!)
A starling, sitting near
Pipes, "Wait a year!"
And marching with the band you go
Just keeping step, now fast, now slow,
    And puffing out the melody
How good it feels!
But look: The column wheels!
    Is it by God's decree?
    Don't give that to me!

And before the year was up and over
I had learnt to take my medicine—by the glass
(Two children round your neck and the price of bread and
what all!)
And when they were through with me, when they were
ready
They had me on my knees and on my ass
(You must get in with people, one good turn deserves
another, don't stick your neck out!)
The starling, sitting near,
Piped: "Less than a year!"
And marching with the band she'd go
Just keeping step, now fast, now slow,
    And puffing out the melody
How good it feels
But look: The column wheels!
    Is it by God's decree?
    Don't give that to me!

Many saw I, sure, the heavens storming,
And no star was bright enough or seemed too high
(Where there's a will there's a way, you can't hold a good
man down!)
Soon they felt—'mid all the shaking of the mountains—
How much strength it takes to lift a straw hat or a fly
(After all you must cut your coat according to the cloth.)
The starling, sitting near,

* Lines in parentheses are spoken.

Pipes, "Wait a year!"
And marching with the band they go
Just keeping step, now fast, now slow,
     And puffing out the melody
How good it feels!
But look: The column wheels!
     Is it by God's decree?
     Don't give that to me!

MOTHER COURAGE. And so I think you should stay here with
your sword drawn if you're set on it and your anger is big
enough. You have good cause, I admit. But if your anger is
a short one, you'd better go.

YOUNG SOLDIER. Aw, shove it!
     He stumbles off, the other soldier following him.

CLERK *sticks his head out.* The captain is here. You can lodge
your complaint.

MOTHER COURAGE. I've thought better of it. I'm not complain-
ing.
     Exit. The CLERK *looks after her, shaking his head.*

5

TWO YEARS HAVE PASSED. THE WAR COVERS
WIDER AND WIDER TERRITORY. FOREVER
ON THE MOVE THE LITTLE WAGON CROSSES
POLAND, MORAVIA, BAVARIA, ITALY, AND
AGAIN BAVARIA. 1631. TILLY'S VICTORY
AT LEIPZIG COSTS MOTHER COURAGE FOUR
SHIRTS.

*The wagon stands in a war-ruined village. Faint military
music from the distance. Two soldiers are being served at a
counter by* CATHERINE *and* MOTHER COURAGE. *One of them
has a woman's fur coat about his shoulders.*

MOTHER COURAGE. What, you can't pay? No money, no
schnapps! They can play a victory march, they should pay
their men.

FIRST SOLDIER. I want my schnapps! I arrived too late for plunder. The Chief allowed one hour to plunder the town, it's a
swindle. He's not inhuman, he says. So I guess they bought
him off.

CHAPLAIN, *staggering in.* There are more in the farmhouse. A
whole family of peasants. Help me someone, I need linen!
The SECOND SOLDIER *goes with him.* CATHERINE *is getting
very excited. She tries to get her mother to bring linen out.*

MOTHER COURAGE. I have none. I sold all my bandages to the
regiment. I'm not tearing up my officer's shirts for these people.

CHAPLAIN, *calling over his shoulder.* I said I need linen!

MOTHER COURAGE, *stopping* CATHERINE *from entering the
wagon.* Not a thing! They have nothing and they pay nothing!

CHAPLAIN, *to a woman he is carrying in.* Why did you stay
out there in the line of fire?

WOMAN. Our farm——

MOTHER COURAGE. Think they'd ever let go of *anything?* And
now I'm supposed to pay, Well, I won't!

FIRST SOLDIER. They're Protestants, why should they be Protestants?

MOTHER COURAGE. Protestant, Catholic, what do *they* care?
Their farm's gone, that's what.

SECOND SOLDIER. They're not Protestants anyway, they're
Catholics.

FIRST SOLDIER. In a bombardment we can't pick and choose.

PEASANT *brought on by* CHAPLAIN.
My arm's gone.

CHAPLAIN. Where's that linen?

MOTHER COURAGE. I can't give you any. With all I have to pay
out—taxes, duties, bribes . . .
CATHERINE *takes up a board and threatens her mother with
it, emitting gurgling sounds.*

Are you out of your mind? Put that board down or I'll fetch you one, you lunatic! I'm giving nothing, I don't dare, I have myself to think of.

The CHAPLAIN *lifts her bodily off the steps of the wagon and sets her down on the ground. He takes out shirts from the wagon and tears them in strips.*

My shirts, my officer's shirts!

From the house comes the cry of a child in pain.

PEASANT. The child's still in there!

CATHERINE *runs in.*

MOTHER COURAGE. Hold her back, the roof may fall in!

CHAPLAIN. I'm not going back in there!

MOTHER COURAGE. My officer's shirts, half a gilder apiece! I'm ruined.

CATHERINE *brings a baby out of the ruins.*

MOTHER COURAGE. Another baby to drag around, you must be pleased with yourself. Give it to its mother this minute!

CATHERINE *is rocking the child and half humming a lullaby.*

CHAPLAIN, *bandaging.* The blood's coming through.

MOTHER COURAGE. There she sits, happy as a lark in all this!

Shouting toward the music.

Stop that music, I can see your victory all right!

Seeing FIRST SOLDIER *trying to make off with the bottle he's been drinking from.*

Stop, you pig, if you want *another* victory you must pay for it!

FIRST SOLDIER. I'm broke.

MOTHER COURAGE, *tearing the fur coat off him.* Then leave this, it's stolen goods anyhow.

CATHERINE *rocks the child and raises it high above her head.*

6

BEFORE THE CITY OF INGOLSTADT IN BA-
VARIA MOTHER COURAGE ATTENDS THE
FUNERAL OF THE FALLEN COMMANDER,
TILLY. CONVERSATIONS TAKE PLACE ABOUT
WAR HEROES AND THE DURATION OF THE
WAR. THE CHAPLAIN COMPLAINS THAT
HIS TALENTS ARE LYING FALLOW AND CATH-
ERINE GETS THE RED BOOTS. THE YEAR IS
1632.

*The inside of a canteen tent. The inner side of a counter at
the rear. Rain. In the distance, drums and funeral music.
The* CHAPLAIN *and the* REGIMENTAL CLERK *are playing
checkers.* MOTHER COURAGE *and her* DAUGHTER *are taking
inventory.*

CHAPLAIN. The funeral procession is just starting out.

MOTHER COURAGE. Pity about the Chief—twenty two pairs,
socks—getting killed that way. They say it was an accident.
There was a fog over the fields that morning, and the fog was
to blame. The Chief called up another regiment, told 'em to
fight to the death, rode back again, missed his way in the
fog, went forward instead of back, and ran straight into a
bullet in the thick of the battle!
*A whistle from the rear. She goes to the counter. To a
soldier.*
It's a disgrace the way you're all skipping your Commander's funeral!
She pours a drink.

CLERK. They shouldn't have handed the money out before the
funeral. Now the men are all getting drunk instead of going
to it.

CHAPLAIN, *to the* CLERK. Don't you have to be there?

CLERK. I stayed away because of the rain.

MOTHER COURAGE. It's different for you, the rain might spoil your uniform.

VOICE FROM THE COUNTER. Service! One brandy!

MOTHER COURAGE. Your money first. No, you *can't* come inside the tent, not with those boots; you can drink outside, rain or no rain. I only let officers in here.
To the CLERK.
The Chief had his troubles lately, I hear. There was unrest in the second regiment because he didn't pay 'em but said it was a holy war and they must fight it for free.

CHAPLAIN, *as music continues.* Now they're filing past the body.

MOTHER COURAGE. I feel sorry for a commander or an emperor like that—when maybe he had something special in mind, something they'd talk about in times to come, something they'd raise a statue to him for. The conquest of the world now, *that's* a goal for a commander, he couldn't do better than *that,* could he? . . . Lord, worms have gone into the biscuit. . . . In short he works his hands to the bone and then it's all spoiled by the common riffraff that only wants a jug of beer or a bit of company, not the higher things in life. The finest plans have always been spoiled by the littleness of them that should carry them out. Even emperors can't do it all by themselves. They count on support from their soldiers and the people round about. Am I right?

CHAPLAIN, *laughing.* You're right, Mother Courage, till you come to the soldiers. They do what they can. Those fellows outside, for example, drinking their brandy in the rain, I'd trust 'em to fight a hundred years, one war after another, two at once if necessary. And I wasn't trained as a Commander.

MOTHER COURAGE. . . . Seventeen leather belts. . . . Then you don't think the war might end?

CHAPLAIN. Because a Commander's dead? Don't be childish, they're a dime a dozen. There are always heroes.

MOTHER COURAGE. Well, I wasn't asking just for the sake of argument. I was wondering if I should buy up a lot of supplies. They happen to be cheap right now. But if the war ended, I might just as well throw them away.

CHAPLAIN. I realize you are serious, Mother Courage. Well, there have always been people going around saying someday the war will end. I say, you can't be sure the war will *ever* end. Of course it may have to pause occasionally—for breath, as it were—it can even meet with an accident—nothing on this earth is perfect—a war of which we could say it left nothing to be desired will probably never exist. A war can come to a sudden halt—from unforeseen causes—you can't think of everything—a little oversight, and the war's in the hole, and someone's got to pull it out again! The someone is the Emperor or the King or the Pope. They're such friends in need, the war has really nothing to worry about, it can look forward to a prosperous future.

A SOLDIER *sings at the counter.*

A schnapps, host, quick, make haste!
A soldier's no time to waste,
Must be for his Kaiser fighting!

Make it a double, this is a holiday.

MOTHER COURAGE. If I was sure you're right . . .

CHAPLAIN. Think it out for yourself, how *could* the war end?

SOLDIER.
Your breast, girl, quick, make haste!
A soldier's no time to waste,
Must be to Moravia riding!

CLERK, *of a sudden.* What about peace? Yes, peace. I'm from Bohemia, I'd like to get home once in a while.

CHAPLAIN. You would, would you? Dear old peace! What happens to the hole when the cheese is gone?

CLERK. In the long run you can't live without peace!

CHAPLAIN. Well, I'd say there's peace even in war, war has its. . . islands of peace. For war satisfies *all* needs, even those of peace, yes, they're provided for, or the war couldn't keep going. In war—as in the very thick of peace—you can take a crap, and between one battle and the next there's always a beer, and even on the march you can catch a nap—on your elbow maybe, in a gutter—something can always be managed. Of course you can't play cards during an attack, but neither can you while plowing the fields in peace-time; it's when the victory's won that there are possibilities. And can't you be fruitful and multiply in the very midst of slaughter—behind a barn or some place? Nothing can keep you from it very long in any event. And so the war has your offspring and can carry on. War is like love, it always finds a way. Why *should* it end?

CATHERINE *has stopped working. She stares at the* CHAPLAIN.

MOTHER COURAGE. Then I *will* buy those supplies, I'll rely on you.

CATHERINE *suddenly bangs a basket of glasses down on the ground and runs out.* MOTHER COURAGE *laughs.*

Lord, Catherine's still going to wait for peace. I promised her she'll get a husband—when it's peace.

Runs after her.

CLERK, *standing up.* I win. You were talking. You pay.

MOTHER COURAGE, *returning with* CATHERINE. Be sensible, the war'll go on a bit longer, and we'll make a bit more money, then peace'll be all the nicer. Now you go into the town, it's not ten minutes walk, and bring the things from the Golden Lion, just the more expensive ones, we can get the rest later in the wagon. It's all arranged, the clerk will go with you, most of the soldiers are at the funeral, nothing can happen to you. Do a good job, don't lose anything, Catherine, think of your trousseau!

CATHERINE *ties a cloth round her head and leaves with the* CLERK.

CHAPLAIN. You don't mind her going with the clerk?

MOTHER COURAGE. She's not so pretty anyone would want to ruin her.

CHAPLAIN. The way you run your business and always come through is nothing short of commendable, Mother Courage— I see how you got your name.

MOTHER COURAGE. Poorer people need courage. They're lost, that's why. That they even get up in the morning is something—in *their* plight. Or that they plow a field—in war time. Or that they have an Emperor and a Pope, what courage *that* takes, when you can lose your life by it! The poor! They hang each other one by one, they slaughter each other in the lump, so if they want to look each other in the face once in a while—well, it takes courage, that's all.

She sits, takes a small pipe from her pocket and smokes it.

You might chop me a bit of firewood.

CHAPLAIN, *reluctantly taking his coat off and preparing to chop wood.* Properly speaking, I'm a pastor of souls, not a wood-cutter.

MOTHER COURAGE. But I don't have a soul. And I do need wood.

CHAPLAIN. What's that little pipe you've got there?

MOTHER COURAGE. Just a pipe.

CHAPLAIN. I think it's a very particular pipe.

MOTHER COURAGE. Oh?

CHAPLAIN. The cook's pipe in fact. Our Swedish Commander's cook.

MOTHER COURAGE. If you know, why beat about the bush?

CHAPLAIN. Because I don't know if you've been *aware* that's what you've been smoking. It was possible you just rummaged among your belongings and your fingers just lit on a pipe and you just took it. In pure absent-mindedness.

MOTHER COURAGE. How do you know that's not it?

CHAPLAIN. It isn't. You *are* aware of it.

He brings the ax down on the block with a crash.

MOTHER COURAGE. What if I was?

CHAPLAIN. I must give you a warning, Mother Courage, it's my duty. You are unlikely ever again to see the gentleman but that's no pity, you're in luck. Mother Courage, he did not impress me as trustworthy. On the contrary.

MOTHER COURAGE. Really? He was such a nice man.

CHAPLAIN. Well! So that's what you call a nice man. I do not.

The ax falls again.

Far be it from me to wish him ill, but I cannot—cannot—describe him as nice. No, no, he's a Don Juan, a cunning Don Juan. Just look at that pipe if you don't believe me. You must admit it tells everything about him.

MOTHER COURAGE. I see nothing special in it. It's been, um, used.

CHAPLAIN. It's bitten half-way through! He's a man of great violence! It is the pipe of a man of great violence, you can see *that* if you've any judgment left!
He deals the block a tremendous blow.

MOTHER COURAGE. Don't bite my chopping block half-way through!

CHAPLAIN. I told you I had no training as a woodcutter. The care of souls was my field. Around here my gifts and capabilities are grossly misused. In physical labor my god-given talents find no—um—adequate expression—which is a sin. You haven't heard me preach. Why, I can put such spirit into a regiment with a single sermon that the enemy's a mere flock of sheep to them and their own lives no more than smelly old shoes to be thrown away at the thought of final victory! God has given me the gift of tongues. I can preach you out of your senses!

MOTHER COURAGE. I need my senses, what would I do without them?

CHAPLAIN. Mother Courage, I have often thought that—under a veil of plain speech—you conceal a heart. You are human, you need . . . warmth.

MOTHER COURAGE. The best way of warming this tent is to chop plenty of firewood.

CHAPLAIN. You're changing the subject. Seriously, my dear Courage, I sometimes ask myself how it would be if our relationship should be somewhat more firmly . . . cemented. I mean, now the wind of war has whirled us so strangely together.

MOTHER COURAGE. The cement's pretty firm already. I cook your meals. And you lend a hand—at chopping firewood, for instance.

CHAPLAIN *going over to her, gesturing with the ax.* You know what I mean by a close relationship. It has nothing to do with eating and woodcutting and such base necessities. Let your heart speak!

MOTHER COURAGE. Don't come at me like that with your ax, that'd be *too* close a relationship!

CHAPLAIN. This is no laughing matter, I am in earnest. I've thought it all over.

MOTHER COURAGE. Dear Chaplain, be a sensible fellow. I like you, and I don't want to heap coals of fire on your head. All I'm after is to bring me and my children through in that wagon. Now chop the firewood and we'll be warm of an evening, which is quite a lot these days. What's that?

She stands up. CATHERINE *enters breathless with a nasty wound above her eye and brow. She is letting everything fall, parcels, leather goods, a drum etc.*

Catherine, what is it? Were you attacked? On the way back? It's not serious, only a flesh wound, I'll bandage it up for you, and you'll be better within the week. Didn't the clerk walk you back? That's because you're a good girl, he thought they'd leave you alone. The wound really isn't deep, it won't show. That's it, now it's all bandaged. Now I have something for you, I've been keeping it, just watch.

She digs YVETTE POTTIER's *red boots out of a bag.*

You see? You always wanted 'em and now you have 'em. Put them on before I think twice about it.

She helps her.

It won't show at all! The boots have kept well, I cleaned them good before I put them away.

CATHERINE *leaves the shoes and creeps into the wagon.*

CHAPLAIN *when she's gone.* I hope she won't be disfigured?

MOTHER COURAGE. There'll be a scar. She needn't wait for peace now.

CHAPLAIN. She didn't let them get any of the stuff from her.

MOTHER COURAGE. Maybe I shouldn't have been so strict with her. If only I ever knew what went on inside her head. One time she stayed out all night, once in all the years. I could never get out of her what happened, I racked my brains for quite a while.

She picks up the things CATHERINE *spilled and sorts them angrily.*

This is war. A nice source of income to have!

Cannon shots.

CHAPLAIN. Now they're lowering the Commander in his grave! A historic moment.

MOTHER COURAGE. It's a historic moment to me when they hit my daughter over the eye. She's all but finished now, she'll get no husband, and she's so crazy for children! Even her dumbness comes from the war. A soldier stuck something in her mouth when she was little. I'll not see Swiss Cheese again, and where my Eilif is the Good Lord knows. Curse the war!

7

A HIGHWAY. THE CHAPLAIN AND CATH-ERINE ARE PULLING THE WAGON.* IT IS DIRTY AND NEGLECTED, THOUGH THERE ARE NEW GOODS HUNG ROUND IT.

MOTHER COURAGE, *walking beside the wagon and drinking heavily from a flask at her waist.* I won't have my war all spoiled for me! It destroys the weak, does it? Well, what does peace do for 'em? Huh?

She sings her song.

So cheer up, boys, the rose is fading
When vict'ry comes you may be dead
A war is just the same as trading
But not with cheese—with steel instead!

> The spring is here, get out of bed
> The snow melts fast, green buds arrive
> You'll sleep forever when you're dead
> But if you're not, then look alive!

And the wagon moves on.†

* The turntable is used as in the Prologue.
† In performance the one intermission comes here.

8

1632. IN THIS SAME YEAR GUSTAVUS ADOL-
PHUS FELL IN THE BATTLE OF LÜTZEN. THE
PEACE THREATENS MOTHER COURAGE WITH
RUIN. HER BRAVE SON PERFORMS ONE
HEROIC DEED TOO MANY AND COMES TO A
SHAMEFUL END.

*A camp. A summer morning. In front of the wagon, an old
woman and her son. The son is dragging a large bag of bed-
ding.*

MOTHER COURAGE, *from inside the wagon.* Must you come at
the crack of dawn?

YOUNG MAN. We've been walking all night, twenty miles it was,
we have to be back today.

MOTHER COURAGE *still inside.* What do I want with bed
feathers? Take 'em to the town!

YOUNG MAN. At least wait till you see 'em.

OLD WOMAN. Nothing doing here either, let's go.

YOUNG MAN. And let 'em sign away the roof over our heads for
taxes? Maybe she'll pay three gilders if you throw in that
bracelet.
Bells start ringing.
You hear, mother?

VOICES *from the rear.* It's peace! The King of Sweden's killed!

MOTHER COURAGE, *sticking her head out of the wagon. She
hasn't done her hair yet.* Bells! What are the bells for, middle of the week?

CHAPLAIN, *crawling out from under the wagon.* What's that
they're shouting?

YOUNG MAN. It's peace.

CHAPLAIN. Peace!?

MOTHER COURAGE. Don't tell me peace has broken out—when I've just gone and bought all these supplies!

CHAPLAIN, *calling, toward the rear.* Is it peace?

VOICE, *from a distance.* Yes, the war stopped three weeks ago!

CHAPLAIN, *to* MOTHER COURAGE. Or why would they ring the bells?

VOICE. A great crowd of Lutherans have just arrived with wagons—they brought the news.

YOUNG MAN. It's peace, mother.

The OLD WOMAN *collapses.*

What's the matter?

MOTHER COURAGE, *back in the wagon.* Catherine, it's peace! Put on your black dress, we're going to church, we owe it to Swiss Cheese!

YOUNG MAN. The people here say so too, the war's over.

The OLD WOMAN *stands up, dazed.*

I'll get the harness shop going again now, I promise you. Everything'll be all right, father will get his bed back. . . . Can you walk?

To the CHAPLAIN.

She felt sick, it was the news. She didn't believe there'd ever be peace again. Father always said there would. We're going home.

They leave.

MOTHER COURAGE, *off.* Give her a schnapps!

CHAPLAIN. They've left already.

MOTHER COURAGE, *still off.* What's going on in the camp over there?

CHAPLAIN. They're all getting together, I think I'll go over. Shall I put my pastor's clothes on again?

MOTHER COURAGE. Better get the exact news first, and not risk being identified as the antichrist.

CHAPLAIN. And who may this be coming down from the camp? Well, if it isn't our Swedish Commander's cook!

COOK, *somewhat bedraggled, carrying a bundle.* Who's here? The Chaplain!

CHAPLAIN. Mother Courage, a visitor!
MOTHER COURAGE *clambers out.*

COOK. Well, I promised I'd come over for a brief conversation as soon as I had time. I didn't forget your brandy, Mrs. Fierling.

MOTHER COURAGE. Mr. Lamp, the Commander's cook! After all these years! Where is Eilif?

COOK. Isn't he here yet? He went on ahead yesterday, he was on his way over.

CHAPLAIN. I *will* put my pastor's clothes on.
He goes behind the wagon.

MOTHER COURAGE. He may be here any minute then.
Calls toward the wagon.
Catherine, Eilif's coming! Bring a glass of brandy for the Cook, Catherine!
CATHERINE *doesn't come.*
Pull your hair over it and have done, the Cook's no stranger. She won't come out. Peace is nothing to her, it was too long coming. Well, one more schnapps!

COOK. Dear old peace!
He and MOTHER COURAGE *sit.*

MOTHER COURAGE. Cook, you come at a bad time: I'm ruined.

COOK. What? That's terrible!

MOTHER COURAGE. The peace has broken my neck. On the Chaplain's advice I've gone and bought a lot of supplies. Now everybody's leaving and I'm holding the bag.

COOK. How ever could you listen to the Chaplain? If I'd had time—but the Catholics were too quick—I'd have warned you against him. He's a windbag. Well, so now he's the big wheel round here!

MOTHER COURAGE. He's been doing the dishes for me and helping with the wagon.

COOK. I'll bet he has. And I'll bet he's told you a few of his jokes. He has a most unhealthy attitude to women. I tried to influence him but it was no good. He isn't sound.

MOTHER COURAGE. Are you sound?

COOK. If I'm nothing else, I'm sound. Your health!

MOTHER COURAGE. Sound! Only one person around here was ever sound, and I never had to slave as I did then. He sold the blankets off the children's beds in autumn. You aren't recommending yourself if you *admit* you're sound.

COOK. You fight tooth and nail, don't you? I like that.

MOTHER COURAGE. Don't tell me you dream of my teeth and nails.

COOK. Well, here we sit, while the bells of peace do ring, and you pour your famous brandy as only you know how.

MOTHER COURAGE. I don't see how they can hand out all this pay that's in arrears. And then where shall I be with my famous brandy? Have you all been paid?

COOK, *hesitating*. Not exactly. That's why we disbanded. In the circumstances, I thought, why stay? For the time being, I'll look up a couple of friends. So here I am.

MOTHER COURAGE. In other words, you're broke.

COOK, *annoyed by the bells*. It's about time they stopped that racket! I'd like to set myself up in some business.

MOTHER COURAGE. Oh, Cook, it's a dog's life.

COOK, *as the* CHAPLAIN *turns up, wearing his old costume*. We'll discuss it.

CHAPLAIN. The coat's pretty good. Just a few moth holes.

COOK. I don't know why you take the trouble. You won't find another job. Who could you incite now to earn an honorable wage or risk his life for a cause? Besides I have a bone to pick with you.

CHAPLAIN. Have you?

COOK. I have. You advised a lady to buy superfluous goods on the pretext that the war would never end.

CHAPLAIN, *hotly.* I'd like to know what business it is of yours?

COOK. It's unprincipled behavior! How can you give unwanted advice? And interfere with the conduct of other people's businesses?

CHAPLAIN. Who's interfering now, I'd like to know?
Haughtily to MOTHER COURAGE.
I had no idea you were such a close friend of this gentleman and had to account to *him* for everything.

MOTHER COURAGE. Now don't get excited. The Cook's giving his personal opinion. You can't deny your war was a lemon.

CHAPLAIN. You mustn't take the name of peace in vain. Remember, you're a hyena of the battlefield!

MOTHER COURAGE. A what!?

COOK. If you insult my girl friend, you'll have to reckon with me!

CHAPLAIN. I am *not* speaking to you, your intentions are only too transparent!
To MOTHER COURAGE.
But when I see *you* take peace between finger and thumb like a snotty old hanky, my humanity rebels! It shows that you want war, not peace, for what you get out of it. But don't forget the proverb: he who sups with the devil must use a long spoon!

MOTHER COURAGE. Remember what one fox said to another that was caught in a trap? "If you stay there, you're just asking for trouble!" There isn't much love lost between me and the war. And when it comes to calling me a hyena, you and I part company.

CHAPLAIN. Then why all this grumbling about the peace just as everyone's heaving a sigh of relief? Is it just for the junk in your wagon?

MOTHER COURAGE. My goods are not junk. I live off them.

CHAPLAIN. You live off war. Exactly.

COOK, *to the* CHAPLAIN. As a grown man, you should know better than to go around advising people.
To MOTHER COURAGE.

Now, in your situation you'd be smart to get rid of certain goods at once—before the prices sink to zero. Get ready and get going, there isn't a moment to lose!

MOTHER COURAGE. That's sensible advice, I think I'll take it.

CHAPLAIN. Because the Cook says so.

MOTHER COURAGE. Why didn't *you* say so? He's right, I must get to the market.
She climbs into the wagon.

COOK. One up for me, Chaplain. You have no presence of mind. You should have said, "I gave you advice? Why, I was just talking politics!" And you shouldn't take me on as a rival. Cockfights are not becoming to your cloth.

CHAPLAIN. If you don't shut your trap, I'll murder you, whether it's becoming or not!

COOK, *taking his boots off and unwinding the wrappings on his feet.* If you hadn't degenerated into a godless tramp, you could easily be quite a success these days. Cooks won't be needed, there's nothing to cook, but there's still plenty to believe, and people'll go right on believing it.

CHAPLAIN, *changing his tone.* Cook, please don't drive me out! Since I bcame a tramp, I'm a somewhat better man. I couldn't preach to 'em any more. So where should I go?
YVETTE POTTIER enters, decked out in black, with a stick. She is much older, fatter, and heavily powdered. Behind her, a servant.

YVETTE. Hullo, everybody! Is this Mother Courage's establishment?

CHAPLAIN. Quite right. And with whom have we the pleasure?

YVETTE. I am Madame Colonel Starhemberg, good people. Where's Mother Courage?

CHAPLAIN, *calling to the wagon.* Madame Colonel Starhemberg wants to speak with you!

MOTHER COURAGE, *from inside.* Coming!

YVETTE, *calling.* It's Yvette!

MOTHER COURAGE, *inside.* Yvette!

YVETTE. Just to see how you're getting on!
> *As the* COOK *turns round in horror.*
> Peter!

COOK. Yvette!

YVETTE. Of all things! How did *you* get here?

COOK. On a cart.

CHAPLAIN. Well! You know each other? Intimately?

YVETTE. I'll say!
> *Scrutinizing the* COOK.
> You're fat.

COOK. For that matter, *you're* no beanpole.

YVETTE. Anyway, nice meeting you, tramp. Now I can tell you what I think of you.

CHAPLAIN. Do that, tell him all, but wait till Mother Courage comes out.

COOK. Now don't make a scene . . .

MOTHER COURAGE *comes out, laden with goods.* Yvette!
> *They embrace.*
> But why are you in mourning?

YVETTE. Doesn't it suit me? My husband, the colonel, died several years ago.

MOTHER COURAGE. The old fellow that nearly bought my wagon?

YVETTE. Naw, not him—his older brother!

MOTHER COURAGE. Good to see one person who got somewhere in the war.

CHAPLAIN. You promised to give us your opinion of this gentleman.

COOK. Now, Yvette, don't make a stink!

MOTHER COURAGE. He's a friend of mine, Yvette.

YVETTE. He's—Peter Piper, that's what!

MOTHER COURAGE. What!?

COOK. Cut the nicknames. My name's Lamp.

MOTHER COURAGE, *laughing.* Peter Piper? Who turned the women's heads? I'll have to sit down. And I've been keeping your pipe for you.

CHAPLAIN. And smoking it.

YVETTE. Lucky I can warn you against him. He's a bad lot. You won't find a worse on the whole coast of Flanders. He got more girls in trouble than . . .

COOK. That's a long time ago, it isn't true any more.

YVETTE. Stand up when you talk to a lady! Oh, how I loved that man! And all the time he was having a little bowlegged brunette. He got *her* in trouble too, of course.

COOK. I seem to have brought *you* luck!

YVETTE. Shut your trap, you hoary ruin! And you take care, Mother Courage, this type is still dangerous even in decay!

MOTHER COURAGE, *to* YVETTE. Come with me, I must get rid of this stuff before the prices fall.

YVETTE *concentrating on* COOK. Miserable cur!

MOTHER COURAGE. Maybe you can help me at army head-quarters, you have contacts.

YVETTE. Damnable whore hunter!

MOTHER COURAGE, *shouting into the wagon.* Catherine, church is all off, I'm going to market!

YVETTE. Inveterate seducer!

MOTHER COURAGE, *still to* CATHERINE. When Eilif comes, give him something to drink!

YVETTE. I've put an end to your tricks, Peter Piper, and one day —in a better life than this—the Lord God will reward me!
She sniffs.
Come, Mother Courage!
Leaves with MOTHER COURAGE. *Pause.*

CHAPLAIN. As our text this morning let us take the saying, the mills of God grind slowly. And you complain of my jokes!

COOK. I have no luck. I'll be frank, I was hoping for a good hot dinner, I'm starving. And now they'll be talking about me, and she'll get a completely wrong picture. I think I should go before she comes back.

CHAPLAIN. I think so too.

COOK. Chaplain, the peace makes me sick. Mankind must perish by fire and sword, we're born and bred in sin! Oh, how I wish I was roasting a great fat capon for the Commander —God knows where *he's* got to—with mustard sauce and those little yellow carrots . . .

CHAPLAIN. Red cabbage—with capon, red cabbage.

COOK. You're right. But he always wanted yellow carrots.

CHAPLAIN. He never understood a thing.

COOK. You always put plenty away.

CHAPLAIN. Under protest.

COOK. Anyway, you must admit, those were the days.

CHAPLAIN. Yes, that I might admit.

COOK. Now you've called her a hyena, there's not much future for you here either. What are you staring at?

CHAPLAIN. It's Eilif!
Followed by two soldiers with halberds, EILIF *enters. His hands are fettered. He is white as chalk.*
What's happened to you?

EILIF. Where's mother?

CHAPLAIN. Gone to town.

EILIF. They said she was here. I was allowed a last visit.

COOK, *to the soldiers.* Where are you taking him?

SOLDIER. For a ride.
The other soldier makes the gesture of throat cutting.

CHAPLAIN. What has he done?

SOLDIER. He broke in on a peasant. The wife is dead.

CHAPLAIN. Eilif, how could you?

EILIF. It's no different. It's what I did before.

COOK. That was in wartime.

EILIF. Shut your hole. Can I sit down till she comes?

SOLDIER. No.

CHAPLAIN. It's true. In war time they honored him for it. He sat at the Commander's right hand. It was bravery. Couldn't we speak with the provost?

SOLDIER. What's the use? Stealing cattle from a peasant, what's brave about that?

COOK. It was just dumb.

EILIF. If I'd been dumb, I'd have starved, smarty.

COOK. So you were bright and paid for it.

CHAPLAIN. At least we must bring Catherine out.

EILIF. Let her alone. Just give me some brandy.

SOLDIER. No.

CHAPLAIN. What shall we tell your mother?

EILIF. Tell her it was no different. Tell her it was the same. Aw, tell her nothing.
The soldiers take him away.

CHAPLAIN. I'll come with you, I'll . . .

EILIF. I don't need a priest!

CHAPLAIN. You don't know—yet.
Follows him.

COOK, *calling after him.* I'll have to tell her, she'll want to see him!

CHAPLAIN. Better tell her nothing. Or maybe just that he was here, and he'll return, maybe tomorrow. Meantime I'll be back and can break the news.
Leaves quickly. The COOK *looks after him, shakes his head, then walks uneasily around. Finally, he approaches the wagon.*

COOK. Hi! Won't you come out? You want to run away from
the peace, don't you? Well, so do I! I'm the Swedish Commander's cook, remember me? I was wondering if you got
anything to eat in there—while we're waiting for your
mother. I wouldn't mind a bit of bacon—or even bread—just
to pass the time.

He looks in.

She's got a blanket over her head.

The thunder of cannon.

MOTHER COURAGE, *running, out of breath, still carrying the
goods.* Cook, the peace is over, the war's on again, has been
for three days! I didn't get rid of this stuff after all, thank
God! There's a shooting match in the town already—with
the Lutherans. We must get away with the wagon. Pack,
Catherine! What's on *your* mind? Something the matter?

COOK. Nothing.

MOTHER COURAGE. But there is, I see it in your face.

COOK. Eilif was here. Only he had to go away again.

MOTHER COURAGE. He was here? Then we'll see him on the
march. I'll be with our side this time. How'd he look?

COOK. The same.

MOTHER COURAGE. He'll *never* change. And the war couldn't
get *him*, he's bright. Help me with the packing.

She starts it.

Did he tell you anything? Is he in good with the captain?
Did he tell you about his heroic deeds?

COOK, *darkly.* He's done one of them over again.

MOTHER COURAGE. Tell me about it later.

CATHERINE *appears.*

Catherine, the peace is all through, we're on the move
again.

To the COOK.

What *is* biting you?

COOK. I'll enlist.

MOTHER COURAGE. A good idea. Where's the Chaplain?

COOK. In the town. With Eilif.

MOTHER COURAGE. Stay with us a while, Mr. Lamp, I need a bit of help.

COOK. This Yvette thing . . .

MOTHER COURAGE. Hasn't done you any harm at all in my eyes. Just the opposite. Where there's smoke, there's fire, they say. You'll come?

COOK. I won't say no.

MOTHER COURAGE. The twelfth regiment's under way. Into harness with you! Maybe I'll see Eilif before the day is out, just think! Well, it wasn't such a long peace, we can't grumble. Let's go!
They move off.

9

THE HOLY WAR HAS LASTED SIXTEEN YEARS AND GERMANY HAS LOST HALF ITS INHABITANTS. THOSE WHO ARE SPARED IN BATTLE DIE BY PLAGUE. OVER ONCE BLOOMING COUNTRYSIDE HUNGER RAGES. TOWNS ARE BURNED DOWN. WOLVES PROWL THE EMPTY STREETS. IN THE AUTUMN OF 1634 WE FIND MOTHER COURAGE IN THE FICHTELGEBIRGE NOT FAR FROM THE ROAD THE SWEDISH ARMY IS TAKING. WINTER HAS COME EARLY AND IS HARD. BUSINESS IS BAD. ONLY BEGGING REMAINS. THE COOK RECEIVES A LETTER FROM UTRECHT AND IS SENT PACKING.

In front of a half-ruined parsonage. Early winter. A grey morning. Gusts of wind. MOTHER COURAGE *and the* COOK *at the wagon in shabby clothes.*

COOK. There are no lights on, no one's up.

MOTHER COURAGE. But it's a parsonage. The parson'll have to leave his feather bed and go ring the bells. Then he'll have himself a hot soup.

COOK. Where'll he get it from? The whole village is starving.

MOTHER COURAGE. The house is lived in. There was a dog barking.

COOK. If the parson has anything, he'll stick to it.

MOTHER COURAGE. Maybe if we sang him something ...

COOK. I've had enough. Anna, I didn't tell you, a letter came from Utrecht. My mother died of cholera, the inn is mine. There's the letter, if you don't believe me.

MOTHER COURAGE, *reading.* Lamp, I'm tired of wandering too. I feel like a butcher's dog taking meat to the customers and getting none myself.

COOK. The world's dying out.

MOTHER COURAGE. Sometimes I see myself driving through hell with this wagon and selling brimstone. And sometimes I'm driving through heaven handing out provisions to wandering souls! If only we could find a place where there's no shooting, me and my children—what's left of 'em—we might rest up a while.

COOK. We could open this inn together. Think about it, Courage. *My* mind's made up. With or without you, I'm leaving for Utrecht. And today at that.

MOTHER COURAGE. I must talk to Catherine, it's sudden.
    CATHERINE *emerges from the wagon.*
    Catherine, I've something to tell you. The cook and I want to go to Utrecht, he's been left an inn. We'd be sure of our dinner: nice, hm? And you'd have a bed, what do you think of *that*? This is a dog's life, on the road, you might be killed any time, even now you're covered with lice ... I think we'll decide to go, Catherine.

COOK. Anna, I must have a word with you alone.

MOTHER COURAGE. Go back inside, Catherine.
    CATHERINE *does so.*

COOK. I'm interrupting because there's a misunderstanding,

ANNA. I thought I wouldn't have to say it right out, but I see I must. If you're bringing *her*, it's all off.

CATHERINE *has her head out of the back of the wagon and is listening.*

MOTHER COURAGE. You mean I leave Catherine behind?

COOK. What do you think? There's no room in the inn, it isn't one of those places with three counters. If the two of us stand on our hindlegs we can earn a living, but three's too many. Let Catherine keep your wagon.

MOTHER COURAGE. I was thinking she might find a husband in Utrecht.

COOK. With that scar? And old as she is?

MOTHER COURAGE. Not so loud!

COOK. Loud or soft, what is, is. That's another reason I can't have her in the inn, the customers wouldn't like it.

MOTHER COURAGE. Not so loud, I said!

COOK. There's a light in the parsonage, we can sing now!
They go over toward the wall.

MOTHER COURAGE. How could she pull the wagon by herself? The war frightens her, she couldn't stand it.

COOK. The inn's too small.
Calling.
Worthy Sir, menials, and all within! We now present the song of Solomon, Julius Caesar, and other great souls who came to no good, so you can see we're law-abiding folk too, and have a hard time getting by, especially in winter.
He sings: THE SONG OF THE GREAT SOULS OF THIS EARTH.
You saw the wise man Solomon
You know his history
So plain to him was all the earth
That in fury he cursed the hour of his birth
And saw that all was vanity
How great and wise was Solomon!
But ere night came and day did go
It all was clear to everyone:
'Twas wisdom that had brought him down so low!
How fortunate the man with none.

For the virtues are dangerous in this world, as our fine song tells. You're better off without, you have a nice life, breakfast included—a good hot soup maybe . . . I'm an example of a man who's not had any, and I'd like some, I'm a soldier, but what good did my bravery do me in all those battles? None at all. I might just as well have wet my pants like a coward and stayed home. For why?

You saw the brave man Caesar too
You know what him befell
He sat, a god upon a throne,
Was murdered, as you know full well,
And just when he was greatest grown
He cried aloud, "You too, my son!"
But ere night came and day did go
It all was clear to everyone:
'Twas brav'ry that had brought him down so low!
How fortunate the man with none

Under his breath.

They don't even look out.

Aloud.

Worthy Sir, menials, and all within! You should say, no, courage isn't the thing to fill a man's belly, try honesty, that should be worth a dinner, at any rate it must have *some* effect. Let's see.

You know the honest Socrates
He always spoke the truth
They owed him thanks for this, you'd think
But in fury they gave him hemlock to drink
And said that he was bad for youth
How honest was the people's greatest son!
But ere night came and day did go
It all was clear to everyone:
'Twas honesty had brought him down so low!
How fortunate the man with none

Yes, we're told to be unselfish and share what we have but what if we have nothing? And those who do share it don't have an easy time either, for what's left when you're through sharing? Unselfishness is a very rare virtue—it doesn't pay.

The good Saint Martin, as you know,
Could not bear others' woes
He met a poor man in the snow
Did half his cloak on him bestow
So both of them to death they froze
Who more unselfish than this man?
But ere night came and day did go
It all was clear to everyone:
Unselfishness had brought him down so low!
How fortunate the man with none*

That's how it is with us. We're law-abiding folk, we keep to ourselves, don't steal, don't kill, don't burn the place down. And in this way we sink lower and lower and the song proves true and there's no soup going. And if we were different, if we were thieves and killers, maybe we could eat our fill! For virtues bring no reward, only vices. Such is the world, need it be so?

You see here law-abiding folk
Commandments ten we heed
It hasn't done much good as yet
You who nightly at warm firesides do sit
O save us in our sorest need!
Yes, goodness we have always shown
But ere night came and day did go
It all was clear to everyone:
'Twas fear of God had brought us down so low!
How fortunate the man with none

VOICE, *from above.* You there! Come up! There's some soup here for you!

MOTHER COURAGE. Lamp, I couldn't swallow a thing. Was that your last word?

COOK. Yes, Anna. Think it over.

MOTHER COURAGE. There's nothing to think over.

COOK. You're going to be silly, but what can I do? I'm not inhuman, it's just that the inn's a small one. And now we must go up, or it'll be no soap here too, and we've been singing in the cold for nothing.
*In the interests of brevity this stanza and the preceding speech can be cut.

MOTHER COURAGE. I'll get Catherine.

COOK. Better stick something in your pocket for her. If there
are three of us, they won't like it.
Exeunt.

  *CATHERINE clambers out of the wagon with a bundle. She
  makes sure they're both gone. Then, on a wagon wheel, she
  lays out a skirt of her mother's and a pair of the COOK's
  pants side by side and easy to see. She has just finished,
  and has picked her bundle up, when MOTHER COURAGE returns.*

MOTHER COURAGE, *with a plate of soup.* Catherine! Stay where
you are, Catherine! Where do you think you're going with
that bundle?
She examines the bundle.

She's packed her things. Were you listening? I told him
there was nothing doing, he can *have* Utrecht and his lousy
inn, what would *we* want with a lousy inn?
She sees the skirt and pants.

Oh, you're a stupid girl, Catherine, what if I'd seen that
and you gone?
She takes hold of Catherine, who's trying to leave.

And don't think I've sent him packing on your account. It
was the wagon. You can't part us, I'm too used to it, *you*
didn't come into it, it was the wagon. Now we're leaving,
and we'll put the cook's things here where he'll find 'em, the
stupid man.
*She clambers up and throws a couple of things down to go
with the pants.*

There! He's fired! The last man I'll take into *this* business!
Now let's you and me be going. Get into harness. This
winter'll pass——like all the others.
*They harness themselves to the wagon, turn it around, and
start out. A gust of wind. Enter the COOK, still chewing. He
sees his things.*

10

On the highway. MOTHER COURAGE *and* CATHERINE *are
pulling the wagon. They come to a prosperous farmhouse.
Someone inside is singing.*

It was a red rose that cheered us
Upon a fair rose tree
With sweet delight it filled us
In March the tree we planted
Then not in vain 'twas tended
How happy with our garden we!
It was a red rose that cheered us

When the north winds are blowing
And bends the green fir tree
There's little to be fearing:
A brave roof we have over us
Its moss and straw, they cover us
How happy with our roof are we
When the north winds are blowing!

MOTHER COURAGE *and* CATHERINE *have stopped to listen.*
Then they start out again.

11

JANUARY, 1636. CATHOLIC TROOPS THREAT-
EN THE PROTESTANT TOWN OF HALLE. THE
STONES BEGIN TO TALK. MOTHER COURAGE
LOSES HER DAUGHTER AND JOURNEYS ON-
WARDS ALONE. THE WAR IS NOT YET NEAR
ITS END.

The wagon, very far gone now, stands near a farmhouse
with a straw roof. It is night. Out of the wood come a LIEU-
TENANT *and* THREE SOLDIERS *in full armor.*

LIEUTENANT. And there mustn't be a sound. If anyone yells,
cut him down.

FIRST SOLDIER. But we'll have to knock—if we want a guide.

LIEUTENANT. Knocking's a natural noise, it's all right, could be
a cow hitting the wall of the cowshed.
The SOLDIERS *knock at the farmhouse door. An old peasant*
woman opens. A hand is clapped over her mouth. Two
soldiers enter.

MAN'S VOICE. What is it?

The SOLDIERS *bring out an old peasant and his son.*

LIEUTENANT, *pointing to the wagon on which* CATHERINE *has appeared.*
There's one.
A soldier pulls her out.
Is this everybody that lives here?

PEASANTS, *alternating.* That's our son. And that's a girl that can't talk. Her mother's in town buying up stocks because the shopkeepers are running away and selling cheap. They're canteen people.

LIEUTENANT. I'm warning you. Keep quiet. One sound and you'll have a sword in your ribs. And I need someone to show us the path to the town.
Points to the YOUNG PEASANT.
You! Come here!

YOUNG PEASANT. I don't know any path!

SECOND SOLDIER, *grinning.* He don't know any path!

YOUNG PEASANT. I don't help Catholics.

LIEUTENANT, *to* SECOND SOLDIER. Show him your sword.

YOUNG PEASANT, *forced to his knees, a sword at his throat.* I'd rather die!

SECOND SOLDIER, *again mimicking.* He'd rather die!

FIRST SOLDIER. I know how to change his mind.
Walks over to the cowshed.
Two cows and a bull. Listen, you. If you aren't going to be reasonable, I'll sabre your cattle.

YOUNG PEASANT. Not the cattle!

PEASANT WOMAN, *weeping.* Spare the cattle, captain, or we'll starve!

LIEUTENANT. If he must be pigheaded!

FIRST SOLDIER. I think I'll start with the bull.

YOUNG PEASANT, *to the old one.* Do I have to?
The OLDER ONE *nods.*
I'll do it.

PEASANT WOMAN. Thank you, thank you, captain, for sparing us, for ever and ever, Amen.
The old man stops her going on thanking him.

FIRST SOLDIER. I knew the bull came first all right!
Led by the YOUNG PEASANT, *the* LIEUTENANT *and the* SOLDIERS *go on their way.*

OLD PEASANT. I wish we knew what it was. Nothing good, I guess.

PEASANT WOMAN. Maybe they're just scouts. What are you doing?

OLD PEASANT, *setting a ladder against the roof and climbing up.* I'm seeing if they're alone.
On the roof.
Things are moving—all over. I can see armour. And a cannon. There must be more than a regiment. God have mercy on the town and all within!

PEASANT WOMAN. Are there lights in the town?

OLD PEASANT. No, they're all asleep.
He climbs down.
There'll be an attack, and they'll all be slaughtered in their beds.

PEASANT WOMAN. The watchman'll give warning.

OLD PEASANT. They must have killed the watchman in the tower on the hill or he'd have sounded his horn before this.

PEASANT WOMAN. If there were more of us . . .

OLD PEASANT. But being that we're alone with that cripple . . .

PEASANT WOMAN. There's nothing we can do, is there?

OLD PEASANT. Nothing.

PEASANT WOMAN. We can't get down there. In the dark.

OLD PEASANT. The whole hillside's swarming with 'em.

PEASANT WOMAN. We could give a sign?

OLD PEASANT. And be cut down for it?

PEASANT WOMAN. No, there's nothing we can do.

To CATHERINE.

Pray, poor thing, pray! There's nothing we can do to stop this bloodshed, so even if you can't talk, at least pray! He hears, if no one else does. I'll help you.

ALL *kneel,* CATHERINE *behind.*

Our Father, which art in Heaven, hear our prayer, let not the town perish with all that lie therein asleep and fearing nothing. Wake them, that they rise and go to the walls and see the foe that comes with fire and sword in the night down the hill and across the fields. God protect our mother and make the watchman not sleep but wake ere it's too late. And save our son-in-law too, O God, he's there with his four children, let them not perish, they're innocent, they know nothing, one of them's not two years old, the eldest is seven.

CATHERINE *rises, troubled.*

Heavenly Father, hear us, only Thou canst help us or we die, for we are weak and have no sword nor nothing; we cannot thrust our own strength but only Thine, O Lord; we are in Thy hands, our cattle, our farm, and the town too, we're all in Thy hands, and the foe is nigh unto the walls with all his power.

CATHERINE *unperceived, has crept off to the wagon, has taken something out of it, put it under her skirt, and has climbed up the ladder to the roof.*

Be mindful of the children in danger, especially the little ones, be mindful of the old folk who cannot move, and of all Christian souls, O Lord.

OLD PEASANT. And forgive us our trespasses as we forgive them that trespass against us. Amen.

Sitting on the roof, CATHERINE *takes a drum from under her skirt, and starts to beat it.*

PEASANT WOMAN. Heavens, what's she doing?

OLD PEASANT. She's out of her mind!

PEASANT WOMAN. Bring her down, quick!

The OLD PEASANT *runs to the ladder but* CATHERINE *pulls it up on the roof.*

She'll get us in trouble.

OLD PEASANT. Stop it this minute, you silly cripple!

PEASANT WOMAN. The soldiers'll come!

OLD PEASANT, *looking for stones.* I'll stone you!

PEASANT WOMAN. Have you no pity, don't you have a heart?
We have relations there too, four grandchildren, but there's
nothing we can do. If they find us now, it's the end, they'll
stab us to death!

CATHERINE *is staring into the far distance, toward the town.
She goes on drumming.*

PEASANT WOMAN, *to the* PEASANT. I told you not to let that
riffraff in your farm. What do *they* care if we lose our cattle?

LIEUTENANT, *running back with soldiers and young peasant.*
I'll cut you all to bits!

PEASANT WOMAN. We're innocent, sir, there's nothing we can
do. She did it, a stranger!

LIEUTENANT. Where's the ladder?

OLD PEASANT. On the roof.

LIEUTENANT, *calling.* Throw down the drum. I order you!

To PEASANTS.

You're all in this, but you won't live to tell the tale.

OLD PEASANT. They've been cutting down fir trees around here.
If we bring a tall enough trunk we can knock her off the
roof . . .

FIRST SOLDIER, *to the* LIEUTENANT. I beg leave to make a suggestion.

He whispers something to the LIEUTENANT, *who nods. To*
CATHERINE.

Listen, you! We have an idea—for your own good. Come
down and go with us to the town. Show us your mother
and we'll spare her.

CATHERINE *replies with more drumming.*

LIEUTENANT, *pushing him away.* She doesn't trust you, no
wonder with your face.

He calls up to CATHERINE.

Hey, you! Suppose I give you my word? I'm an officer, my
word's my bond!

CATHERINE *again replies with drumming—harder this time.*
Nothing is sacred to her.

FIRST SOLDIER. This can't go on, they'll sure as hell hear it in
the town.

LIEUTENANT. We must make another noise with something.
Louder than that drum. What can we make a noise with?

FIRST SOLDIER. But we mustn't make a noise!

LIEUTENANT. A harmless noise, fool ,a peacetime noise!

OLD PEASANT. I could start chopping wood.

LIEUTENANT. That's it!
The PEASANT *brings his ax and chops away.*
Chop! Chop harder! Chop for your life! It's not enough.
To FIRST SOLDIER.
You chop too!

OLD PEASANT. I've only one ax.

LIEUTENANT. We must set fire to the farm. Smoke her out.

OLD PEASANT. That's no good, Captain, when they see fire from
the town, they'll know everything.
CATHERINE *is laughing now and drumming harder than ever.*

LIEUTENANT. She's laughing at us, that's too much, I'll have
her guts if it's the last thing I do. Bring a musket!
Two soldiers off.

PEASANT WOMAN. I have it, Captain. That's their wagon over
there, Captain. If we smash that, she'll stop. It's all they
have, Captain.

LIEUTENANT, *to the* YOUNG PEASANT. Smash it!
Calling.
If you don't stop that noise, we'll smash up your wagon!
The YOUNG PEASANT *deals the wagon a couple of feeble
blows with a board.*

PEASANT WOMAN *to* CATHERINE. Stop, you little beast!
CATHERINE *stares at the wagon and pauses. Noises of distress come out of her. She goes on drumming.*

LIEUTENANT. Where are those sonsofbitches with that gun?

FIRST SOLDIER. They can't have heard anything in the town or we'd hear their cannon.

LIEUTENANT, *calling.* They don't hear you. And now we're going to shoot you. I'll give you one more chance: throw down that drum!

YOUNG PEASANT, *dropping the board, screaming to* CATHERINE. Don't stop now! Go on, go on, go on . . .
The SOLDIER *knocks him down and stabs him.* CATHERINE *starts crying but goes on drumming.*

PEASANT WOMAN. Not in the back, you're killing him!
The SOLDIERS *arrive with the gun.*

LIEUTENANT. Set it up!
Calling while the gun is set up on forks.
Once for all: stop that drumming!
Still crying, CATHERINE *is drumming as hard as she can.*
Fire!
The SOLDIERS *fire.* CATHERINE *is hit. She gives the drum another feeble beat or two, then collapses.*

LIEUTENANT. That's an end to the noise.
But the last beats of the drum are lost in the din of cannon from the town. Mingled with the thunder of cannon, alarm-bells are heard in the distance.

FIRST SOLDIER. She made it.

12

Toward morning. The drums and pipes of troops on the march, receding. In front of the wagon MOTHER COURAGE *sits by* CATHERINE's *body. The peasants of the last scene are standing near.*

PEASANTS, *one sentence apiece.* You must leave. There's only one regiment to go. You can never get away by yourself.

MOTHER COURAGE. Maybe she's asleep.
She sings.

Lullaby baby
What's that in the hay?
The neighbor's child's crying
But mine, he is gay!
Neighbor's child's in tatters
But silk is your due
From the robe of an angel
Made over for you
Not a crust has the neighbor's child
You have a cake
If it's too stale for you
Pray, do but speak!
Lullaby baby
What's rustling there?
Neighbor's child's in Poland
Mine's who knows where

You shouldn't have told her about the children.

PEASANTS. If you hadn't gone off to the town to get your cut, maybe it wouldn't have happened.

MOTHER COURAGE. I'm glad she can sleep.

PEASANTS, *one sentence apiece.* She's not asleep, it's time you realized. She's through. You must get away. There are wolves in these parts. And the bandits are worse.

MOTHER COURAGE, *standing up.* That's right.

PEASANTS. Have you no one now?

MOTHER COURAGE. Yes. My son Eilif.

PEASANTS. Find him then. Leave *her* to us. We'll give her a proper burial. You needn't worry.

MOTHER COURAGE. Here's a little money for the expenses.
Harnessing herself to the wagon.
I hope I can pull the wagon by myself. Yes, I'll manage, there's not much in it now.
Another regiment passes with pipe and drum.

MOTHER COURAGE. Hey! Take me with you!!
She starts pulling the wagon. A chorus is heard.

The stage is completely bare as before, and this time Mother Courage is quite alone. The wagon, though empty, is sometimes too much for her and sways dangerously. Slowly toiling round the periphery of the stage, Courage seems lost in space. She does not sing. The turntable does not turn.

With all its luck, with all its danger
The war moves slowly 'cross the plains
Whether it's thirty years or longer
The common soldier nothing gains
His food is filth, his coat he plunders
The regiment steals half his pay
But there is always time for wonders:
The holy war won't end today

> *The spring is here, get out of bed*
> *The snow melts fast, green buds arrive*
> *You'll sleep forever when you're dead*
> *But if you're not, then look alive!*

NOTES

FANTASIO (1834) is first published in this English version by Jacques Barzun in this volume. There was an earlier translation by Maurice Baring in 1929; a version which first appeared in America in *From the Modern Repertoire,* Series One, edited by Eric Bentley (Denver, 1949). Still earlier versions are to be found in *Comedies of Musset,* ed. and tr. S. L. Gwynn, London, 1890; *Barberine and other Comedies,* Chicago, 1892; and *The Complete Writings of Musset,* New York, 1905.

THE DIARY OF A SCOUNDREL (1868) became part of the repertoire of the Moscow Art Theatre in 1910 and, as such, was seen in America a dozen years later. At the same time (1923) a translation was published by Brentanos under the title *Enough Stupidity in Every Wise Man* (translator: Polya Kasherman). A British version by David Magarshack and entitled *Even a Wise Man Stumbles* is included in *Easy Money and Two Other Plays* by Alexander Ostrovsky (London, 1944). The Ackland version was published in London in 1948; it is first published in America in the present volume.

LA RONDE (1896–97) first appeared in America as *Hands Around* (New York, 1920); the translation is unsigned, the introduction is initialled by "F.L.G." and "L.D.E.," and the copyright is in the name of A. Koren. This edition was privately printed. The second American appearance of *Reigen* came in 1929 with the printing of a version by Keene Wallis. A little later an anonymous version was included in a Schnitzler volume in the Modern Library (1933). The Keene Wallis version was reprinted with a few editorial changes in *From the Modern Repertoire,* Series One, edited by Eric Bentley (Denver, 1949). The first British edition appeared in 1953 as *Merry Go Round* (translators: Frank and Jacqueline Marcus). The Bentley version is first published in the present volume.

PURGATORY was included in the *Last Poems and Plays* by W.B. Yeats (New York, 1939) and reprinted in the *Collected Plays* (1953). It is somewhat obscure until the poet provides us with a couple of clues: one is in the poem itself in the form of references to the remorse of evildoers which drives them, after death, back to the scene of their sins*; the other is in a statement which Yeats gave to the press when the play was produced at the Abbey Theatre: "In my play a spirit suffers because of its share, when alive, in the destruction of an honored house. The destruction is taking place all over Ireland today." Donald Pearce has discussed this national aspect of the play in *Journal of English Literary History*, March, 1951. T. S. Eliot writes: "I wish he had not given it this title because I cannot accept a purgatory in which there is no hint of, or at least no emphasis upon, Purgation. But, apart from the extraordinary theatrical skill with which he has put so much action within the compass of a very short scene of but little movement, the play gives a masterly exposition of the emotions of an old man. . . . What is most astonishing is the virtual abandonment of blank verse meter in *Purgatory*. . . . The course of improvement [in Yeats' later plays] is towards a greater and greater starkness. The beautiful line for its own sake is a luxury dangerous even for the poet who has made himself a virtuoso of the technique of the theatre."—The First Annual Yeats Lecture, 1940 (reprinted in *The Permanence of Yeats*, MacMillan, 1950). In *Poetry and Drama* (1951), Mr. Eliot goes yet further: "It was only in his last play *Purgatory* that he solved his problem of speech in verse, and laid all his successors under obligation to him."

* See also his *Words Upon the Window Pane:* "Some spirits are earthbound—they think they are still living and go over and over some action of their past lives, just as we go over some painful thought, except that where they are thought is reality . . . Sometimes a spirit relives . . . some passionate or tragic moment of life . . . the murderer repeats his murder, the robber his robbery, the lover his serenade, the soldier hears the trumpet once again. If I were a Catholic I would say that such souls were in Purgatory. In vain do we write *requiescat in pace* on the tomb, for they must suffer, and we in our turn must suffer until God gives peace."

MOTHER COURAGE was written in German just before the Second World War but first published in English, in *New Directions in Prose and Poetry 1941* (translator: H. R. Hays). The world première took place in Zurich just after the war, and the first German edition was published in 1949. The English version first published in the present volume was made by Eric Bentley while working on Mr. Brecht's staff at the Munich production of the play (1950). It is therefore based on a production script, not on the longer, published text. The style of the dialogue having no counterpart in English, Mr. Bentley has often relied on his knowledge of the performance: the aim has been to help American actors get the same effects that the German actors got. The reader could acquire some notion of the remarkable visual effects of the play from the many published photographs of productions: the largest collection is in the anthology *Theaterarbeit* (Leipzig, 1952); there are also a couple of pictures in Eric Bentley's *In Search of Theatre*. The lyrics of the Bentley version were written for the Paul Dessau score, a piano reduction of most of which is provided below. Some of the songs were recorded in German by the original cast (Eterna Records). There is a single LP disk of *Mother Courage* music among the records of Germaine Montero who played the part of Mother Courage in France; this is distributed by Chant du Monde, Paris, and Vanguard Records, New York. The Bentley version of the play was first produced by the San Francisco Drama Guild, during the winter and spring of 1956.

In view of the fact that this play has loosely been said to be "based on" this or that, it may be well to add that there is a German work of the seventeenth century entitled *The Life of the Arch-Impostor and Adventuress Courage*. But from this work Brecht has taken only a very few hints. If Grimmelshausen, the author of *Adventuress Courage*, has influenced Brecht more broadly, it is through another work: *Simplicissimus the Vagabond.** Brecht's main character, as well as the incidents of her story, are, so far as anyone knows, his own invention.

* Tr. A. T. S. Goodrick, London, 1912.

ADAPTATION VS. TRANSLATION

In the theatrical business, the term translation is applied to a first, rough English draft prepared by a linguist with no gift for writing; the term adaptation being reserved for the final stage version which is made by a "playwright."

Both conceptions are fraught with fallacy. The fallacy of the translation is that you might still claim to be accurate when you have translated a beautiful phrase with an ugly one. The adaptor, on the other hand, tends to make the opposite mistake, and assume that the more changes he makes the better. Sometimes the changes do show the adaptor to be a very smart fellow, but is his smartness *apropos?* If you paid your money to see Giraudoux, you may not be willing to settle for Mr. Behrman.

Obviously, there is no fixed rule. If an adaptor is a much better writer than his author, we should be glad to have him show the latter a due disrespect: some of Shakespeare's plays are adaptations. Or there may be a relationship of parity, as when an Anouilh comes to us through the mediation of a Fry.

But these cases are the exceptions, not the rule. Normally one wishes to believe one is reading a version *of an original:* God (not Lancelot Andrewes), Plato (not Jowett), Proust (not Scott Moncrieff). Is not the job of an Andrewes, a Jowett, or a Scott Moncrieff noble enough? Coleridge was modest in his rendering of Schiller, Shelley in his rendering of Goethe; they did not adapt.

In short, commercial usage has made of both terms—translation and adaptation—a downright derogation. That is why the editor of this volume has freed his writers from either imputation by calling each text, noncommittally and incontrovertibly, an "English version." This is not to say that they all approach their material in the same way. Temperaments —as well as circumstances—alter cases. When the editor had a choice of version he did not on principle go for the more literal or the more free. To repeat: there is no fixed rule. Mr. Barzun's version of *La Parisienne* is more literal than Mr. Ashley Dukes's; it is also better English dialogue. Mr. Ackland's version of *Enough Stupidity in Every Wise Man* is less literal than either of the earlier versions; yet it is the only one of the three that impresses the reader as a drama at all. Not one or two but a dozen or so factors are involved: and, at that, not only such things as the talent of the translator but such things as the distance at which another culture stands from ours. Moscow is further off than Paris; he who would bring us a Russian play may have more work to do. Then there is the *relation* between the author's temperament and his translator's. There is the question of differing theatrical conventions. There is the question of . . . perhaps a dozen is too low an estimate. It must be left to the scholarly and polyglot to refer each "version" here reprinted to the original and judge how much has successfully been imported and also if anything has successfully been added to make up for what has inevitably been lost.

APPENDIX

Paul Dessau's music to
*Mother Courage**

Paul Dessau writes, "This music was composed in California, 1946, in the closest collaboration with Brecht. It consists of nine songs, several marches, a short overture, and a finale which combines three distinct march themes that have played a part in the drama. The principal item is the Song of Mother Courage (see the prologue etc.) the music of which is derived from an old French ballad.* * The idea of adapting old tunes is not exactly new to the history of music. "For Brecht's other texts, I tried to invent music which, though influenced by folk elements, goes beyond the folk song in rhythmic and harmonic complexity.

"A composer usually wishes to follow the Mozartian tradition of poetry 'the obedient daughter of music.' But I have tried to begin and end with the words—though to be sure there are musical features, such as the musical caesura in the first line of the Song of Fraternization, which the text did not dictate. Brecht's words themselves have great musicality. The musical ornaments I have used (see the Song of Fraternization again) do not, I think, obfuscate either Brecht's style or his meaning; I aim at making of music-and-words a unity. (Incidentally, the decorative elements, I know, are somewhat foreign to folk music; I was trying to give to folk music the character of finished art work.)

"The orchestra consists of seven musicians. Thumb tacks are placed on the hammers of a piano so that it sounds rather like a spinet (not a harpsichord)—or perhaps a better comparison would be a giant guitar. Combined with accordian, two flutes, an almost always muted trumpet, and percussion, this prepared piano will create the right kind of sound for the play. The audience will have the impression of hearing old, familiar music in a new form."

* Reproduced here by permission of Therese Pol Dessau. Copies of the full score may be obtained from the Suhrkamp Verlag, Schaumainkai 53, Frankfort on Main, Germany. The score here reproduced is a piano reduction of the songs only, not intended for use in the theatre.

* * It had been printed by Brecht in 1927 to the words of another song—in *Die Hauspostille*.

The Songs will sound better if thumb tacks are placed on the hammers of the piano (at the point, of course, where hammer and string make contact).—Paul Dessau

see pp. 237, 287 (this time starting on the fifth line of the stanza) and 313.

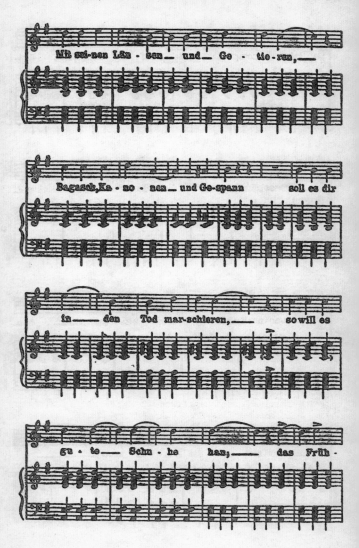

DIE BALLADE VON WEIB UND DEM SOLDATEN
The Ballad of the Soldier Boy

see pages 252-253

auf und das Spieß-mes-ser fängt er, ___

___ und das Spieß - messer fängt er mit Hän - den

auf ___ sag - ten zum Weib ___

die Sol - da - ten.*

* For the second stanza, not printed here in the German,
return to the beginning of the song.

geht wie der Rauch,   und die Wärme geht auch

Ihr ver-

und es wärmen uns nicht eure Taten,   ach, wie

LIED VON FRATERNISIEREN, *Song of Fraternization*

see pages 256-257

das Re - gi - ment stand im Ge - viert,

dann wurd' ge - trommelt, wie's der Brauch,

dann nahm der Feind uns hinterm Stranch

und hat fra - ter - ni - siert.

LIED VON DER GROSSEN KAPITULATION
Song of the great Capitulation

see pages 275–277

SOLDATENLIED, *Soldier's Song*

Ein Schnaps, Wirt, schnell, sei ge - scheit! Ein
Rei - ter hat kein Zeit.___ Muß für sein
Kai - ser strei - - ten,___ muß für sein
Kai - ser strei - - ten.___ Dein

see page 282

LIED DER GROSSEN GEISTER
Song of the Great Souls of This Earth

see pages 301-303

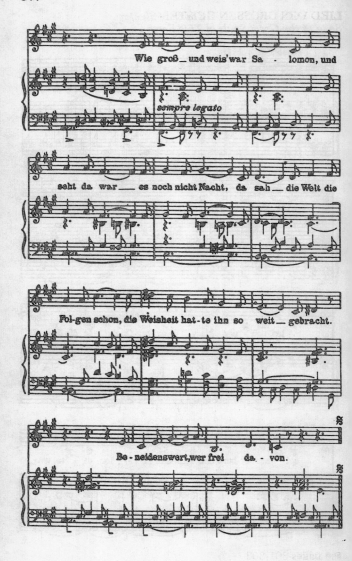

Wie groß_ und weis'war Sa - lomon, und

seht da war_ es noch nicht Nacht, da sah_ die Welt die

Fol-gen schon, die Weisheit hat-te ihn so weit_ gebracht.

Be - neidenswert,wer frei da - von.

LIED VON DER BLEIBE, *Song of Shelter*

see page 305

WIEGENLIED, *Cradle Song*

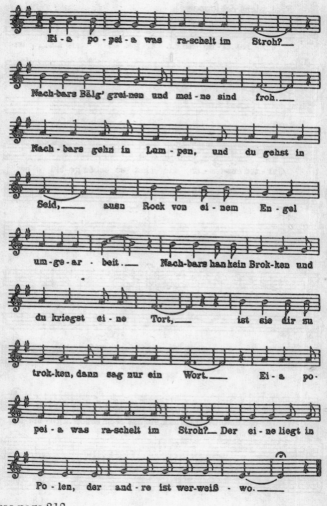

Ei - a po - pei - a was ra-schelt im Stroh?

Nach-bars Bälg' grei-nen und mei-ne sind froh.

Nach - bars gehn in Lum - pen, und du gehst in

Seid, ausn Rock von ei - nem En - gel

um-ge-ar - beit. Nach-bars han kein Brok-ken und

du kriegst ei - ne Tort, ist sie dir zu

trok-ken, dann sag nur ein Wort. Ei - a po-

pei - a was ra-schelt im Stroh? Der ei - ne liegt in

Po - len, der and - re ist wer-weiß - wo.

see page 312